T0305453

An Employment-Targeted Economic Program for Kenya

A project of the International Poverty Centre in Brasilia (IPC),
United Nations Development Programme

An Employment-Targeted Economic Program for Kenya

Robert Pollin
Mwangi wa Gĩthĩnji
James Heintz

*Department of Economics and Political Economy Research Institute (PERI),
University of Massachusetts–Amherst, USA*

COUNTRY STUDY SUPPORTED BY THE INTERNATIONAL POVERTY CENTRE
*This is an independent report produced by a team of international and national consultants supported
by the International Poverty Centre in Brasilia (IPC). This report is part of a wider global research
program encompassing several other countries. The views in this report are the authors' and not
necessarily IPC's. However, the IPC regards this report as an important contribution to the debate on
economic policies and employment programs in Kenya as well as in other countries in Africa.*

Edward Elgar
Cheltenham, UK • Northampton, MA, USA

Published by
Edward Elgar Publishing Limited
Glensanda House
Montpellier Parade
Cheltenham
Glos GL50 1UA
UK

Edward Elgar Publishing, Inc.
William Pratt House
9 Dewey Court
Northampton
Massachusetts 01060
USA

A catalogue record for this book
is available from the British Library

Library of Congress Control Number: 2008927708

ISBN 978 1 84844 030 2

Printed and bound in Great Britain by MPG Books Ltd, Bodmin, Cornwall

Contents

Tables

Figures

Acknowledgments

In September 2005, Robert Pollin and James Heintz conducted an initial series of interviews with numerous representatives at Government of Kenya Ministries, policymakers, academic researchers, donor agencies, and non-government organizations. In March 2006, our expanded team of researchers and consultants, now including Mwangi wa Gĩthĩnji, Jacob Omolo, and Eduardo Zepeda, proceeded through another round of discussions. These discussions included many people with whom we met initially in September 2005, but also added many more people. Finally, the three authors of this study returned to Nairobi in October 2006 to present a preliminary version of this study in a series of seminars.

We are extremely grateful to all of the people who gave of their time to provide us with their insights and perspectives. The meetings and seminars were invaluable for understanding the workings of the Kenyan economy and identifying many of the policy challenges highlighted in this report. The seminars, moreover, gave us an opportunity to test our preliminary ideas with groups of highly knowledgeable and committed people, who provided us with innumerable insights that have added immeasurably to the quality of this present work.

The individuals and organizations with whom we consulted include: Rosemary Ateino (IDS-Nairobi), Professor Michael Chege (UNDP), Noah Chanyisa Chune (COTU), Terry Davidon (Kenya Commercial Bank), H. Ade Freeman (ILRA), Dr. Wahome Gakuru (National Economic and Social Council), James Gatungu (Central Bureau of Statistics), Anne Gikonyo (Horticultural Crops Development Authority), Ambassador Bo Göransson (Embassy of Sweden), Jan Hansen (European Union Commission), Kalle Hellman (Embassy of Sweden), Musa Kathanje (Central Bank of Kenya), Peter Kebati (Mumias Sugar Factory), David Kiboi (Ministry of Water and Irrigation — Principal Economist), Anthony Kilele (Central Bureau of Statistics), Leonard N. Kimani (National Economic and Social Council), David K. Kimani (KTDA), Romano Kiome (Ministry of Agriculture), Dr. Moses Kiptui (Central Bank of Kenya), Nancy Kirui (Ministry of Labor), William K. Kirwa (Agricultural Development Corporation), Dr. Gem Kodhek (Ministry of Agriculture), Gershon N. Konditi (Federation of Kenyan Employers), Wellingtone A. Lubira (Ministry of Agriculture), Dr. Moses Makayoto (KIRDI), Damiano Kulundu Manda (KIPPRA), Dr. Benjamin O. Maturu (Central Bank of Kenya), Michael Mbeka (Ministry of Cooperative Development and Marketing), Dr. Dorothy McCormick (IDS-Nairobi), Andrew Mude (ILRI), Eng. J.M. Munene (formerly, ICDC), John Muriuki (Leather Development Centre), Monica Musau (COTU), Musabi Muteshi (DFID, Kenya), Richard Mutei (Kenya National Federation of Jua Kali Associations), Stephen

Muthua (ASIST Africa), David Nalo (Ministry of Trade and Industry), Njuguna Ndung'u (AERC), Rose Ngugi (KIPPRA), James M.N. Nguku (Horticultural Crops Development Authority), John Njenga (Kenya Flower Council), Dishon M. Njere (Department of MSE Development, Ministry of Labour), Edward Ntalami (Capital Markets Authority), James Nyatich (Ministry of Cooperative Development and Marketing), Walter Odero (DFID, Kenya), Aloys O. Ojiambo (Department of MSE Development, Ministry of Labour), Seth Otieno (Ministry of Trade and Industry), Raphael Owino (Central Bank of Kenya), Nelson Rutto (Central Bank of Kenya), Benjamin Sogomo (Horticultural Crops Development Authority), Dr. Wilson Songa (Ministry of Agriculture), Lerionka S. Tiampati (KTDA), Dr. Kamau Thugge (Ministry of Finance), J.K. Wanyela (Kenya Bankers Association), Mary M. Wanyonyi (Central Bureau of Statistics), Solomon W. Waweru (Coffee Board of Kenya), and the International Labour Organization office in Nairobi.

In addition, the staff of the UNDP country office in Nairobi were invaluable in providing logistical support, substantive inputs, and useful suggestions. In particular, Paul André de la Porte (Resident Representative), Nardos Bekele-Thomas (Deputy Resident Representative), Kelly Ki Jeong Lee, Fortunatus Okwiri, Marcello Giordani, and Dorothy Mongi were instrumental in supporting this work.

Dankit Nassiuma, Vivian Nyarunda, and Robert Nderitu of the Kenya National Bureau of Statistics came to the University of Massachusetts-Amherst for two weeks in February/March 2007 to work through with us a range of technical problems relating to the 2005-06 Kenya Integrated Household Budget Survey. This was a tremendous learning experience for us. It also provided us with the most up-to-date high quality data on a range of crucial aspects of the Kenyan economy. We are grateful to Dankit, Vivian, and Robert for both the professional collaboration and friendships.

We would like to acknowledge the work of five consultants who made important contributions to this project: Aziz Khan (University of California-Riverside), Jacob Omolo (IPAR), Mbui Wagacha, Jeannette Wicks-Lim (PERI), and Eduardo Zepeda (UNDP International Poverty Centre, Brasilia). Jerry Epstein and Richard Anker of PERI both offered insightful perspectives and critiques at various stages of the project. We would also like to thank Terry McKinley (UNDP International Poverty Centre) for facilitating this project and his sharp, no-holds-barred, critiques. We also acknowledge the financial support of the UNDP International Poverty Centre, which made this project possible.

Adam Hersh and Lynda Pickbourn, both advanced Economics Ph.D. students at the University of Massachusetts Amherst, provided excellent research assistance. Heidi Garrett-Peltier, Jeannette Wicks-Lim, and Debbie Zeidenberg of PERI did fine work copyediting this manuscript at record speed, and Kim Weinstein has done her customary outstanding job in designing and producing the book. Judy Fogg, the Administrative Director of PERI, has been, as always, incomparable in making this project happen.

Brief Highlights of Major Proposals

The principal focus of our study is to develop effective policies for greatly expanding decent employment opportunities in Kenya. As we use the term, "decent employment" means a work situation that enables people to at least maintain him/herself and his/her family above a reasonable poverty line.

The government of Kenya has committed itself to generating 500,000 new jobs per year at least through 2007. We certainly embrace this goal. At the same time, there are wide disparities in the types of employment opportunities available in Kenya. A high proportion of people working full time at jobs are still unable to support themselves and their families above a poverty-line level. This is why it is crucial to not simply focus on employment alone, but the quality of employment.

EMPLOYMENT CONDITIONS AND LIVING STANDARDS

Labor Force and Unemployment

At the time of the most recent labor force survey in 2005–06, the total labor force—including all people employed and unemployed—totaled 13.5 million. Among the 18.8 million in their economically active years, this means a labor force participation rate of 72 percent. Of the 13.5 million participating in the labor force in some way, 12.1 million are counted as employed and 1.4 million are openly unemployed. Thus, the open unemployment rate is 10.5 percent.

Division of Employment and Incomes by Sectors

We can divide the total number of jobs in the Kenyan economy into three broad categories—agricultural self-employment, the informal sector, and the formal sector. The breakdown of total employment by these three sectors is 50 percent in agricultural self-employment, 36 percent in the informal sector, and only 14 percent in the formal sector.

At the time of writing, Kenya's National Bureau of Statistics (KNBS) has not yet been able to release income data for those who are self-employed agricultural workers. This means that we cannot report income data for fully half of all working people in Kenya. Nevertheless, we are able to report wage incomes for those working in the informal and formal sectors and net business earnings for self-employed workers in non-agricultural enterprises.

Incomes, on average, are much higher in the formal than informal sector. There are also significant income disparities between the categories of workers within each sector. Finally, there are also large disparities by region. Allowing for differences by employment categories, most private sector urban workers earn about twice as much as rural workers in the same job category. The urban/rural income disparities are small only between public sector employees.

Labor Incomes and Poverty

Of all Kenyans who are participating in the labor force but are unemployed, roughly 65 percent live in poverty, based only on earnings from employment. However, the proportion living in poverty are basically the same if a Kenyan is employed and working up to 39 hours per week. Specifically, for those working 1–27 hours per week, nearly 70 percent live in poverty. Among those working 28–39 hours per week, about 66 percent live in poverty.

Among the labor force participants working 40 hours or more per week, the percentage living in poverty does go down, to 46.1 percent. Still, this percentage remains very high. It means that, even among workers employed 40 hours or more per week, nearly 50 percent of them live in poverty.

The most serious problem facing Kenyans in the labor market today is not unemployment per se or even low hours per se. It is that, even among those Kenyans (outside the agricultural self-employed) who are working long hours—i.e. 40 hours or more—the chances are very high that one will be living in poverty.

PROFILE OF NON-AGRICULTURAL HOUSEHOLD ENTERPRISES

Based on the 2005–06 Kenya Integrated Household Budget Survey (KIHBS), we find that there are a total of 2.1 million non-agricultural household enterprises in Kenya. Roughly 90 percent are informal enterprises and 10 percent are formal. In terms of employment, about 5.2 million people are working in non-agricultural household enterprises, including contributing family workers.

Household Enterprises by Industrial Sectors

The overwhelming majority of non-agricultural household enterprises—82 percent of the total number of firms—are in the business of providing some sort of service. Of these service enterprises, 73.8 percent are informal and 8.2 percent are formal.

Profile of Employment in Household Enterprises

The largest category of employment in the household enterprise sector is unpaid family members, accounting by itself for 37 percent of all household enterprise employment. Own-account workers—people working alone for themselves—represent another 34 percent of all household enterprise employment. Thus, own-account workers and unpaid family members together account for more than 70 percent of all employment in household enterprises.

Costs of Operating Household Enterprises

The two largest categories of costs are the purchasing of goods that are resold—i.e. inventory purchases—and raw materials. In addition, there are large disparities between informal and informal enterprises in terms of the proportions they pay for licenses and taxes. Informal firms are paying an average of 3.8 percent of their total costs in licenses and taxes, while formal enterprises pay 8.5 percent. Thus, informal firms would have to increase their licenses and tax obligations quite significantly in order to operate as formal enterprises and receive the benefits from being a formal sector firm.

Sources of Start-Up Credit

The great majority of non-agricultural household enterprises rely on either their own savings or funds from family members to provide the initial financing for their businesses. Savings and Credit Cooperatives (SACCOs) provide start-up funds to only 3.2 percent of household enterprises. The formal commercial banks appear to play almost no role whatsoever in helping household enterprises to begin operations.

Earnings from Household Enterprises

Most household enterprises in Kenya are informal and very small scale. The earnings that these firms receive, on average, are very low—not sufficient, on average, to maintain the people working in them above the official poverty line. If household enterprises are formal and relatively large in size, their earnings are dramatically higher.

Considerations for Policy Proposals

Three separate factors would seem crucial considerations for policy:

1. raising productivity and expanding the domestic market in general, but also shaping policies so that household enterprises specifically will benefit from these overall economic gains;

2. improving access to credit for household enterprises; and
3. reducing the overall number of people relying on informal household enterprises, so as to reduce the excessive competition among them that keeps earnings at a poverty level. To do this will mean increasing opportunities for formal sector employment.

LABOR COSTS, LABOR MARKET INSTITUTIONS, AND EMPLOYMENT EXPANSION

It is frequently argued that a primary cause of insufficient employment opportunities is excessive labor costs that discourage businesses from hiring more workers. This perspective is prominent, for example, in the recent Concept Note written by the World Bank as a preliminary document to its ongoing *Jobs in Kenya* study (World Bank 2005a).

There are four possible ways in which the costs to businesses of hiring workers could fall: 1) workers receive lower overall compensation, including wages and benefits; 2) the industrial relations system and labor market regulations—including laws and regulations regarding workers' right to organize, conflict resolution, and hiring and firing—operates with more flexibility for business; 3) workers perform their workplace operations at a higher level of productivity; or 4) the government absorbs some portion of the costs of hiring workers.

In the World Bank's Concept Note, the focus appears to be on the first two ways to reduce business costs, i.e. to lower wages and benefits for workers and to increase the flexibility of the Kenyan formal labor market. We focus on these two considerations in this section of our study. We consider productivity and government employment subsidies later.

Lowering Formal Sector Wages to Increase Employment

- We roughly estimate the amount of wage reductions needed to increase private formal sector employment by 25 percent, i.e. increasing employment in this sector by about 190,000 jobs, from 770,000 to 960,000. We find that average wages in the formal private sector would have to fall by approximately 42 percent.
- According to our calculations, cutting an average formal private sector worker's monthly wage by 42 percent would mean that the worker and his/her family income would fall to between 10 and 23 percent below their respective urban or regional poverty lines.
- About 400,000 Kenyans would experience a large increase in income. This would include both the 190,000 workers newly hired into formal sector jobs and the roughly 210,000 people who live off of the incomes of these

workers. Despite these people enjoying rising incomes, they would, on average, also still be living between 10 and 23 percent below their respective urban or regional poverty lines.

Beyond these immediate effects, the fact that 1.7 million people would experience a declining living standard would of course generate social unrest. This, in turn, would create an unstable atmosphere for private investors. The decline in private investment would, in turn, lead to a contraction in job opportunities.

Industrial Relations and Labor Market Rigidities

To what extent has the expansion of decent employment opportunities in Kenya been hindered by the country's system of industrial relations, including regulations concerning hiring, hours, and firing; the extent and strength of union power in labor markets; and minimum wage standards? The World Bank's 2005 Concept Note suggests that these factors may be playing an important role in holding back employment growth in the private formal sector.

Yet the evidence is mixed at best, including data from the World Bank's own studies. It is reasonable to conclude from the most extensive World Bank study by Alby, Azam, and Rospabé (2005) that most business representatives in Kenya consider labor market regulations around hiring, firing, and hours to be relatively minor barriers to expansion, if they are barriers at all.

The Impact of Labor Unions

The World Bank's Concept Note suggests that labor unions may be operating as a significant source of labor market rigidities in Kenya. But the evidence suggests that this is unlikely to be a significant barrier to the expansion of decent employment. If for no other reason, this is because unions represent a small and diminishing portion of Kenya's labor force. Consistent with this, the Alby et al. study reports that in 2003, 93.6 percent of firms surveyed in Kenya reported losing zero work days due to strikes and labor unrest.

Minimum Wage Laws

Kenya operates with a wide array of minimum wage orders that apply to different sectors, regions of the country, and job categories. However, in August 2007, the Ministry of Labor proposed abolishing all minimum wage standards.

• As of June 2006, the minimum wage laws are exerting little influence on actual wage-setting within the formal private sector. For example, between 43–50 percent of formal private sector workers were earning wages below the lower-range average for the statutory minimum wage.

- Despite this lack of enforcement, the 2005 minimum wage laws have been serving a useful function in at least defining a decent standard that would enable working people and their families to live above the poverty line. Thus, to conclude that the minimum wage should be eliminated or significantly reduced from its current levels is to therefore also conclude that the Kenyan economy is unable to pay even those workers with jobs in the formal private sector a wage that will keep them and their families out of poverty.
- Labor market conditions in Kenya would probably benefit from a simplification of the elaborate system of minimum wage standards that are presently in place.

THE RURAL SECTOR: INSTITUTIONAL REFORM FOR DEVELOPMENT

We consider specific conditions that prevail with Kenya's major crops, including tea and coffee, horticulture, maize and wheat, millet and sorghum, sugar cane and rice. We also discuss the livestock sector. These detailed discussions form the basis for our policy recommendations aimed at raising productivity and international competitiveness in the agricultural sector. The seven themes that we develop out of our discussions on the various agricultural sectors are these:

1. *Learning from successes.* Kenya has experienced successes in agriculture in a number of important areas. In terms of sectors, tea, horticulture, and wheat stand out. We can extract valuable lessons from these successes. First, improvements have occurred when there is proper infrastructure and support for farmers or where farmers have sufficient capital to overcome structural impediments. Second, in some sectors it is possible for individual farmers or firms to exploit returns to scale to overcome impediments.
2. *Adaptation rather than replication of past successes.* Kenya's agricultural sector was broadly successful from independence until about 1980. But this doesn't mean that simply recreating the institutional environment or policies of the early independence years will be adequate for recreating a positive agricultural growth path. The aim of policy now should be to combine the management successes of the early independence years with a continued effort to promote the well-being of smallholders.
3. *Understanding the resources and capabilities of smallholders.* Most of Kenya's rural population has few assets in terms of resources or education. But the return to primary education for rural agricultural households is between 8 and 12 percent per year. Assuring access to education for poor households would thus raise their agricultural productivity substantially.

4. *Designing effective extension services for smallholders.* A policy that aims to privatize extension is not likely to succeed with poor smallholders because they lack both the physical and human capital to make effective use of a private, demand-driven, extension service. Demand-driven extension works best for medium- and large-scale farmers who have specific problems to be solved. Poor farmers tend to have a broader range of problems that need more than a single visit and require systematic training.

5. *Returns to scale and agricultural cooperatives.* Two crucial changes need to occur for cooperatives to play a successful role in agricultural development. The first is to create an effective regulatory body overseeing the operations of cooperatives and similar institutions. The second is increased public funding, probably through the Ministry of Cooperatives, to support the government's regulatory efforts, and to give positive guidance and support to these institutions.

6. *Infrastructure improvements.* We discuss elsewhere in the study proposals for improving Kenya's road and water infrastructure. Beyond these basic needs, there are also lessons to be learned from industries that have managed to absorb the increased costs imposed by poor infrastructure—particularly in terms of transportation and energy supplies—by taking advantage of returns to scale. This is particularly evident within the flower industry and the Kenya Tea Development Authority (KTDA).

7. *Cost of capital and access to credit.* The cost of and access to capital has long been a problem for smallholders. Apart from the high cost and difficulty of obtaining credit in the past, there has been a bias against smallholders in terms of the amount and the duration of loan. One approach to this situation is to dramatically increase the provision of affordable credit through rural-based SACCOs and other microfinance enterprises, through a program of credit subsidies, a topic that we consider at some length below.

INVESTING IN ROADS AND WATER INFRASTRUCTURE

Infrastructure investments are central to raising productivity and thereby people's incomes. Improving the country's infrastructure is equally important in terms of promoting trade competitiveness. Finally, increased public spending in these areas can serve as a major source of job growth within the country's formal economy, as has traditionally been the case in Kenya as well as many other countries:

- We argue for increased government spending on roads and water infrastructure at about 40 billion Kenyan shillings (Ksh) above present medium-term budget strategy paper (MTBSP) commitments.

- This level of additional spending will bring major improvements in productivity. We also estimate that it will create roughly 350,000 new formal sector jobs.

MONETARY POLICY, INFLATION CONTROL, AND INTEREST RATES

The Government of Kenya's 2003 *Economic Recovery Strategy for Wealth and Employment Creation* states that its focus will be on four goals:

- to contain inflation to below 5.0 percent;
- to maintain a competitive exchange rate consistent with an export-driven economic recovery;
- to maintain an interest rate structure that promotes financial savings and ensures efficient allocation of the same; and
- to ensure adequate growth in credit to the private sector.

These are all important goals that are worthy in their own right. At the same time, in our view, this list of goals raises a set of serious concerns that require careful attention.

What is the Relationship between Inflation and Growth?

No professional consensus exists on the relationship between inflation and economic growth. At the same time, two basic conclusions are evident:

- Virtually all research finds no clear negative relationship between growth and *single-digit* inflation specifically for the developing countries.
- This suggests that for Kenya, setting an inflation target below 5 percent is not likely to offer benefits in terms of the economy's growth performance.

Supply Shocks and Kenyan Inflation Control

- Supply-side shocks have a major impact on inflationary dynamics in Kenya. As one important example, food price inflation, due to droughts or other breakdowns in the country's food production, raises the country's overall inflation rate and lowers living standards, particularly of poorer households. The same holds for oil price shocks.
- Tightening monetary policy in response to such events in order to maintain low inflation rates runs the risks of worsening the economic impact of these shocks. As such, it is important to try to observe how a shock to one

component of the CPI affects other components. For example, how does a spike in food or energy prices affect other prices in the economy? Are these effects transitory or long-lived?

- We estimated a vector autoregression (VAR) model of the overall effects of supply-shock inflation. The findings from our VAR model suggest the following policy implications:
- *Food price shocks* do have a major direct impact on overall "headline" inflation in the short run. And because food prices constitute over 50 percent of the overall CPI basket, these effects can impose serious hardships, especially for lower-income households. The most effective approach would be for the government to utilize its existing grain storage facilities throughout the country to provide an effective food buffer stock.
- *Energy price shocks* have a more sustained impact on inflation in Kenya. However, Kenya, acting alone, cannot do much to lessen the negative consequences of adverse movements in global oil prices, which feed into consumer energy prices. This is because Kenya imports all of its oil, and because building an oil buffer stock would likely be far more expensive than what could be developed for a food supply.
- *Transportation price shocks*, which partially reflect changes in fuel prices but also other components of transportation, such as bus and matatu fares, also appear to have a sustained impact on overall inflation in Kenya. In this case, the Kenyan government could take measures to lower transportation costs. One measure would be to improve the country's transportation infrastructure. It is also important for the government to try to counteract short-term spikes in transportation prices.

We propose four basic changes in the conduct of monetary policy in Kenya:

1. *Use a core short-term real interest rate as an intermediate monetary target.* The Central Bank of Kenya should move away from targeting the growth rates of monetary aggregates. The Bank has little direct control over monetary aggregates and the links between monetary growth and macroeconomic performance, as defined by the quantity theory of money, are too weak to form the basis of a development-oriented monetary policy. Targeting real interest rates will have a more direct influence over interest rates and the exchange rate.

2. *Remove the anti-growth bias in monetary policy.* This involves a shift in the ways in which monetary policy is conducted. Specifically, monetary policy should be prepared to (1) provide economic stimulus during a contraction; and (2) distinguish between demand-pull and cost-push inflation. The effectiveness of a counter-cyclical monetary policy will be enhanced if financial reforms insure that monetary policy has a direct impact on real economic performance.

3. *Diversify the toolkit for addressing inflation in Kenya.* Using monetary policy alone may be a costly way of reducing inflation in Kenya. This is particularly likely to be true when inflation is the result of supply-side shocks. Multiple tools are needed to simultaneously control inflation and support a poverty-reducing development agenda.

4. *Institute reforms to the financial sector to channel credit to socially productive uses.* The Kenyan banking sector has substantial excess capacity that could be mobilized to facilitate the attainment of development objectives, such as employment creation, increasing productivity, enhancing investments, and supporting poverty reduction. However, at present, the financial structure does not channel credit to socially productive uses to a sufficient extent.

EXCHANGE RATE POLICY AND FOREIGN TRADE

The analysis in this section leads to the following policy conclusions:

- A targeted exchange rate policy is an important macroeconomic instrument for ensuring the competitiveness of Kenya's exports. It could also provide an appropriate economic environment for diversifying Kenya's export base.
- Kenya should focus on developing regional trade within the African continent. Kenya remains a net exporter to the continent and should remain competitive in this region as long as the appropriate policies are in place. Moreover, regional growth can have important positive feedback effects in the Kenyan economy.
- Targeted interventions aimed at promoting industrial expansion are needed to generate employment that reduces poverty in a way that is sustainable in the long run.

RESTRUCTURING KENYA'S FINANCIAL SYSTEM

The combination of a strong commercial banking sector and a widespread, vibrant but badly undercapitalized microfinance system suggests a clear policy approach: to bring into much closer alliance the formal commercial banking system and the microfinance institutions (MFIs).

- We propose to create a pool of subsidized credit at a level equal to roughly 20 percent of the current level of private investment in Kenya. These funds would be made available to commercial banks, on condition that they in turn make loans to SACCOs and other MFIs. The MFIs would then be far more capable of making large amounts of loans to small businesses, informal enterprises, and agricultural smallholders.

- We propose that guarantees be set at 75 percent of the loans that commercial banks make to MFIs. We demonstrate that, even assuming default rates on these guaranteed loans as high as 30 percent, the total accruals on these government contingent liabilities would amount to no more than Ksh nine billion, i.e., about 5 percent of the national budget.

FISCAL POLICY: HOW TO PAY FOR NEW PRO-EMPLOYMENT INITIATIVES

- We propose three major new areas of public expenditure beyond what has already been budgeted, in the areas of transport and water infrastructure; credit subsidies, especially for small businesses and rural smallholders; and improvements in marketing support, again, especially for small businesses and rural smallholders.
- According to our estimates, these three proposals should require expenditures of about Ksh 50 billion per year in 2005 prices, which is equal to about 3 percent of Gross Domestic Product (GDP).
- We propose these additional funds come primarily from two sources. The most important new source is tax revenues that should result from increased formalization of the economy. As a supplemental source of funds, the Treasury is well-situated to maintain its current level of borrowing from domestic sources, rather than following through on its current plan to significantly cut domestic borrowing. Other countries at similar levels of development carry more debt from domestic sources than the Kenyan Treasury; and many of these other countries have experienced successful growth trends in recent years, despite having higher domestic debt levels than Kenya.
- Possible external sources of increased government revenues include external borrowing, debt relief, and foreign aid. Each may be useful in generating small supplemental streams of revenue.

Summary of Major Findings and Proposals

The principal focus of our study is to develop effective policies for greatly expanding decent employment opportunities in Kenya. The term "decent work" has recently been embraced as an organizing principle by the International Labor Organization, and we believe the term has resonance for considering the situation in Kenya today. As we use the term in the Kenyan context, decent employment means a work situation that enables a worker to at least maintain him/herself and his/her family above a reasonable poverty line.

The government of Kenya has committed itself to generating 500,000 new jobs per year at least through 2007. We certainly embrace this goal. At the same time, there are wide disparities in the types of employment opportunities available in Kenya. A high proportion of people working full time at jobs are still unable to support themselves and their families above a poverty line level. This is why it is crucial to not simply focus on employment alone, but the quality of employment.

We are also not simply focused on improving employment opportunities for those near the poverty line. Among its sub-Saharan African neighbors, Kenya has a relatively highly educated population. There are also sectors of the Kenyan economy that are dynamic and generating healthy numbers of skilled, middle-class employment and business opportunities. Our proposals aim to expand opportunities for the poor and near poor in a manner that concurrently creates a wide range of employment and business opportunities. This includes all types of business owners—especially small and medium-sized enterprises, in the informal as well as formal sector, agricultural smallholders, as well as well-trained workers operating at high productivity levels.

Our program is in the spirit of the UN Millennium Development Goals, as they apply in Kenya. The MDGs are focused on raising standards of individual human welfare. The goals include the eradication of extreme poverty and hunger, universalizing primary education, equalizing opportunities for women, and improving a range of key health outcomes. Our own focus is less on these ends themselves than on the most effective means of accomplishing them.

Following an introductory Chapter 1, the main body of this work consists of nine chapters. The topics of these chapters are as follows: 2) Employment

Conditions and Living Standards; 3) Profile of Non-agricultural Household Enterprises; 4) Labor Costs, Labor Market Institutions and Employment Expansion; 5) The Rural Sector: Institutional Reform for Development; 6) Investing in Roads and Water Infrastructure; 7) Monetary Policy, Inflation Control, and Interest Rates; 8) Exchange Rate Policy and Foreign Trade; 9) Restructuring Kenya's Financial System; and 10) Fiscal Policy: How to Pay for New Pro-employment Initiatives. We also present a brief concluding chapter that brings together our various proposals that are all aimed, in combination, toward promoting a large-scale expansion of decent employment in Kenya.

INTRODUCTION

Kenya's overall economic performance has been poor since the early 1980s, after having been generally positive in the first 15 years or so since the country became independent in 1964. We observe this shift in the country's economic trends through examining some basic evidence on GDP per capita, investment as a share of GDP, agricultural value added per worker, and the trade balance. Since 2004, there have been signs of improvement—including more rapid GDP growth per capita and higher rates of investment, and we consider this most recent evidence as well.

Why did the Kenyan economy descend into a long period of stagnation beginning in the early 1980s? Kenya's stagnation coincides closely with the 24-year presidential reign, between 1978 and 2002, of Daniel Arap Moi. As of this writing, President Mwai Kibaki has been in power for nearly five years. It is too early to render a judgment as to how successful the Kibaki administration has been in nurturing a more successful economic growth path. In any case, it is not our purpose to focus on the role of any single political figure or party in contributing to Kenya's economic decline.

Kenya's economic decline also correlates closely with the implementation of so-called "Structural Adjustment" policies under the auspices of the International Monetary Fund (IMF) and the World Bank. These policies included: 1) fiscal policies targeted at keeping deficits low and reducing the overall level of spending; 2) monetary policy aimed at maintaining a low inflation environment as opposed to balancing the goals of inflation control and employment promotion; 3) liberalizing trade and capital flows; 4) the privatization of publicly-owned enterprises; and 5) the deregulation of the private business sector. This is not the place for a broad examination of the overall merits of this policy approach. However, we will consider how specific features of Kenya's structural adjustment program have affected the country's economic performance. We will also propose changes in the country's policy approach based on the evidence we present.

Another factor that is widely seen as contributing to Kenya's economic stagnation is the high level of government corruption. Operating on a large scale, corruption can prevent vital policy initiatives from being carried out effectively. There is no doubt that for any positive policy initiatives to succeed, the level of corruption and mismanagement in Kenya's economy will have to be controlled more effectively. We offer suggestions, as appropriate in the context of our specific proposals, to consolidate advances already made toward controlling corruption.

Whatever factors have been responsible for Kenya's long economic stagnation, the severity of the country's economic problems were underscored during late 2005 and early 2006, when a severe drought in the northern part of the country drastically reduced food production and put 2–3 million people at risk of starvation. The drought and consequent humanitarian crisis was very much a regional phenomenon. Food supplies dropped to extremely low levels in the north, while agricultural production of such staple crops as maize was abundant in the west of Kenya. Kenya exported basic food crops to other African countries despite the acute food shortage in the arid and semi-arid regions in the north. The response of the Kenyan government and the international community was to increase emergency relief. However, a lack of food security and extreme volatility in agricultural production are perennial features of Kenya's agricultural sector that will not be addressed by a once-off disbursement of emergency aid. Kenya's food and water insecurity and the risk of famine are structural issues, rooted in a lack of transportation, communication, and water infrastructure.

Amid these serious economic difficulties, there are also many positive features of Kenya's economy today which need to be recognized. Indeed, one of our strategies in formulating new policy approaches has been to build from these many areas of achievement and future promise. These successful areas include:

- *Exports*. Kenya has continued to be among the world's leading exporters of tea. Moreover, the tea sector is characterized by a successful integration of smallholders along with large-scale farmers and processors. More recently, Kenya has also emerged as a leading horticultural exporter. We recognize that wages for workers in these sectors have not been consistently improving commensurate with the gains in export sales. This is clearly an important area for improvement.
- *Administration of infrastructure*. Though there is much evidence of governmental agencies failing to deliver on their procurement projects, the Kenya Roads Board (KRB) has recently managed to successfully spend virtually their full road maintenance budget.
- *A vibrant financial system*. Kenya has a strong combination of institutions. At one level, sophisticated commercial banks operate along with emerging

securities markets, with the country increasingly becoming a regional financial center. At another level, Kenya has the largest network of microfinance institutions in sub-Saharan Africa. The aim of policy should be to bring these two sets of institutions together.

- *Macroeconomic stability.* Kenya has never had a serious problem of inflation control. It has also succeeded in maintaining a fairly high level of tax revenue collections, which is all the more remarkable because most private economic activities are performed informally. Finally, Kenya has maintained a relatively low level of public debt. These are all positive achievements as far as they go. These should be seen as foundations on which to establish policies focused on promoting decent employment.

EMPLOYMENT CONDITIONS AND LIVING STANDARDS

In examining broad economic conditions and living standards, we have been fortunate to receive early access to the 2005–06 Kenya Integrated Household Budget Survey, produced by Kenya's National Bureau of Statistics. We are grateful to our colleagues at the KNBS for this opportunity to utilize this invaluable resource.

Working with these 2005–06 KIHBS data, we observe these basic patterns. To begin with, total labor force participation—including all people employed and unemployed—is 13.5 million. Among the 18.8 million people in their economically active years, this means a labor force participation rate of 72 percent. Of the 13.5 million participating in the labor force in some way, 12.1 million are counted as employed and 1.4 million are openly unemployed. Thus, the open unemployment rate is 10.5 percent.

As is true in any economy, the figures on open unemployment provide a very limited picture of labor market conditions. This is because the open unemployment rate does not take into account underemployment, or more importantly, poverty-level employment—that is, people who are employed but are still bringing home low incomes. This could result from some combination of two factors: 1) receiving very low hourly income from employment; or 2) being employed involuntarily for a low number of hours. We therefore consider in Chapter 2 evidence on poverty-level employment, along with data on open unemployment, sectoral employment, wages, and earnings.

Division of Employment by Sectors

We can divide the total number of jobs in the Kenyan economy into three broad categories—agricultural self-employment, the informal sector, and the formal sector. The breakdown of total employment by these three sectors is 50 percent in agricultural self-employment, 36 percent in the informal sector, and only 14 percent in the formal sector.

Open Unemployment by Region, Gender, and Age

There are large disparities in open unemployment by region, age, and educational levels, while differences by gender are negligible. Thus, there is far more open unemployment in urban than rural regions—17.3 percent versus 8.5 percent. By age, the largest proportion of unemployed are those between 15 and 39 years old. In terms of educational attainment, the highest proportion of openly unemployed are those who have completed primary education, at 11.6 percent. It is notable that unemployment is not most severe among the least educated. Moreover, the percentage of openly unemployed among the most educated— i.e. those who have received higher education—is 8.5 percent, which is roughly on par with the 9.6 percent of those who have not completed primary education. In short, these figures show us that open unemployment is not a problem concentrated among the least advantaged groups in Kenyan society. It is rather a problem that is spread fairly evenly across different social groupings.

Incomes from Employment

In considering these data, it is unfortunate that, at the time of writing, the KNBS has not yet been able to release income data for those who are self-employed agricultural workers. This means that we cannot report income data for fully half of all working people in Kenya. Nevertheless, we are able to report wage incomes for those working in the informal and formal sectors and business revenues for self-employed workers in non-agricultural enterprises.

We see from these data that, incomes, on average, are much higher in the formal than informal sector. There are also significant income disparities among the categories of workers within each sector. Finally, there are also large disparities by region. Allowing for differences by employment categories, most private sector urban workers earn about twice as much as rural workers in the same job category. The urban/rural income disparities are small only between public sector employees.

Labor Incomes and Poverty

The most recent poverty figures have been developed by the KNBS from the same 2005–06 Integrated Budget Household Survey, and are presented in their publication, *Basic Report on Poverty in Kenya* (Government of Kenya, 2007a). Recognizing that the KNBS poverty thresholds are based on consumption rather than income levels, we proceed cautiously with these most recent poverty threshold figures to provide perspective on the median earnings figures for informal and formal sector workers in Kenya.

To begin with, the urban poverty line of Ksh 2,913 per month is about 25 percent below the Ksh 4,000 in median monthly earnings of both paid employees and self-employed own-account workers in the urban informal sector. Paid employees in the formal sector earn about three times the level of the Ksh 2,913 urban poverty line.

Now, of course, a high proportion of income earners have to support not only themselves with their earnings, but other family members as well. We assume for illustrative purposes that, for example, the average working person in Kenya supports one other person through his/her earnings, and we consider the implications of this in terms of poverty outcomes. First, for urban informal paid employees, dividing their Ksh 4,000 monthly earnings among two people means that each person lives on Ksh 2,000 per month. This is about one-third below the urban poverty line of Ksh 2,913. Even with urban formal paid employees, dividing Ksh 9,000 per month among two people means that both people are living on Ksh 4,500 per month. This amount is only slightly more than 50 percent above the urban poverty line. The story is similar in comparing the incomes of rural workers with the Ksh 1,562 rural poverty line.

Sources of Poverty-Level Employment: Low Hours and Low Earnings

We have found that, of all labor force participants for whom we have household income estimates, roughly 65 percent of the unemployed live in poverty, based on employment earnings alone. However, the proportions living in poverty are basically the same if a Kenyan is employed and working up to 39 hours per week. Specifically, for those working 1–27 hours per week, nearly 70 percent live in poverty. Among those working 28–39 hours per week, about 66 percent live in poverty.

Among those who report working 40 hours or more per week, the percentage living in poverty does go down to 46.1 percent. Still, this percentage remains very high. It means that, even among workers employed 40 hours or more per week, nearly 50 percent of them live in poverty. But it is also important here to recognize that a large majority of Kenyans do work 40 hours or more per week. This means, in turn, that even though the chances of living in poverty in Kenya do go down somewhat if one works 40 hours or more per week, it is still the case that the overwhelming proportion of labor force participants in Kenya who live in poverty are also working 40 hours or more per week.

Considering these data overall, a key message emerges, both for our study and for economic policy discussions in Kenya more generally. It is that the most serious problem facing Kenyans in the labor market today is not unemployment per se or even low hours per se. It is that, even among those Kenyans (outside the agricultural self-employed) who are working long hours—i.e. 40 hours or more—the chances are very high that one will be living in poverty.

PROFILE OF NON-AGRICULTURAL HOUSEHOLD ENTERPRISES

Non-agricultural household enterprises are a basic foundation of the Kenyan economy. Any strategy for expanding decent employment and reducing poverty in Kenya will have to focus on the non-agricultural household enterprise sector—to expand opportunities for people working in the sector, either by improving conditions within the sector itself or by creating more opportunities for decent employment outside this sector.

The 2005–06 KIHBS provides access to an unprecedented statistical portrait of this sector—its size, employment patterns, costs, sources of funds for financing expansion, and earnings. In Chapter 3, we present some of the most important statistical evidence that is now available.

There are a total of 2.1 million non-agricultural household enterprises in Kenya. Roughly 90 percent are informal enterprises and 10 percent are formal. In terms of employment, about 5.2 million people total are working in non-agricultural household enterprises, including contributing family workers. Of the 5.2 million employed in non-agricultural household enterprises, 4.1 million, or 79 percent, are working in informal enterprises, and 1.1 million, or 21 percent, in formal enterprises.

The domestic market within Kenya itself is by far the most important source of sales for Kenyan household enterprises, both the informal and formal firms. Almost no Kenyan household enterprise—less than one-tenth of 1 percent of the more than 2 million firms—sell a significant fraction of their goods and services on export markets. With respect to the domestic market itself, roughly 90 percent of non-agricultural household enterprises sell directly to consumers. Most of the remaining 10 percent of these firms sell to private businesses within Kenya. Almost no household enterprises sell their products to the public sector.

Household Enterprises by Industrial Sectors

The overwhelming majority of non-agricultural household enterprises—82 percent of the total number of firms—are in the business of providing some sort of service. Of these service enterprises, 73.8 percent are informal and 8.2 percent are formal. Most of the remaining household enterprises are in manufacturing. Among the service-providing enterprises in this sector, the overwhelming majority are in retail trade. Retail trade itself accounts for a total of about 63 percent of all non-agricultural household enterprises.

Profile of Employment in Household Enterprises

The largest category of employment in the household enterprise sector is unpaid family members, accounting by itself for 37 percent of all household enterprise employment. Own-account workers—people working alone for themselves—represent another 34 percent of all household enterprise employment. Thus, own-account workers and unpaid family members together account for more than 70 percent of all employment in household enterprises. The next largest category, 19.5 percent of all household enterprise workers, consists of employees working for someone else. Employers, those who are running household enterprises that include paid employees, represent only 3 percent of household enterprise employment.

Costs of Operating Household Enterprises

The two largest categories of costs are the purchasing of goods that are resold—i.e. inventory purchases—and raw materials. Across sectors, wages, and salaries are not nearly as large a cost element as are inventories and raw materials, accounting, on average, for only 5.7 percent of total costs. There are large disparities in the relative size of the wage/salary bill when we move from considering informal to formal enterprises. With informal enterprises, wages and salaries account for only 4.8 percent of total costs, while, with formal household enterprises, wages and salaries rise to almost 14 percent of total costs.

One other important set of figures is the disparity between informal and formal enterprises in terms of the proportions they pay for licenses and taxes. Informal firms are paying an average of 3.8 percent of their total costs in licenses and taxes, while formal enterprises pay 8.5 percent. Thus, informal firms would have to increase their licenses and tax obligations quite significantly in order to operate as formal enterprises and receive the benefits from being a formal sector firm. Observing this large cost differential between informal and formal enterprises raises an obvious policy-related point: what are the benefits that would accrue to informal firms from joining the formal sector? Unless there are clear and significant benefits for firms in the formal sector, it will be to their obvious advantage to remain informal and face significantly lower costs in terms of licensing and taxes.

Sources of Start-Up Credit

The great majority of non-agricultural household enterprises rely on either their own savings or funds from family members to provide the initial financing for their businesses. Moreover, the differences between informal and formal enterprises are not large in this case. Overall, 52.3 percent of all household enterprises rely on their own savings, and another 21.8 percent rely on family gifts or loans. Savings and Credit Co-operatives (SACCOs) provide start-up funds to only 3.2 percent of household enterprises. The formal commercial banks appear to play almost no role whatsoever in helping household enterprises to begin operations.

Earnings from Household Enterprises

In Chapter 2, we review earnings figures for individuals in the labor force. In this chapter, we consider earnings from the perspective of the household enterprises as entities, as opposed to the people who are working in these enterprises, or other types of enterprises, in Kenya.

The median level of monthly earnings for all non-agricultural household enterprises is Ksh 2,370. This figure is 50 percent above the overall rural poverty line, and is 19 percent below the overall urban poverty line. What makes this low figure especially notable is that, as we saw, the largest single category of workers within household enterprises is "unpaid family members." This means that, in a significant number of household enterprises, the overall earnings in the range of Ksh 2,400 per month is meant to supply a livelihood for more than one person working at the enterprise. Beyond these median earnings figures, there are also significant differences in earnings based on different factors. Earnings for informal sector firms are consistently lower than those for formal sector firms.

In general, we find that most household enterprises in Kenya are informal and very small scale. The earnings that these firms receive, on average, are very low—not sufficient, on average, to maintain the people working in them above the official poverty line. If household enterprises are formal and relatively large in size, their earnings are dramatically higher. However, it is obviously a great challenge for household enterprises to grow beyond operating as a small-scale firm since these firms have almost no access to credit. Moreover, the very large number of household enterprises in operations means that competition among them is necessarily strong.

Factors Influencing Household Enterprise Earnings

As part of our use of the 2005–06 KIBHS data set, we have conducted a formal statistical analysis of the factors that influence the levels of earnings for non-agricultural household enterprises. The key findings are as follows:

1. As noted at the outset of this chapter, household enterprises in Kenya sell almost exclusively within the domestic Kenyan market. But, within this framework, the enterprises that are able to sell to businesses within Kenya have higher earnings than the enterprises that are able to sell only to other households or to individuals on the streets. Therefore, forming linkages

among household enterprises and other domestic businesses in Kenya should raise average earnings of household enterprises.

2.   If an enterprise obtains start-up capital from a SACCO, this has a large and significant positive impact on earnings. This finding is especially important, given that, as we have observed above, less than 4 percent of household enterprises are currently receiving start-up credit from SACCOs.

3.   If a household enterprise is involved in contingent or seasonal activities—that is, it operates for only a fraction of the year—this has a significant negative impact on the enterprise's average monthly earnings.

4.   The educational level attained by the manager/owner of a household enterprise will have a significant positive impact on earnings.

5.   Women operating household enterprises on their own earn less than men in equivalent situations. This suggests that gender biases exist in the operations of household enterprises.

Considerations for Policy Proposals

Based on the findings we report in this chapter, three separate factors would seem crucial as considerations for policy:

1.   Raising productivity and expanding the domestic market in general, but also shaping policies so that household enterprises specifically will benefit from these overall economic gains.

2.   Improving access to credit for household enterprises. From the evidence we have presented, the level of involvement by the SACCOs, to say nothing of commercial banks, can be improved by a great amount.

3.   Reducing the overall number of people relying on informal household enterprises, so as to reduce competition among them that keeps earnings below the poverty level. To do this will also mean increasing opportunities for formal sector employment.

LABOR COSTS, LABOR MARKET INSTITUTIONS, AND EMPLOYMENT EXPANSION

An explanation that economists frequently make as a cause of inadequate employment growth is that excessive labor costs are discouraging businesses from hiring more workers. This perspective is prominent, for example, in the Concept Note written by the World Bank as a preliminary document to its ongoing *Jobs in Kenya* study (2005a).

There are four possible ways in which the costs to businesses of hiring workers could fall: 1) workers receive lower overall compensation, including wages and benefits; 2) the industrial relations system and labor market regulations—

including laws and regulations regarding workers' rights to organize, conflict resolution, and hiring and firing—operate with more flexibility for business; 3) workers perform their workplace operations at a higher level of productivity; or 4) the government absorbs some portion of the costs of hiring workers.

In the World Bank's preliminary Concept Note, the focus appears to be on the first two ways to reduce business costs, i.e. to lower wages and benefits for workers and to increase the flexibility of the Kenyan formal labor market. We focus on these two considerations in this section of our study. But we also provide some brief discussion in this section on raising productivity and government employment subsidies—i.e. using government subsidies as a way of reducing labor costs for business. We then also take up these latter two concerns in more depth later in the study.

Lowering Formal Sector Wages to Increase Employment

To evaluate the net welfare effects of reducing wages in Kenya's formal economy, we need to begin by estimating how many new formal sector jobs are likely to be created through reducing wages. Once we have such an estimate, we can then assess the net benefits of such wage cuts. Let us assume for the purposes of this exercise that our aim is to increase private modern employment by 25 percent. From the 2005–06 KIHBS survey data, this would mean increasing employment in this sector by about 190,000 jobs, from 770,000 to 960,000 million jobs.

Economists estimate the relationship between relative changes in wage rates and employment levels through calculating a "wage elasticity of employment." Wage elasticities measure by how much we would expect employment to rise as a result of wage levels going down. We work with an elasticity of -0.6 for Kenya, which means that if wages were to fall by 10 percent, employment would rise by 6 percent. This means that to generate an additional 190,000 private sector formal economy jobs strictly through a strategy of wage-cutting, wages in the formal sector would have to fall by about 42 percent.

The median monthly wage level in the modern private sector as of 2005–06 was roughly Ksh 6,160. The breakdown between the urban and rural regions is an urban median wage of Ksh 9,000 per month, and a rural median wage of Ksh 4,800. This means that, for the urban formal sector, the median monthly wage would have to fall to Ksh 5,220. For the rural formal sector, the median monthly wage would have to fall to Ksh 2,784.

This means that, to generate an additional 25 percent increase in these jobs, the average monthly wage in the sector would have to fall to about Ksh 4,100. How significant would this wage cut be for workers and their families? According to our calculations, cutting an average worker's monthly wage to Ksh 4,100 would mean that the worker and his/her family income would fall to roughly 15 percent below the poverty line.

What would be the overall effects of this combination of wage cuts in the range of 40 percent for existing formal sector workers, with an expansion of about 190,000 jobs in the formal sector at the new, lower wage level? We calculate the net effect of the wage-cutting scenario—including all the workers receiving either wage cuts or wage increases and the additional people who live off of these workers' incomes—would be as follows:

1. Nearly 1.7 million Kenyans would see their living standard fall sharply. This would include both the 770,000 workers and the roughly 900,000 additional people who live off of the wages of these workers. These 1.7 million people would see their income levels fall, on average, to between 10 percent and 23 percent below their respective urban or rural poverty lines.

2. About 400,000 Kenyans would experience a large increase in income. As above, this would include both the 190,000 workers newly hired into higher-paying formal sector jobs and the roughly 210,000 people who live off of the income of these workers. Despite these people enjoying rising incomes, they would, on average, also still be living between 10 and 23 percent below their respective urban or rural poverty lines.

Beyond these immediate effects, the fact that 1.7 million people would experience a declining living standard will of course generate social unrest. This, in turn will create an unstable atmosphere for private investors. The decline in private investment will in turn lead to a contraction in job opportunities.

Industrial Relations and Labor Market Rigidities

To what extent has the expansion of decent employment opportunities in Kenya possibly been hindered by the country's system of industrial relations, including regulations concerning hiring, hours, and firing; the extent and strength of union power in labor markets; and minimum wage standards? The World Bank's *Jobs in Kenya: Concept Note* (2005a) suggests that these factors may be playing an important role in holding back employment growth in the private formal sector. Yet the evidence informing these policy concerns is mixed, including data from the World Bank's own studies.

The most extensive set of evidence that relates to these issues comes from the World Bank's 2005 study, "Labor Institutions, Labor-Management Relations, and Social Dialogue in Africa," by Alby et al. This study presents results from surveys of businesses throughout Africa, and also offers comparative statistics from other regions of the world.

Alby et al. report findings on the views of business owners and managers on "difficulty of hiring," "rigidity of hours," and "difficulty of firing," as well as broader evidence on the costs of hiring and firing procedures. According to some of their findings, Kenya ranks very low in terms of the rigidity of employment conditions, at least as perceived by the country's business owners and managers. However, by other measures, Kenya ranks higher in terms of the costs associated with hiring and firing procedures. Overall then, the findings are mixed in terms of Kenya's rankings relative to other countries in the sample.

However, if we focus only on the results where Kenya comes out poorly in the rankings, the survey findings still do not support a conclusion that labor market rigidities in Kenya operate as significant barriers to employment expansion. Thus, even the figures where Kenya comes out least favorably—that is, in the findings on the number of firms citing layoffs and labor market regulations as significant obstacles—we still see only 21–22 percent of business owners citing this as a problem. This means that close to 80 percent of firm owners/managers do not see labor market regulations as a significant problem.

Thus, considering the overall weight of evidence presented by the Alby et al. study, and evaluating these findings in light of the propensity for some upward bias that is inherent in surveying business owners and managers on these questions, it is reasonable to conclude that most business representatives in Kenya consider labor market regulations around hiring, firing, and hours to be relatively minor barriers to expansion, if they are barriers at all.

The Impact of Labor Unions

The World Bank's Concept Note suggests that labor unions may be operating as a significant source of labor market rigidities in Kenya. But the evidence suggests that, as with the regulations on hiring, firing, and hours, this is unlikely to be a significant barrier to the expansion of decent employment. If for no other reason, this is because unions represent a small and diminishing portion of Kenya's labor force. The same 2005 World Bank study by Alby et al. reports that union membership in Kenya fell from 700,000 in 1985 to 436,036 in 2000, a decline of 38 percent.

The decline in union membership since the mid-1980s suggests that, to the extent that unions may have the capacity to operate as a rigidity in Kenya's formal labor market, the disruptive force of this rigidity should clearly have diminished sharply, not increased, since the mid-1980s. Consistent with this, the Alby et al. study reports that in 2003, 93.6 percent of firms surveyed in Kenya reported losing zero work days due to strikes and labor unrest.

The 2005–06 KIHBS provides some more recent figures on the extent of unionization in Kenya. We observe from this survey data that 1) membership in unions and welfare associations are concentrated in Kenya's formal public sector; 2) it is likely that about 70 percent of public sector employees are unionized, with the largest grouping being teachers and civil servants below the senior level;

and 3) union membership in the private formal sector is probably around 20 percent of total employment in that sector.

A careful 2005 econometric study by Manda, Bigsten and Mwabu concludes that Kenyan unions do help formal sector workers obtain a wage premium in addition to getting protection from excessively long hours of work and from arbitrary job loss. At the same time, they find that elite-level workers in Kenya do not join unions, and thus, the gains generated by unions are received primarily by less-skilled production level workers.

As a general matter, relatively high rates of unionization do not necessarily serve as a barrier to expanding decent employment opportunities in Kenya or promoting the country's overall economic progress. Indeed, in 1995, the World Bank's own *World Development Report* noted that it is "possible to identify the conditions and policies under which free trade unions can advance rather than impede development." Following up on this, a more recent World Bank publication of 2003, *Unions and Collective Bargaining*, recognized that "high unionization rates lead to lower inequality of earnings and can improve economic performance in the form of lower unemployment and inflation, higher productivity and speedier adjustment to shocks."

Minimum Wage Laws

Kenya operates with a wide array of minimum wage orders that apply to different sectors, regions of the country, and job categories. In all, there are 45 separate minimum wage standards. However, in August 2007 the Minister of Labour, Dr. Newton Kulundu, announced that the government was planning to eliminate minimum wage standards.

What has been the impact of minimum wage standards on the actual wage levels paid in the formal private sector? We can obtain a sense of this by examining the data we report in Chapter 4 on actual wage levels as of 2005–06 relative to the statutory minimum wage standards. From these figures, we see that for workers paid hourly, about 73 percent are paid below the lowest average figure for the statutory minimum wage. Considering workers paid either on a daily or monthly basis—who constitute the overwhelming majority of paid employees—between 43 and 50 percent of private formal sector workers are earning wages below the lower-range average for the statutory minimum wage. These findings suggest that, as of 2005–06, the minimum wage laws are exerting little influence in actual wage-setting within the formal private sector.

Given their current ineffectiveness in setting actual wage floors, should the minimum wage laws be repealed, as is currently being proposed by the Labour Minister? In fact, the 2005 minimum wage laws have been serving a useful function in at least defining a decent standard that would enable working people and their families to live above the poverty line. Thus, to conclude that the minimum wage should be eliminated or significantly reduced from its current levels is to therefore also conclude that the Kenyan economy is unable to pay even those workers with jobs in the formal private sector a wage that will keep them and their families out of poverty. Rather than seek to eliminate or weaken a minimally decent wage standard in an effort to promote employment growth, it would seem preferable, at least as an initial endeavor, to pursue alternative policy approaches for expanding decent employment, including raising productivity, increasing access to credit, improving marketing capacity, and maintaining a more competitive exchange rate. At the same time, labor market conditions in Kenya would probably benefit from a simplification of the elaborate system of minimum wage standards that are presently in place.

THE RURAL SECTOR: INSTITUTIONAL REFORM FOR DEVELOPMENT

Any attempt at significantly improving employment opportunities and reducing poverty in Kenya cannot help but focus on the role of the rural population and the agricultural sector. Agriculture is of course a foundation of the Kenyan economy. Moreover, in the last two years, there seems to have been a clear upswing in agricultural production, accompanying the economy's general growth upswing. According to the government's *2006 Economic Survey*, the overall economy grew at 5.4 percent in 2005 while agriculture grew at 6.7 percent (Government of Kenya 2006c). This is in sharp contrast to the long-term stagnation and decline in agricultural productivity since the early 1980s. Will the agricultural sector be able to sustain its relatively positive growth of the past two years? In Chapter 5, we consider specific conditions that prevail with Kenya's major crops, including tea and coffee, horticulture, maize and wheat, millet and sorghum, sugarcane and rice. We also discuss the livestock sector. These detailed discussions form the basis for our policy recommendations aimed at raising productivity and international competitiveness in the agricultural sector. The seven themes that we develop out of our discussions on the various agricultural sectors are these:

1. *Learning from Successes.* Kenya has experienced successes in agricultural in a number of important areas. In terms of sectors, tea, horticulture, and wheat stand out. The sugarcane producer Mumias is an important success story. From these successes we can extract a number of valuable lessons that may be useful in thinking about agricultural policy. First, improvements have occurred when there is proper infrastructure and support for farmers or where farmers have sufficient capital to overcome structural impediments. Second, in some sectors it is possible for individual farmers or firms to exploit returns to scale to overcome impediments. This has been true, for example, in the

flower sector among farmers who are sufficiently capitalized. Among smallholders, for this to occur, either a collective farmer organization such as the Kenyan Tea Development Authority or a firm such as Mumias has to harness the returns to scale. But nurturing additional organizations of this type will require some form of government subsidy or participation.

2. *Adaptation rather than Replication of Past Successes.* Kenya's agricultural sector was broadly successful from independence until about 1980. But this doesn't mean that simply recreating the institutional environment or policies of the early independence years will be adequate for recreating a positive agricultural growth path. Many of the main supporting institutions, including the Kenya Meat Commission and the Kenya Cooperative Creameries, were formed in the colonial era and structured to support big farmers. These institutions did not change substantially after independence. And while it is true that many of the reforms that were pursued in the 1980s and 1990s were poorly conceived, planned or implemented, or pushed by an overtly political objective, some of them were guided by a positive agenda of addressing the previous bias toward large-scale producers. The aim of policy now should be to combine the management successes of the early independence years with a continued effort to promote the well-being of smallholders.

3. *Understanding Resources and Capabilities of Smallholders.* Most of Kenya's rural population has little in terms of resources or education. These are the farmers who need to become small commercial producers in order for poverty to drop significantly in the short- to medium-term in the rural areas. In order to service these farmers better it is important for policymakers to recognize their capabilities and needs. The key point here is that most smallholders have had very limited formal schooling. The lack of formal education puts smallholders at a distinct disadvantage in comparison to other participants in agricultural markets. Husbands, Pinckney, and Konyaugoh (1996) estimated that returns to primary education for rural agricultural households were between 8 to 12 percent per year. Assuring access to education for poor households would thus raise their agricultural productivity tremendously.

4. *Designing Effective Extension Services for Smallholders.* The need for increased educational opportunities becomes clear in terms of improving the access to markets of smallholders. There is certainly a need for improvements in market access, as many observers in government and among donor agencies emphasize. At the same time, it is equally important to recognize that taking full advantage of the market opportunities that exist (for example, to export horticultural produce) requires a fair amount of human capital. In fact one of the reasons given for the failure of rural cooperatives is the low literacy of their members (Government of Kenya 2004). This point be-

comes relevant also in terms of designing improvements in extension services. For example, a policy that aims to privatize extension is not likely to succeed with poor smallholders because they lack both the physical and human capital to make effective use of a private, demand-driven, extension service. Demand-driven extension works best for medium-scale and larger farmers who have specific problems to be solved (Schwartz 1994). Poor farmers tend to have larger problems that need more than a single visit and require systematic training.

5. *Returns to Scale and Agricultural Cooperatives.* The traditional collective organization for Kenyan farmers, both large and small, has been cooperatives. While the early cooperatives catered mainly to larger farmers in the 1950s and immediately after independence, the government encouraged smallholders to organize themselves into cooperatives for marketing and the purchase of inputs. By 2005 there were over 1.1 million members of 4,304 agricultural cooperatives. Cooperatives in Kenya have been closely associated with coffee farmers, with close to 50 percent of all members of an agricultural cooperative belonging to a coffee society. Both the early successes and more recent failures of the coffee cooperatives have been taken to be representative of the experiences with cooperatives and their prospects for the future. This is particularly true with respect to the failures of the coffee cooperatives.

Two crucial changes need to occur for cooperatives to play a successful role in agricultural development. The first is to create an effective regulatory body overseeing the operations of cooperatives and similar institutions. The second is increased public funding, probably through the Ministry of Cooperatives, to support the government's regulatory efforts, and to give positive guidance and support to these institutions. The 1997 Cooperative Act enabled farmers to obtain complete control over cooperatives, without any government regulatory oversight. It was the subsequent absence of any effective regulatory structure that encouraged mismanagement of the cooperatives, and the collapse of the coffee cooperatives.

6. *Infrastructure Improvements.* We discuss in Chapter 6 some proposals for improving Kenya's road and water infrastructure. Beyond these basic needs, there are also lessons to be learned from industries that have managed to absorb the increased costs imposed by poor infrastructure—particularly in terms of transportation and energy supplies—by taking advantage of returns to scale. This is particularly evident within the flower industry and KTDA. KTDA maintains a fleet of trucks that guarantees access to markets for its members, accepting that the costs of this measure are high. In the short term, one approach to dealing with the transportation problem and increasing market access for small farmers could be the organization of transport collectives. These cooperatives could be responsible for trans-

porting smallholder crops to major urban areas and to bring back to the farmers the major inputs—seed, fertilizer, pesticides—which are generally more available and cheaper in the major urban areas.

7. *Cost of Capital and Access to Credit.* The cost and access to capital has long been a problem for smallholders. Apart from the high cost and difficulty of obtaining credit in the past there has been a bias against smallholders in terms of the amount and the duration of loan. For example, between 1980 and 1986, the most recent period for which data are available, large farmers received most of their loans with relatively long-term maturities of over seven years as long-term loans. By contrast, smallholders virtually never received long-term loans. One approach out of this situation is to dramatically increase the provision of affordable credit through rural-based SACCOs and other microfinance enterprises, a topic that we consider at some length below.

INVESTING IN ROADS AND WATER INFRASTRUCTURE

Infrastructure investments are central for raising productivity and thereby people's incomes. Improving the country's infrastructure is equally important in terms of promoting trade competitiveness. Finally, increased public spending in these areas can serve as a major source of job growth within the country's formal economy, as has traditionally been the case in Kenya as well as many other countries.

Recognizing the centrality of investing in the country's infrastructure, the 2006 MTBSP commits to increasing the share of government resources going to physical expenditures from 19.2 percent in 2005–06 to 21.6 percent in 2008–09. The MTBSP states its priority areas as being the expansion and improved maintenance of road networks and other public works. It has also prioritized increasing access to water resources, along with the provision of affordable energy. This increased level of spending for the country's infrastructure is certainly needed. However, we believe that these expenditure commitments need to increase significantly beyond even these enhanced projected levels. To illustrate this point, in Chapter 6 we focus on the areas of transport and water infrastructure because these are the two most urgent areas of need.

Roads

Road transportation accounts for roughly 80 percent of all transport in Kenya. It is also the form of transportation with the most straightforward fiscal implications. The impact of improvements in the rural road infrastructure is potentially large.

Kenya currently has 28,500 km of national and urban roads and an additional 150,000 of rural (mostly dirt or gravel) roads. According to the KRB, a 2002 survey found that approximately one-third of Kenya's national and urban roads are in poor repair. The estimated cost of rehabilitating all these poor roads is Ksh 228 billion. Suppose that we set a goal of rehabilitating all of these poor quality roads within 12 years. The real annual cost (not factoring in inflation or the cost of other repair activities) would be roughly Ksh 19 billion per year—i.e. approximately twice the current budget of the KRB. This suggests that, despite the significant budget reprioritization to support road infrastructure, Kenya's roads will remain substandard in the foreseeable future unless additional resources are made available.

Lack of financial resources is only one of two basic problems that Kenya must overcome if it is going to significantly improve its transportation infrastructure. The other, equally serious concern, is the government's capacity to complete projects that already have received adequate funding allocations, with the funds at the Treasury, waiting to be spent. The single largest budgetary item here is for road maintenance. For 2004–05, Ksh 8.6 billion was allocated for maintenance, and virtually all of these funds were spent. The country's road maintenance program is evidently operating at a high level of efficiency. However, road construction programs, as well as the smaller planning and design programs, were unable to spend a high proportion of their allocations.

A few important points emerge from these figures. The first is that, because the maintenance program is operating so much more effectively than the other programs, it should therefore continue to receive the largest share of budgetary allocations. Second, in order to improve efficiency in the road building areas, the successes in the road maintenance program should be examined carefully for lessons that may be applicable to the construction projects. Finally, and related, the government needs to initiate measures to raise productivity linked to the completion of new road projects. Such measures could be regarded as one significant component of an overall program to "mainstream productivity" in all areas of the country's economic management.

Water

Kenya is a water-scarce country. Renewable freshwater endowments currently stand at 600–700 m^3 per person per year. A country is categorized as "water scarce" if it has less than 1,000 m^3 per capita in renewable freshwater resources. In addition, water resources are unequally distributed across geographical regions in Kenya. The arid and semi-arid lands, which cover a large part of the land surface in northern Kenya, are particularly vulnerable due to a lack of water security. Water insecurity was the single greatest problem associated with the recent famine in 2005–06.

Currently, Kenya has irrigation infrastructure in place to service about 105,000 hectares of agricultural land. This is less than one fifth of the estimated full irrigation potential of the country—about 540,000 hectares. The cost of expanding irrigation infrastructure to meet the country's full potential is high—involving physical infrastructure, compensation for the employees working on these projects, and purchase of land for the construction of irrigation facilities.

In addition to the deficiencies in the irrigation system, water storage facilities are also in poor condition in Kenya. Excluding hydroelectric facilities, the per capita water storage capacity in Kenya stood at just 4.3 m^3 per person in 1999. In 1969, three decades earlier, the estimated water storage capacity was three times higher, at 11.4 m^3. This 1969 level of storage capacity was itself low. But the fact that capacity has diminished in absolute terms since 1969 is a major matter of concern.

To raise the country above the threshold for water security, another 350 m^3 in water storage capacity would be needed. Financing an increase in water storage at this level would cost an additional Ksh 37.5 billion per year for 30 years, equal to about 2.5 percent of GDP. We conduct a costing exercise in which we allow for a budget at roughly this level, which would mean increasing the already planned budget by about Ksh 20 billion per year. Of course, the issue of whether the funds will be utilized efficiently cannot be assumed away. As with the road construction projects, the successful completion of projects that have already received their funding allocation may be at least as much, if not more, of a problem than receiving the budgetary allocation itself. Actual spending falls short of budgeted spending in a number of areas. However, the efficiency of delivery varies from one category of water infrastructure to the next. For example, planned and actual expenditures are reasonably well matched for the construction and rehabilitation of dams, pans, and dykes and flood control projects.

Employment Effects of Expanding Roads and Water Infrastructure Spending

We conduct an exercise in which we assume that all the road and water projects operate at a budgetary allocation as we have described in the foregoing discussions—i.e at a funding level of roughly Ksh 40 billion greater than the current allocation levels projected through 2008-09 in the MTBSP. What would be the impact of this increased level of spending in terms of employment within the country? According to our estimate, this amount of increased spending will directly produce 333,000 jobs, assuming that workers on these projects receive an average wage rate of Ksh 5,000 per month. In addition, we roughly estimate that another 20,000 jobs in wage employment will be indirectly generated through multiplier effects—i.e. the increase in employment that comes from the 333,000 newly employed workers spending their wage income in Kenya's economy.

MONETARY POLICY, INFLATION CONTROL AND INTEREST RATES

The government's *Economic Recovery Strategy for Wealth and Employment Creation* (Government of Kenya 2003c) states that its focus will be on four goals:

1. Contain inflation to below 5.0 percent;
2. Maintain a competitive exchange rate consistent with an export-driven economic recovery;
3. Maintain an interest rate structure that promotes financial savings and ensures efficient allocation of the same; and
4. Ensure adequate growth in credit to the private sector.

These are all important goals that are worthy in their own right. At the same time, in our view, this list of goals raises a set of serious concerns that require careful attention. Our concerns, as described in Chapter 7, are as follows:

1. Containing inflation below 5.0 percent could operate as a significant obstacle to promoting economic growth, employment expansion, and poverty reduction.
2. Maintaining a competitive exchange rate and promoting export growth is highly desirable. However, the economy of Kenya at present is heavily dependent on imports in the areas of energy products, chemicals, equipment, and machinery. Thus, the goal of promoting exports must be advanced within the framework of also reducing import-dependency in these areas.
3. Promoting an efficient allocation of financial savings and ensuring an adequate growth in credit to the private sector are crucial to the country's growth prospects. But it is not likely that monetary policy by itself can reconcile these two goals, especially in the context of also attempting to maintain inflation below 5.0 percent. Other policy interventions will be needed to encourage an efficient allocation of credit to the private sector.

We address each of these issues in this and the following chapters. In Chapter 7, we focus on inflation control and the operating procedures for monetary policy. In Chapter 8 we consider the exchange rate and trade, and in Chapter 9, we propose ways to restructure the financial system to promote growth and employment expansion.

Inflation Control and Economic Growth

We first review some relevant literature on the relationship between inflation and growth. We then consider the evidence in Kenya that relates the effects of supply shocks—in particular large spikes in the prices of energy, food, and transportation—on overall inflation in the country. We finally discuss alternatives to tight monetary policy as an approach to inflation control.

What is the relationship between inflation and growth? Answers to this question vary widely in the professional literature. Some of the most influential recent studies were those produced by the late Michael Bruno, who was Chief Economist at the World Bank at the time he conducted his studies.

Considering the findings from all the studies reviewed in this chapter, it is clear that no consensus exists on the relationship between inflation and economic growth. At the same time, a few basic conclusions from these various studies that are relevant for the Kenyan case do seem warranted. One major conclusion is that regardless as to whether researchers observe a negative growth/inflation relationship emerging in the low or high double-digit range for developing countries, only one study found a clear negative relationship between growth and *single-digit* inflation specifically for the developing countries. This suggests that for Kenya, setting an inflation target below 5.0 percent is not likely to offer benefits in terms of the economy's growth performance. If Kenya chooses to follow the low-end finding within the professional literature on the inflation/growth trade-off, that would still suggest an inflation target in the range of 8–9 percent.

Supply Shocks and Kenyan Inflation Control

Supply-side shocks have a major impact on inflationary dynamics in Kenya. As one important example, food price inflation, due to droughts or other breakdowns in the country's food production, raises the country's overall inflation rate and lowers living standards, particularly of poorer households. Rapid increases in global oil prices have similar effects on the Kenyan economy. Tightening monetary policy in response to such events in order to maintain low inflation rates runs the risks of worsening the economic impact of these shocks. As such, it is important to try to observe how a shock to one component of the Consumer Price Index affects other components. For example, how does a spike in food or energy prices affect other prices in the economy? Are these effects transitory or long-lived?

To investigate these questions, we estimated a vector autoregression (VAR) model that includes the ten components of the Kenyan CPI as variables. Overall, the findings from our VAR model suggest the following policy implications:

1. Food price shocks do have a major direct impact on overall "headline" inflation in the short run. And because food prices constitute over 50 percent of the overall CPI basket, these effects can impose serious hardships, especially for lower-income households. At the same time, these effects are tran-

sitory. The most effective approach would be for the government to utilize its existing grain storage facilities throughout the country to provide an effective buffer stock of food that is readily accessible.

2. Transportation and communication price shocks—which, according to the Kenyan CPI, includes petrol, diesel, car service, insurance, tax fares, matatu fares, postage, and phone calls—have systemic effects on other prices in the Kenyan economy, even though they constitute only 5.7 percent of the overall CPI. These prices are, of course, heavily affected by global oil prices. The most direct channel is through the petrol and diesel price components. But car service, taxi fares, bus fares, and matatu fares will also be affected by an oil shock. In the short term, the most effective means of counteracting the effect of global oil price shocks would be for the government to quickly increase its subsidy for public transportation, including bus and matatu fares. Over the longer term, investments in the country's transportation infrastructure, especially its roads system, will lower the overall share of transportation costs in the CPI, and thereby mitigate the effects on the overall CPI of a short-term oil price shock.

3. Energy price shocks—including here, electricity, water, paraffin, cooking gas, and charcoal prices—also have a sustained, systemic impact on inflation in Kenya. As with the transportation and communications component of the CPI, the only way that the government can counteract the effects of a global oil price spike would be to subsidize the prices of these components of the CPI in the short run. This would short-circuit the long-lasting effects of these price increases on the overall CPI.

Additional Inflation Control Tools

The weight of the professional literature suggests that, as Kenya continues to advance an aggressive program of employment expansion, it should not weaken the program as long as inflation remains moderate. But what happens if inflation accumulates momentum, such that a rise to a 10 percent inflation rate leads to still greater inflationary pressures? Should Kenya then revert to stringent growth in the money supply as a means of raising interest rates? In fact, other policy tools are available for their use, through which Kenya could contain inflation within a moderate range, without having to rely on high interest rates as its primary control mechanism.

One tool would be to pursue so-called "incomes policies." Incomes policies have been developed in various specific ways, but the basic idea is straightforward: that wage and price increases are negotiated on an economy-wide basis between labor and business in the formal economy. The most basic critique of incomes policies is that, in order for the approach to have any chance of success, it is necessary that a country operate with a high level of organization among workers, and that there be some reasonable degree of common ground between workers and business. Otherwise, there will be no realistic prospect for economy-wide bargaining to yield results that will be honored widely. In the case of Kenya, the establishment of the Productivity Centre offers a real possibility that incomes policies could be broadly agreed upon as a tool for dampening inflationary pressures before they reach dangerous levels.

Retargeting Monetary Policy

We focus here on three concerns: 1) the specific procedures and policy tools being used in Kenya; 2) how some of these procedures may contribute to worsening cyclical fluctuations rather than dampening them; and 3) how the focus on controlling inflation may contribute to excessively high interest rates. Based on our discussions of these points, we then propose five basic changes in the conduct of monetary policy in Kenya. These are:

1. *Use a core short-term real interest rate as an intermediate monetary target.* The Central Bank of Kenya should move away from targeting the growth rates of monetary aggregates. The Bank has little direct control over monetary aggregates and the links between monetary growth and macroeconomic performance are too weak to form the basis of a development-oriented monetary policy. Targeting real interest rates will have a more direct influence over critically important macroeconomic prices.

2. *Remove the anti-growth bias in monetary policy.* This involves a shift in the ways in which monetary policy is conducted. Specifically, monetary policy should be prepared to (a) provide economic stimulus during a contraction and (b) distinguish between demand–pull and cost–push inflation. The effectiveness of a counter-cyclical monetary policy will be enhanced if financial reforms insure that monetary policy has a direct impact on real economic performance.

3. *Diversify the toolkit for addressing inflation in Kenya.* Using monetary policy alone may be a costly way of reducing inflation in Kenya. This is particularly likely to be true when inflation is the result of supply-side shocks. Multiple tools are needed to simultaneously control inflation and support a poverty-reducing development agenda. Monetary policy should not be expected to operate effectively on its own.

4. *Institute reforms to the financial sector to channel credit to socially productive uses.* The Kenyan banking sector has substantial excess capacity that could be mobilized to facilitate the attainment of development objectives, such as employment creation, increasing productivity enhancing investments, and supporting poverty reduction. However, at present, the financial structure fails to channel sufficient credit to socially productive uses.

EXCHANGE RATE POLICY AND FOREIGN TRADE

Over the past several decades, Kenya has moved towards increasingly market-determined trade and exchange rate regimes. The import-substitution strategy of the 1960s and 1970s, with its protectionist measures to encourage domestic production, has been gradually replaced by a stronger export orientation, with reductions in tariffs and quantitative restrictions. At the same time, Kenya's fixed exchange rate regime was replaced by a crawling peg which, in turn, was eventually replaced by a floating regime. Despite an expansion of trade in the early 1990s, these reforms have not been successful in addressing Kenya's structural problems, including sustained trade and current account deficits. In addition, Kenya's productive structure has remained relatively unchanged throughout this period, apart from a few significant developments, including the growth of horticultural exports and the expansion of trade among other African countries. Moreover, trade liberalization appears to have had a net negative impact on employment opportunities, with important implications for poverty reduction.

The evidence suggests that, after the shift to a market-determined rate, the shilling has recently become overvalued. This runs contrary to the predictions of the proponents of non-intervention in the foreign exchange market. Although overvaluation may make imported inputs cheaper and could reduce inflation, it has had an adverse effect on exports. While the precise degree of overvaluation is difficult to assess, the analysis presented here suggests that impact of overvaluation has not yet been severe. However, the degree of overvaluation may be stronger with respect to Kenya's major trading partners in Africa. This could be a barrier preventing Kenya from capturing the benefits of greater regional trade integration.

There are reasons to think that overvaluation may be a bigger concern in the future. Inflows of capital and remittances into Kenya appear to have increased recently, including inflows of so-called "hot money." In addition, the world boom in commodity prices may produce so-called "Dutch disease" effects, in which the shilling becomes increasingly overvalued with negative consequences for the domestic economy. The data presented here suggests that the shilling was relatively more competitive when Kenya was targeting its real exchange rate using a managed regime, such as a crawling peg.

Analysis of the determinants of export performance and import penetration indicate that exports tend to respond more strongly to changes in prices as opposed to changes in incomes within the economies of Kenya's main trading partners. The reverse holds true for imports. Kenya's imports rise and fall sharply along with increases and declines in Kenya's own national income. However, price increases in imported products such as oil do little to reduce the demand for oil imports. Therefore, managing the real exchange rate through active policy interventions may be important for promoting new and more diverse types of exports. However, exchange rates appear to have less of an impact on imports. This raises the question of how Kenya's excessive dependence on imported inputs and capital goods could be reduced. Targeted policies such as the credit allocation schemes discussed above that actively underwrite the country's industrial expansion could be instrumental in addressing these structural problems.

Three broad directions for policy emerge from the analysis presented in Chapter 8:

1. A targeted exchange rate policy is an important macroeconomic instrument for ensuring the competitiveness of Kenya's exports. It could also provide an appropriate economic environment for diversifying Kenya's export base.
2. Kenya should focus on developing regional trade within the African continent. Kenya remains a net exporter to the continent and should remain competitive in this region as long as the appropriate policies are in place. Moreover, regional growth can have important positive feedback effects in the Kenyan economy.
3. Targeted interventions aimed at promoting industrial expansion are needed in order to generate employment that reduces poverty in a way that is sustainable in the long run.

RESTRUCTURING THE FINANCIAL SYSTEM

As noted above and in Chapter 9, Kenya's financial system already has some important positive features. These include:

1. Kenya's commercial banking system is generally well-developed, and by some standard performance measures, is more focused on lending to the private sector than is the case in other sub-Saharan African countries.
2. Kenya is developing as a regional financial center, with emerging securities markets.
3. Kenya has a widespread system of microfinance institutions (MFIs) already in place and operating. SACCOs are the most important of these institutions. But there are others, both formal and informal, client- and member-based. These include the Kenya Rural Enterprise Program (KREP) bank (formal, client-based) and ROSCAs (Rotating Savings and Credit Associations, which are informal, member-based).

Despite these positive features, the contributions of the financial system to promoting economic growth, employment expansion, and poverty reduction are inadequate. In our view, the main reasons for this inadequate performance are as follows:

1. Interest rate levels are high in *nominal* terms—that is, before making any adjustments for inflation. Rates are not necessarily high in *real* terms—i.e. after subtracting the inflation rate from the nominal interest rate. But knowing whether *real* interest rates are high or low depends on movements in the rate of inflation. This creates considerable uncertainty in the financial system.
2. More significant than problems with interest rate levels are the spreads between deposit and lending rates, which are extremely wide. Again, depending on how one calculates a real interest rate, most deposit rates are actually negative. There is therefore no incentive to save in formal financial markets. These wide interest rate spreads indicate lack of competition in the commercial banking system.
3. The commercial banking system lends more than one-third of its deposit base to the government. This of course reduces the availability of funds for businesses, especially Small and Medium-sized Enterprises (SMEs) and small farmers.
4. More generally, the farming, SME and informal sectors are starved for credit. This is due to the fact that a) commercial banks do not generally lend to these sectors; and b) the SACCOs and other MFIs do not have sufficient resources to provide large-scale funds. Moreover, the largest share of the lending done by the MFIs is for personal household purposes or family emergencies.

Given this combination of positive and negative features of the Kenyan financial system, the solution to the problem, at a fundamental level, seems straightforward: to somehow bring into much closer alliance the formal commercial banking system and the MFIs. In fact, proposals along these lines have been suggested by, among others, the International Monetary Fund in a more general 2005 study on sub-Saharan African finance (Sacerdoti 2005). This idea has also been raised in some previous research papers by Kenyan scholars (e.g. Atieno 2001). What remains is to flesh out a large-scale program that could be realistically implemented on a short-term basis, but that is also capable of enabling a longer-term transformation of the Kenyan financial system.

The proposal that we present in Chapter 9 will create a pool of subsidized credit at a level equal to roughly 20 percent of the current level of private investment in Kenya. These funds would be made available to commercial banks, on condition that they in turn make loans to SACCOs and other MFIs. The MFIs would then be far more capable of making large amounts of loans to small businesses, informal enterprises, and agricultural smallholders. We propose that guarantees be set at 75 percent of the loans that commercial banks make to MFIs. We demonstrate that, even assuming default rates on these guaranteed loans as high as 30 percent, the total accruals on these government contingent liabilities would amount to no more than Ksh 9 billion, i.e., about 5 percent of the fiscal budget.

We also briefly discuss other complementary initiatives in this chapter. These include: reviving cooperative-type institutions to build collateral for SMEs and smallholders; revitalizing the public investment banks, such as the Industrial and Commercial Development Corporation and the Agricultural Development Bank, perhaps as private/public partnerships; utilizing the Postbank as a lender to SMEs, an idea that has already passed the Parliament; and indexing loans so as to shift, at least in part, inflation risk from lenders to borrowers.

FISCAL POLICY: HOW TO PAY FOR NEW PRO-EMPLOYMENT INITIATIVES

As we have seen, we are proposing three major new areas of public expenditure beyond what has already been budgeted—for road and water infrastructure; credit subsidies, especially for small businesses in the formal and informal sectors, and smallholders; and for marketing, cooperatives, extension services, and grain storage. According to our estimates, these three proposals should require expenditures of about Ksh 52 billion per year in 2005 prices, which is equal to about 3 percent of GDP.

For the fiscal year 2007–08, the Treasury has estimated total expenditures at 25.5 percent of GDP and revenues of 20.9 percent of GDP. This implies a deficit of 4.6 percent of GDP, with the projection that this deficit will fall to 4.2 percent of GDP in 2008–09.

How would we propose to finance these existing expenditures? We need to consider this question in the context of two other important considerations: 1) the Treasury is committed to reducing its level of outstanding debt, which now stands at 41.4 percent of GDP, of which 18.2 percent is domestic debt while 23.1 percent is external debt; and 2) the current budget projections assume donor support, in the form of grants and loans, amounting to about 4.3 percent of GDP as of 2007–08 and 2008–09. It is probably not prudent to assume that this figure could or should rise much higher.

Given these considerations, the question that arises is how the Treasury would finance the additional spending programs we are proposing. There are five ways in which additional public revenues could be made available to finance the policies that we are suggesting. They are:

1.   increased collection of taxes from domestic sources;
2.   increased domestic borrowing;
3.   increased external borrowing;
4.   debt relief or complete forgiveness by foreign creditors; and
5.   overseas development assistance providing direct budget support.

In our view, the two most viable sources for generating increased tax revenues in both the short and longer term are the two domestic sources, i.e. higher domestic tax revenues and maintaining, rather than cutting, existing levels of domestic borrowing. For various reasons that we discuss briefly at the end of Chapter 10, the three external sources are all less promising. Still, they each may be useful in generating small supplemental streams of increased government revenue.

The largest potential for increasing tax revenues will be through increased formalization of the economy. The programs we are proposing—in the areas of credit subsidies, export promotion, and infrastructure investments—all aim to increase the share of the formal sector of Kenya's economy. Moreover, over a relatively short time period, the expansion of the formal sector would need to be only modest to fully cover the costs of the programs we have proposed. We show that a relative shift of Kenya's economy in favor of the formal sector from 15 to 20 percent of total employment would itself more than pay for the increased expenditures we are proposing.

Maintaining the government's current level of domestic borrowing would be a viable supplemental measure to finance the additional expenditure. The impact of this increase in government borrowing on the government's long-term fiscal program would be modest. Thus, the Treasury has projected that domestic debt will fall from 18.6 to 16.5 percent of GDP between 2006–07 and 2008–09. The measures we are proposing would entail that domestic debt would remain basically at its current level relative to GDP rather than to fall. Over 1997–2004, the government's average level of domestic debt was 21.8 percent of GDP. This is a relatively modest figure, seen in comparison with a sample of other countries. Our sample includes Swaziland, Rwanda, Burundi, Sierra Leone, Cameroon and Mauritius from sub-Saharan Africa; and, additionally, Honduras, Costa Rica, Malaysia, India, and Sri Lanka. Of course, many of this latter group of countries have experienced successful growth trends in recent years, despite many having higher domestic debt levels than Kenya.

1. Introduction

Following the overarching programmatic commitments of the United Nations Development Programme (UNDP) in the field of economic policy, our project is an effort to outline a pro-poor economic policy framework for Kenya today. We aim to develop a program that will be coherent and workable within the current political and economic framework, while also being effective as a tool for expanding decent employment opportunities, reducing poverty and spreading well-being as broadly as possible.

The principal focus of our study is to develop effective policies for greatly expanding decent employment opportunities in Kenya. The term "decent work" has recently been embraced as an organizing principle by the International Labour Organization (ILO), and we believe the term has resonance for considering the situation in Kenya today.[1] As we use the term in the Kenyan context, decent employment means a work situation that enables a worker to at least maintain him/herself and his/her family above a reasonable poverty line. It also refers to the physical conditions and the rights that workers enjoy at their workplaces. But for our purposes here, we wish to emphasize, in using the term "decent employment," workplace situations that will maintain families above a poverty threshold and offer opportunities for rising living standards over time.

The government of Kenya has committed itself to generating 500,000 new jobs per year at least through 2007. We certainly embrace this goal. At the same time, there are wide disparities in the types of employment opportunities available in Kenya. A high proportion of people working full time at jobs are still unable to support themselves and their families above a poverty line level. This is why it is crucial to not simply focus on employment alone, but the quality of employment.

We are also not simply focused on improving employment opportunities for those around or below the poverty line. Among its sub-Saharan African neighbors, Kenya enjoys a relatively highly educated population. There are also sectors of the Kenyan economy that are dynamic and generating healthy numbers of skilled, middle-class employment and business opportunities. Our proposals aim to expand opportunities for the poor and near-poor in a manner that concurrently creates a wide range of employment and business opportunities. This includes all types of business owners—especially small and medium-sized enterprises—in the informal as well as formal sector, agricultural smallholders, as well as well-trained workers operating at high productivity levels.

Our program is certainly in the spirit of the UN MDGs, as they apply in Kenya. The MDGs are focused on raising standards of individual human welfare. The goals include the eradication of extreme poverty and hunger, universalizing primary education, equalizing opportunities for women, and improving a range of key health outcomes. Our own focus is less on these ends themselves than on the most effective means of accomplishing them.

And here we return to our fundamental concern. Employment is the most important source of income for the overwhelming majority of Kenyans. This fact forges a strong link between decent employment and the MDGs: that deficiency in the availability of decent employment opportunities is the single greatest cause of mass poverty and, correspondingly, that expanding decent employment would be the single most effective means of reducing poverty. Expanding decent employment opportunities will also be the most effective tool for increasing the government's fiscal prospects, since workers with decent formal sector jobs and owners of successful formal sector businesses are also reliable taxpayers. When the base of such taxpayers rises, the government's budgetary commitments for health, education, and other vital goals associated with the MDGs are much more readily able to increase as well.[2]

BASIC ECONOMIC TRENDS

Kenya's overall economic performance has been poor since the early 1980s, after having been generally positive in the first 15 years or so since the country became independent in 1964. We can see this shift in the country's economic trends through examining some basic evidence on GDP per capita, investment as a share of GDP, agricultural value added per worker, the trade balance, and the rise of urbanization. In the next section of this study, we will present more detailed data pertaining to employment and poverty.

In Figure 1.1, we see the movements in the level of per capita income from 1965–2005. As the figure shows, per capita income rose rapidly and consistently from the initial years after independence, when average annual income was about Ksh 28,000 per person in 2005 shillings to 1980, when average annual incomes had risen to about Ksh 46,500, a 66 percent gain in average incomes. However, since the early 1980s, average incomes had basically stopped growing, at least through 2003. In 2004 and 2005, as Figure 1.1 indicates, average incomes did rise at a healthy pace, at an average of about 3 percent per year. Final per capita income statistics for 2006 are not yet available, and thus are not presented in the figure. But the preliminary data show that the roughly 3 percent average annual growth rate did continue. These are certainly positive developments. At the same time, even with this positive trend, average real incomes as of 2005 remain only slightly higher than the level attained in 1980. Certainly a primary goal for eco-

Figure 1.1 Real GDP per Capita in Kenya, 1965–2005 (expressed in 2005 Ksh)

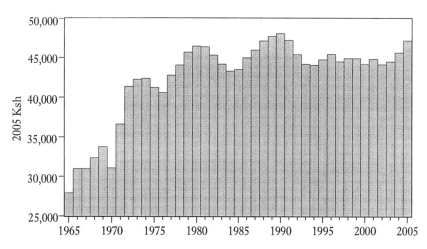

Source: World Bank (2007).

nomic policymakers is to maintain the positive growth momentum of the past three years.

Corresponding with this long-term stagnation of average incomes has been the decline in public and private investment over this same period. We see this in Figure 1.2. At independence, overall investment amounted to about 13 percent of GDP. This figure then rises sharply for the next 14 years, to a peak of nearly 25 percent in 1978. However, investment then begins its long descent through the 1980s and 1990s, reaching as low as 15.4 percent in 1997. As of 2005, there have been some small gains, with the 2005 figure at 18.6 percent of GDP. Still, investment as a share of GDP over the recent period remains at roughly the low level around the time the country became independent.

In Figure 1.3, we can observe a similar pattern in terms of overall agricultural value added per worker, that is, a measure of labor productivity in the agricultural economy. According to the World Bank, as of 2004, the average agricultural laborer in Kenya was creating $326 in value-added (expressed in U.S. dollars for the year 2000). This is 11 percent less than what a similar worker was producing in 1982.

Figure 1.4 shows the trend in Kenya's trade balance. As the figure shows, Kenya has run an annual trade deficit every year since independence, ranging between 3 and 15 percent of the country's GDP on an annual basis. Most significant for our purposes, the deficit has been growing fairly steadily since 1993.

Figure 1.2 Gross Investment as a Percentage of GDP in Kenya, 1965–2005

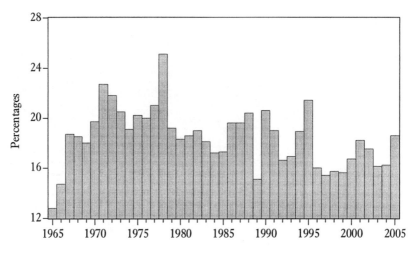

Source: World Bank (2007).

In 1993, the deficit was 5.8 percent of GDP. As of 2005, it had grown to its largest level since independence, of 15.2 percent of GDP. This persistent and growing trade deficit forces policymakers to cover the gap through some combination of capital inflows, foreign aid, and a drawing down of the country's assets. As such, other possible policy initiatives become constrained by the necessity of managing the trade deficit.

These basic economic trends have been occurring alongside a gradual, but significant transformation of Kenya's economic and social order. That is the increase in the share of the country's urban population. We can see this pattern in Figure 1.5. As we see, in 1965, more than 90 percent of Kenya's population lived in the countryside. But the share of urban population has risen since then, reaching 21 percent as of 2005. A transition is clearly taking place in Kenya to becoming an increasingly urbanized country. But this transition has been slow, with the rural-to-urban migration falling significantly after 1980. As such, Kenya remains a predominantly rural society and economy by 2005.

WHAT CAUSED ECONOMIC STAGNATION?

Why did the Kenyan economy experience this long period of stagnation from the early 1980s through at least 2003? There is no avoiding the fact that Kenya's stagnation coincides closely with the 24-year presidential reign, between 1978–

Figure 1.3 Agricultural Value-Added per Worker in Kenya, 1965–2004
(expressed in U.S. dollars in 2000)

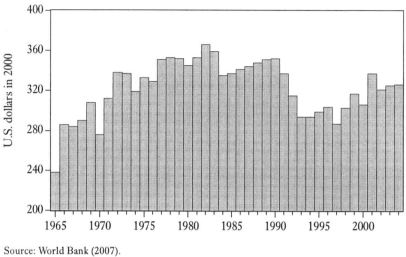

Source: World Bank (2007).

Figure 1.4 Kenya's Imports, Exports and Trade Deficit, 1965–2005
(expressed as percentages of GDP)

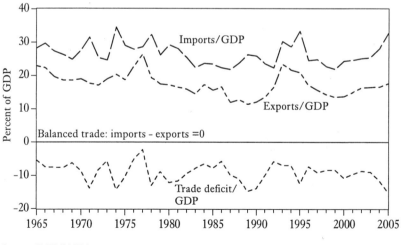

Source: IMF (2007a).

Figure 1.5 Kenya's Urban Population as a Share of Total Population, 1965–2005

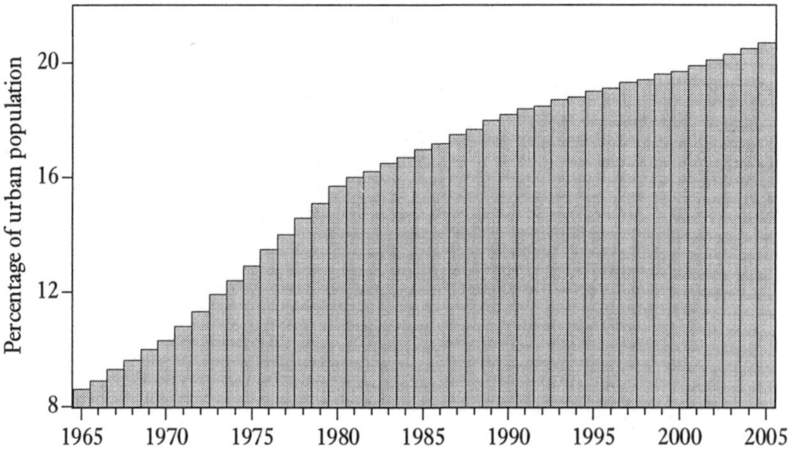

Source: World Bank (2007).

2002, of Daniel Arap Moi. As of this writing, Moi's successor, President Mwai Kibaki has been in power for nearly five years. It is too early to render a judgment as to how successful his administration has been in nurturing a more successful economic growth path. As we have just seen, there is some evidence of a recent improvement in the trend in Kenya's economic growth path. Opinions vary widely on the merits of President Kibaki's economic policies relative to those of the Moi government. In any case, it is not our purpose to focus on the role of any single political figure or party in contributing to Kenya's economic decline. At the simplest level, to do so would neglect other factors that were also present over this same time period.

  Kenya's economic decline correlates closely not only with the tenure in office of the Moi government, but also with the implementation of so-called "structural adjustment" policies under the auspices of the International Monetary Fund and World Bank. These policies, which were put in place not only in Kenya in this period but throughout the developing world, focused on a few basic policy changes. These included 1) fiscal policies targeted at keeping deficits low and reducing the overall level of spending; 2) monetary policy aimed at maintaining a low inflation environment as opposed to balancing the goals of inflation control and employment promotion; 3) liberalizing trade and capital flows; 4) privatization of publicly-owned enterprises; and 5) deregulation of private business. This is not the place for a broad examination of the overall merits of this policy approach, either in Kenya or elsewhere.[3] However, we will consider in some detail how specific features of Kenya's structural adjustment program have affected the country's economic performance. We will also propose changes in the country's policy approach based on the evidence we present here.

Another factor that is widely seen as contributing to Kenya's economic stagnation is the high level of government corruption. Operating on a large scale, corruption can prevent vital policy initiatives, such as the construction of transportation infrastructure, from being carried out effectively. There is no doubt that for any positive policy initiatives to succeed, the level of corruption and mismanagement in Kenya's economy will have to be controlled more effectively. We are encouraged by the positive measures recently implemented by the government, and will offer suggestions, as appropriate in the context of our specific proposals, to consolidate these advances.

DROUGHT AND FAMINE

Whatever factors have been responsible for Kenya's long economic stagnation, the seriousness of the country's economic problems were underscored during late 2005 and early 2006, when a severe drought in the northern part of the country drastically reduced food production and put 2–3 million people at risk of starvation. The drought and consequent humanitarian crisis was very much a regional phenomenon. Food supplies dropped to extremely low levels in the north, while agricultural production of such staple crops as maize was abundant in the west of Kenya. Kenya exported basic food crops to other African countries despite the acute food shortage in the arid and semi-arid regions in the north. During the famine, some farmers in the west were refusing to sell their output to the government as part of the country's relief efforts.

The impact of the food shortages was severe. Deaths due to diarrhea, malaria, and other illnesses increased as people, weakened by lack of food, were unable to fight off infections. Children, the elderly, and individuals with compromised health were particularly vulnerable. Access to food was only part of the problem. Many communities also lacked sufficient water resources and dehydration was a significant risk.

The response of the Kenyan government and the international community was to increase emergency relief. The Kibaki government declared a national state of emergency and set aside financial resources to purchase food amounting to millions of U.S. dollars. International donors and relief agencies pledged additional funds. However, a lack of food security and extreme volatility in agricultural production are perennial features of Kenya's agricultural sector that will not be addressed by a once-off disbursement of emergency aid. Kenya's food and water insecurity and the risk of famine are structural issues, rooted in a lack of transportation, communication, and water infrastructure. The drought was a proximate cause of the crisis in Kenya, but the structural features of the agricultural economy were at the root of the problem.

Such negative shocks to the agricultural sector can have long-lasting consequences. Unable to sustain their livestock, individuals in the north sold off their animals, artificially driving down the price by flooding the market. The wealth of individual producers evaporated as a consequence, leaving households much poorer in terms of both income and assets. Those who were unable to sell their livestock also lost their wealth as their animals died.

At the same time, the price of scarce food rose dramatically. Between October 2005 and March 2006, food prices in Kenya increased by 44 percent in five months, equivalent to 140 percent on an annual basis. The short-term spike in food prices reduced real incomes and contributed to an overall increase in prices. Food inflation has since subsided in Kenya and the shock of the drought appears to have had little long-run impact on inertial inflation. However, the consequences of the drought in terms of household livelihoods have been more severe and long-lasting.

POSITIVE ECONOMIC DEVELOPMENTS

Amid these serious economic difficulties, there are also many positive features of Kenya's economy today which need to be recognized. Indeed, one of our strategies in formulating new policy approaches has been to build from these many areas of achievement and future promise. These successful areas include:

- *Exports.* Kenya has continued to be among the world's leading exporters of tea. Moreover, the tea sector is characterized by a successful integration of smallholders along with large-scale farmers and processors. More recently, Kenya has also emerged as a leading horticultural exporter.
- *Administration of infrastructure.* Though there is much evidence of governmental agencies failing to deliver on their procurement projects, the Kenya Roads Board (KRB) managed to successfully spend virtually their full 2004–05 road maintenance budget. The organizational structure of the KRB is unique and may provide a useful model for other governmental entities.
- *A vibrant financial system.* There are serious problems with Kenya's financial system, as we will discuss. At the same time, the country now operates with a strong combination of institutions. At one level, sophisticated commercial banks operate along with emerging securities markets, with the country increasingly becoming a regional financial center. At another level, Kenya has the largest network of microfinance institutions (MFIs) in sub-Saharan Africa. The aim of policy should be to bring these two sets of institutions

together, for the benefit of both, as well as to promote a more successful development path.

- *Macroeconomic stability.* Kenya has never had a serious problem of inflation control. It has also succeeded in maintaining a fairly high level of tax revenue collections, which is all the more remarkable because most private economic activities are performed informally. That is, most small businesses and rural smallholders do not register with governmental authorities and pay little, if any, taxes. Finally, Kenya has maintained a relatively low level of public debt. These are all positive achievements as far as they go. At the same time, they are not ends in themselves—e.g. low inflation itself cannot be equated with better living standards and greater opportunities. These macroeconomic achievements should therefore been seen as foundations on which to establish policies more focused on promoting decent employment.

STRUCTURE OF STUDY

We proceed in the remaining sections of the study as follows:

In Chapter 2, we present basic data on employment conditions and poverty in Kenya. To do this, we have been fortunate to have been granted early access to the 2005–06 Kenya Integrated Household Budget Survey (KIHBS) data. We are grateful to our colleagues at Kenya's National Bureau of Statistics (KNBS) for sharing this invaluable data source with us.[4] Because we have had the opportunity to work with this rich data set, we have also been able to develop a much clearer picture of working conditions throughout the country than would have been otherwise possible. We present our main findings in Chapter 2. In particular, drawing on the poverty thresholds established by the KNBS itself, we show in Chapter 2 the extent of poverty and near-poverty among those who are employed as well as unemployed outside of agricultural self-employment.

Still working with the KIHBS data set, in Chapter 3, we provide a profile of non-agricultural household enterprises in Kenya. The 2005–06 KIHBS survey provides access to an unprecedented statistical portrait of this sector—its size, employment patterns, costs, sources of funds for financing expansion, and earnings. In this chapter, we present some of the most important statistical evidence that is now available. We then draw from that evidence to begin exploring policy ideas for both improving conditions within this sector and opening opportunities for people working in this sector to enter into more formal employment arrangements.

Having focused in Chapters 2 and 3 on providing a statistical foundation for our analysis and policy recommendations, in Chapter 4 we begin to examine policy questions more fully. In this chapter, our focus is the relationship between labor costs, labor market institutions, and decent employment opportunities. The question is being raised in Kenya, as it has been raised elsewhere, as to whether the underlying force inhibiting employment growth in the formal sector is that unit labor costs are too high. The main factors causing high unit labor costs, in turn, are said to be excessively high wages and labor market rigidities, including unions and minimum wage mandates. Seen from this perspective, the solution to the problem of low employment growth is also straightforward: to lower wages and reduce labor market rigidities. However, we argue in this chapter that the evidence linking stagnant employment growth in the formal sector to labor market rigidities is weak. We also argue that wage-cutting as a policy approach is self-defeating from a welfare standpoint, since it will mean forcing millions of people to a sub-poverty living standard. A wage-cutting approach is also certain to elicit strong resistance, which will worsen the country's investment climate. At the same time, we do support measures to maintain wage increases in line with productivity growth and to improve the efficiency of the industrial relations system. We also briefly introduce here our proposal for a hybrid program of credit and employment subsidies as a means through which the government will effectively absorb a share of businesses' labor costs.

Chapter 5 focuses on the country's rural sector. Any attempt at significantly improving employment opportunities and reducing poverty in Kenya needs to pay careful attention to developments and opportunities in the rural sector. After all, a majority of Kenya's overall population and its poor population in particular continue to reside in rural areas. Moreover, as we saw above, a basic feature of the country's economic stagnation has been the decline in agricultural labor productivity. However, as we discuss in some detail, the reality behind this productivity decline is complex once one breaks down the issue on a sub-sector by sub-sector basis. Moreover, some sub-sectors, notably tea and horticulture, have not experienced a decline at all. As such, we consider here the specific conditions that prevail with Kenya's major crops, including tea and coffee, horticulture, maize and wheat, millet and sorghum, sugarcane and rice. We also discuss livestock. These detailed discussions then form the basis for our policy recommendations aimed at raising productivity and international competitiveness.

Chapter 6 discusses measures to significantly increase investment in roads and water infrastructure beyond what is targeted in the 2006 Medium-Term Budget Strategy Paper. Infrastructure investments are central for raising productivity and thereby people's incomes. Improving the country's infrastructure is equally important in terms of promoting trade competitiveness. Finally, increased public spending in these areas can serve as a major source of job growth within the formal economy. We focus our discussion on the areas of road and water infrastructure because these are the two most urgent areas of need. We specifically sketch a program to increase spending in these areas by around Ksh 40 billion per year. We also show that this program is capable of itself creating around 350,000 new formal sector jobs.

Chapter 7 is concerned with the issues of monetary policy and inflation control. The *Economic Recovery Strategy* (Government of Kenya 2003c) states that its focus will be on four goals: containing inflation to below 5 percent; maintaining a competitive exchange rate consistent with an export-driven economic recovery; maintaining an interest rate structure that promotes financial savings and ensures efficient allocation of the same; and ensuring adequate growth in credit to the private sector. These are all important goals. At the same time, we argue in this chapter that this list of goals raises a set of serious concerns that require careful attention. We first review some relevant literature on the relationship between inflation and growth. As we discuss, there is virtually no evidence demonstrating that developing countries such as Kenya will improve their economy's growth path by holding down inflation within the range of 5 percent or lower. We then consider the evidence in Kenya that relates the effects of supply shocks—in particular large spikes in the prices of food, energy, and transportation—on overall inflation in the country. As we will see, food price shocks can be devastating in the short run, but have little impact longer term. By contrast, energy and transportation price shocks do get embedded in Kenya's economy over a longer time period. We propose different ways of mitigating the negative effects of these supply shocks. We then discuss some alternatives to tight monetary policy, including incomes policies, as an approach to inflation control. We finally then focus on the issues relating to the specifics of how Kenya conducts monetary policy. We examine three major issues: 1) monetary policy operating procedures; 2) how some procedures may contribute to worsening cyclical fluctuations rather than dampening them; and 3) how the focus on controlling inflation may contribute to excessively high interest rates. We then propose some basic changes in the conduct of monetary policy. These include shifting to a core short-term interest rate as an intermediate monetary target and removing what we see as the anti-growth bias in the way policy is current practiced.

Chapter 8 considers trade and exchange rate policy in Kenya. We particularly focus on the effects of the country's structural adjustment programs in the early 1980s. As we show, although trade volumes expanded after liberalization, the structural trade deficit was not reduced. Exports did expand, but the increase in imports offset these gains. In terms of new policy directions, we advocate a targeted exchange rate policy to promote competitiveness and encourage diversification of Kenya's export base. We also suggest that Kenya should focus on developing regional trade within the African continent. Finally, we argue that targeted interventions, such as our loan guarantee program, could also be used to promote the country's exports, especially within Africa, along with viable import substitutes.

Chapter 9 discusses Kenya's financial system. In the first part of the chapter, we describe the major features of the system, including the operations of both the commercial banks and the SACCOs (Savings and Credit Cooperatives) and other microfinance institutions. We then describe a new program of large-scale government-financed loan guarantees for commercial banks. To receive these guarantees, the banks would need to form partnerships with the country's extensive set of microfinance institutions, to provide credit for small- and medium-sized enterprises and rural smallholders. We show how this system can be made to operate with relatively modest overall costs, while also giving large incentives to the banking system to combine with microfinance entities. We conclude the policy discussion of this chapter by briefly considering some other initiatives, including the creation of reliable credit-rating operations; indexing bond rates to inflation; and revitalizing the country's public investment banks.

In Chapter 10, we bring together our various proposals and observe how they might be financed, along with the country's other needs. We are proposing four major new areas of public expenditure beyond what has already been budgeted, in the areas of transport and water infrastructure; credit subsidies, especially for small businesses and rural smallholders; and improvements in marketing support, again, especially for small businesses and rural smallholders. According to our estimates, these four proposals should require expenditures of about Ksh 45 billion per year in 2005 prices, which is equal to about three percent of GDP. How would we propose to finance these existing expenditures? We consider a variety of sources, focusing primarily on the favorable prospects for expanding Kenya's base of taxpayers. Bringing more working people within the formal sector will itself offer a major opportunity for steady expansion of the government's tax revenue base. We also think there is some room for Kenya to roughly maintain its current level of borrowing from domestic lenders, rather than follow the government's current plan of cutting back on this source of funds. We think these two sources of funds offer more promise than three other possibilities, including increased external borrowing, debt relief, and overseas development assistance.

In the concluding Chapter 11, we bring together our various proposals that are all aimed, in combination, toward promoting a large-scale expansion of decent employment in Kenya. Together these proposals represent a coherent program that is workable within the current economic context, while also being effective in reducing poverty and spreading well-being as broadly as possible.

NOTES

1. The ILO explains its commitment to "decent work" as follows: "The overarching objective of the ILO has been re-phrased as the promotion of opportunities for women and men to obtain decent and productive work in conditions of freedom, equity, security and human dignity. De-

cent work is the converging focus of the four strategic objectives, namely rights at work, employment, social protection and social dialogue. Decent work is an organizing concept for the ILO in order to provide an overall framework for action in economic and social development." See http://www.ilo.org/public/english/bureau/integration/decent/index.htm. We also recognize that our study proceeds very much in the tradition advanced by Professor Hans Singer and his collaborators in their classic 1972 work for the ILO, *Employment, Incomes, and Equality: A Strategy for Increasing Productive Employment in Kenya*. It was in writing this study—probably still the most widely distributed piece of research ever published by the ILO—that Professor Singer first developed the crucial distinction between "informal" and "formal" forms of employment.

2. Our purpose is certainly also consistent with the 2005 contribution of Susanna Lindström and Per Roonäs of Sweden's Society for International Development (SIDA), *An Integrated Analysis for Pro-Poor Growth in Kenya*. We have benefited from this study, and from personal discussions with Dr. Roonäs in preparing our own work.

3. Pollin (2003, 2006) has provided some broad perspectives on the experience of neoliberalism globally.

4. In particular, we wish to acknowledge the collaborative work we conducted with National Bureau of Statistics researchers Dankit Nassiuma, Vivian Nyarunda, and Robert Nderitu during their visit to our University of Massachusetts-Amherst offices in February/March 2007.

2. Employment Conditions and Living Standards

In this chapter, we provide a brief portrait of the employment situation in Kenya. The data we present are based on the 2005–06 KIHBS. We have also examined carefully data from the previous 1998–99 Integrated Labour Force Survey. But because of the differences in the methodologies used between the 2005–06 and 1998–99 surveys, the possibilities are very limited for making valid comparisons and drawing reliable conclusions about changes in the Kenyan economy between the two survey periods. As such, for the present discussion, we have focused on the most recent, and more reliable, 2005–06 survey.

We begin, in Table 2.1, with the most basic data on labor conditions in Kenya. As the table shows, as of 2006, the total population of Kenya was 35.6 million. Of this total population, there are 15.5 million, 43.5 percent of the total, who are between 0–14 years of age. The primary working age population (15-64) is 18.8 million, or 52.8 percent of the total population. There are 1.3 million people who are 65 years old or more, accounting for 3.8 percent of the total population.

Focusing on the 18.8 million Kenyans between the ages of 15–64, the total number of these primary working age people participating in the labor force — including all people employed and unemployed—is 13.5 million. This means a labor force participation rate among the primary working age population of 71.5 percent (i.e. 13.5/18.8 million = 71.5 percent).

DIVISION OF EMPLOYMENT BY SECTORS

We can initially divide the total number of employed people in the Kenyan economy into three broad categories. They are:

1. *agricultural self-employed*—These are agricultural workers who are not employed as wage-laborers in agricultural enterprises.
2. *informal sector*—This includes self-employment in non-agricultural unregistered household enterprises and wage-laborers of informal employers.
3. *formal sector*—This includes the entire public sector, self-employed in reg-

Table 2.1 Population and Labor Force in Kenya

Population	35.6 million
Age distribution of population	
0-14 years	15.5 million (43.5%)
15-64 years	18.8 million (52.8%)
65+	1.3 million (3.8%)
Labor force participation rate of primary working-age population (15-64 years)	13.5 million (71.5%)
Total employment	12.1 million
Distribution of employment by sectors	
Agricultural self-employed	6.0 million (50.0%)
Informal (includes non-agricultural self-employed, paid employees, and other employees)	4.3 million (35.7%)
Formal (includes non-agricultural self-employed, paid employees, and other employees)	1.7 million (14.0%)
Undetermined	0.04 million (0.3%)
Open unemployment (relaxed definition)	1.4 million
Open unemployment rate	10.5% (1.4 million/13.5 million)

Source: Authors' calculations based on 2005–06 KIHBS.

istered non-agricultural private enterprises, and wage laborers of formal employers.[1]

As we see in Table 2.1, the largest category of employment, by far, consists of the agricultural self-employed. This category accounts for roughly half of the working-age population. The next largest category consists of those employed in the informal sector, accounting for nearly 36 percent of employment in Kenya. Kenya's formal sector in total accounts for the remaining 14 percent of employment.

Of the 13.5 million people participating in Kenya's labor force, as we can see, 12.1 million are counted as employed and 1.4 million are openly unemployed.[2] Thus, the open unemployment rate is 10.5 percent.

It is important to emphasize immediately two points about this unemployment rate figure. The first concerns the usefulness of the open unemployment statistics themselves. Open unemployment rates are widely cited, in Kenya and elsewhere, as the best-known indicator of the relative robustness or weakness in any given labor market. The 10.5 percent open unemployment rate for Kenya in 2005–06 does indeed convey some useful information. At the same time, it is not nearly adequate as a measure of the overall employment situation in Kenya, just as it would not be in other countries.

This is because the open unemployment rate figure does not take into account underemployment, or more importantly, poverty-level employment—that is, people who are employed but are still bringing home low incomes. This could result from some combination of two factors: 1) receiving very low hourly income from employment; or 2) being employed involuntarily for a low number of hours. We will examine some evidence on poverty-level employment later in this chapter, after we introduce data on wages and earnings.[3]

The second point to emphasize is a point we have mentioned above—the issue of comparability of the unemployment rate statistics from the 2005–06 survey with the figures coming from the 1998–99 survey. In fact, data from the two surveys cannot be compared directly, even though it would be desirable to do so, in order to provide some picture on employment conditions in Kenya over time. More precisely, it is tempting to try to develop some trend line analysis as to whether unemployment has gone up or down in Kenya between the 1998–99 and 2005–06 survey periods. But we have resisted that temptation, since there is no possibility of developing reliable and useful comparisons.

OPEN UNEMPLOYMENT BY REGION, GENDER, AND AGE

In Table 2.2, we present data on open unemployment by region, gender, and age. To begin with, we see that there is far more open unemployment in urban than rural regions—17.3 percent versus 8.5 percent. There is almost no difference in unemployment rates between men and women. But differences are also large according to age groups. By far the largest proportion of the unemployed are those between 15 and 39 years old. In terms of educational attainment, the highest proportion of openly unemployed consists of those who have completed primary education, at 11.6 percent. It is notable that unemployment is not most severe among the least educated. Moreover, the percentage of openly unemployed among the most educated—i.e. those who have received higher education—is 8.5 percent, which is roughly on par with the 9.6 percent of those who have not completed primary education.

In short, these figures show us that open unemployment is not a problem concentrated among the least advantaged groups in Kenyan society. It is rather a problem that is spread fairly evenly across different social groupings. This fact further supports the idea that we need to look beyond the unemployment figures alone to understand the labor market difficulties experienced by Kenyans.

Table 2.2 Open Unemployment by Region, Gender, Age, and Educational Attainment

	Percent unemployed
Region	
Urban	17.3%
Rural	8.5%
Gender	
Male	10.2%
Female	10.8%
Age	
5-14	7.3%
15-39	13.4%
40-64	4.4%
65+	2.2%
Educational attainment	
Primary incomplete	9.6%
Primary completed	11.6%
Secondary completed	5.1%
Higher	8.5%

Source: Authors' calculations based on 2005–06 KIHBS.

BREAKDOWN OF PAID EMPLOYMENT

To get a better understanding of the Kenyan workforce, it will be useful to examine the data according to how people are paid—that is, whether they are paid in wages or are self-employed in some fashion. We present these figures in Table 2.3.

Agricultural Self-employed

To begin with, as Table 2.3 shows, the six million Kenyans—50 percent of the country's employed workforce—that are employed in agricultural self-employment are, by definition, self-employed and therefore do not receive wage income. Their income comes directly from their ability to sell their agricultural products themselves or to pay themselves in kind by consuming their own agricultural produce.

Table 2.3 Composition of Kenyan Work Force by Sectors

		By region		By gender	
	Total	Urban	Rural	Male	Female
A. AGRICULTURAL SELF-EMPLOYED					
Self-employed	6.0 million (50.0%)	96,220 (0.8%)	5.9 million (49.2%)	2.5 million (20.9%)	3.5 million (29.0%)
B. INFORMAL SECTOR					
All employees	4.3 million (35.7%)	1.6 million (13.1%)	2.7 million (22.6%)	2.5 million (20.6%)	1.8 million (15.1%)
Paid employee	2.2 million (18.0%)	776,530 (6.4%)	1.4 million (11.6%)	1.5 million (12.3%)	693,696 (5.8%)
Self-employed, own-account worker	1.4 million (11.7%)	523,432 (4.3%)	883,012 (7.3%)	700,543 (5.8%)	705,902 (5.9%)
Self-employed, unpaid family worker	228,028 (1.9%)	57,100 (0.5%)	170,928 (1.4%)	95,714 (0.8%)	132,314 (1.1%)
Self-employed, working employer	116,753 (1.0%)	66,077 (0.5%)	50,676 (0.4%)	77,795 (0.6%)	38,958 (0.3%)
Other	397,162 (3.1%)	161,142 (1.3%)	218,021 (1.8)	133,186 (1.1%)	245,598 (2.1%)
C. FORMAL SECTOR					
All employees	1.7 million (14.0%)	838,642 (7.0%)	852,550 (7.1%)	1.2 million (9.7%)	525,303 (4.4%)
Paid employee, private	771,078 (6.4%)	418,840 (3.5%)	352,237 (2.9%)	584,781 (4.9%)	186,297 (1.5%)
Paid employee, public	518,858 (4.3%)	207,878 (1.7%)	310,980 (2.6%)	341,017 (2.8%)	177,841 (1.5%)
Paid employee, semi-public	128,304 (1.1%)	66,871 (0.6%)	61,432 (0.5%)	90,275 (0.7%)	38,029 (0.3%)
Self-employed, own-account worker	114,869 (1.0%)	54,696 (0.5%)	60,173 (0.5%)	60,521 (0.5%)	54,348 (0.5%)
Paid employee, non-profits	61,084 (0.5%)	43,008 (0.4%)	18,077 (0.1%)	33,169 (0.3%)	27,915 (0.2%)
Self-employed, working employer	36,915 (0.3%)	24,876 (0.2%)	12,038 (0.1%)	28,495 (0.2%)	8,419 (0.1%)
Self-employed, unpaid family member	26,452 (0.2%)	12,867 (0.1%)	13,585 (0.1%)	11,082 (0.1%)	15,370 (0.1%)
Other	33,632 (0.4%)	9,604 (0.1%)	24,028 (0.2%)	16,547 (0.1%)	17,085 (0.1%)

Source: Authors' calculations, based on the 2005–06 KIHBS.

Considering these figures according to regional and gender breakdowns, it is not surprising, first of all, that the agricultural self-employed are overwhelmingly rural—5.9 million rural as opposed to slightly less than 100,000 urban. The majority of the agricultural self-employed are women—3.5 million women as opposed to 2.5 million men.

Informal Sector Workers

Turning now to the 4.3 million workers—36 percent of the employed labor force—that are in the informal sector, we see that the largest number of these workers are paid employees. Informal paid employees account for 2.2 million people total, which is 18 percent of the total Kenyan workforce.

The next largest category in Kenya's informal sector is the self-employed own-account workers. There are 1.4 million Kenyans working in this category, representing 11.7 percent of Kenya's total workforce.

Beyond these two categories within the informal sector, the numbers drop off substantially. The remaining categories include unpaid family members and self-employed working employers. These two groupings account for about 3 percent of the Kenyan workforce.[4]

In terms of regional and gender breakdown, there are about twice as many informal sector workers in the rural areas as in the urban areas. There are also about 40 percent more men as women working in the informal sector. However, men are disproportionately included as paid employees in the informal sector. In terms of own-account informal sector workers, there is roughly an equal number of men and women.

Formal Sector Workers

We finally turn to Kenya's formal sector workforce. As we have seen, Kenya's formal sector overall employs only 14 percent of the employed people in Kenya. Of that number, the largest grouping is those working as paid employees in the private sector. They account for about 770,000 people, or six percent of Kenya's employed workforce. The public sector accounts for roughly another 4 percent of Kenya's workforce. All other types of employment in the formal sector add up to another 3.5 percent of the total employed workforce.

In terms of regional breakdowns, there is a fairly even split of formal sector workers in both the urban and rural areas. With respect to gender, there are more than twice as many men holding formal sector jobs as women—about 1.2 million men versus 520,000 women.

Table 2.4 Incomes from Informal and Formal Sectors Employment

	Number and percentages of workforce (total= 12.1 million)	Median monthly incomes—wages or net enterprise earnings (in Ksh)	Median monthly incomes by region (in Ksh)	
			Rural	Urban
A. INFORMAL SECTOR				
Paid employee	2,174,563 (18.0%)	2,880	2,000	4,000
Self-employed, own-account worker	1,406,445 (11.7%)	2,600	2,000	4,000
Self-employed, unpaid family worker	228,028 (1.9%)	0	0	0
Self-employed, working employer	116,753 (1.0%)	6,000	4,083	7,800
B. FORMAL SECTOR				
Paid employee, private	771,078 (6.4%)	6,160	4,800	9,000
Paid employee, public	518,858 (4.3%)	15,375	14,672	16,132
Paid employee, semi-public*	28,304 (1.1%)	12,800	4,600	18,700
Self-employed, own-account worker	114,869 (1.0%)	6,000	4,857	6,755

Note: * includes employees of state-owned and majority-controlled enterprises.
Source: Authors' calculations, based on 2005–06 KIHBS.

INCOMES FROM EMPLOYMENT

We now consider evidence on income levels for the various job categories. In considering these data, it is unfortunate that, at the time of writing, the National Bureau of Statistics has not yet been able to release income data for self-employed agricultural workers. This means that we cannot report income data for fully half of all working people in Kenya.

Nevertheless, we are able to report wage incomes for those working in the informal and formal sectors and business revenues for self-employed workers in non-agricultural enterprises. These figures are shown in Table 2.4, which reports median income figures for the largest categories of these workers in both the informal and formal sectors, then also breaks down these median income figures based on whether people live in rural or urban regions of Kenya.

As Table 2.4 shows, incomes, on average, are much higher in the formal than informal sector. There are also significant income disparities among the categories of workers within each sector. Finally, there are also large disparities by region. Allowing for differences by employment categories, most private sector urban workers earn about twice as much as rural workers in the same job category. The urban/rural income disparities are small only between public sector employees.

In the informal sector, the median income for the overwhelming majority of those employed in the sector is between Ksh 2,600 and 2,900 per month. This is the pay level for both paid employees and self-employed own-account workers. By region, as we see, rural workers earn a median of Ksh 2,000 per month, while urban workers receive 4,000. By definition, unpaid family workers receive no income. The self-employed working employers earn twice as much—6,000 per month. But this category of people accounts for only 1 percent of the Kenyan workforce.

In the formal sector, private sector workers also earn about Ksh 6,000 per month, with rural workers getting a median of Ksh 4,800 while urban workers receive Ksh 9,000. Public sector workers earn more than twice that amount—averaging Ksh 15,375 in the public sector itself, and 12,800 in the semi-public sector.

In short, the most remunerative place of employment in Kenya, on average, is in the formal public or semi-public sectors. But these two categories of workers constitute only 5 percent of total employment in Kenya.

LABOR INCOMES AND POVERTY

To gain some perspective on the earnings figures reported in Table 2.4, it will be helpful to compare them with the most recent estimates of poverty thresholds in Kenya.

The most recent poverty figures have been developed by the KNBS from the same 2005–06 KIHBS, and are presented in the 2007 publication, *Basic Report on Poverty in Kenya* (Government of Kenya 2007a). The report establishes poverty thresholds based on individual consumption levels, rather than defining poverty based on income levels. The report argues that "consumption is a more satisfactory measure of well-being for both theoretical and practical reasons," (p. 24). In comparing consumption versus income as a poverty standard, the report finds, for one thing, that consumption levels are more stable than income levels. In addition, it is more difficult for people to give an accurate accounting of their income than to identify the goods and services they regularly consume.

Table 2.5 Consumption Poverty Lines in Kenya (monthly levels of spending, in Ksh)

	Food poverty line	Overall poverty line
Rural poverty line	988	1,562
Urban poverty line	1,474	2,913

Source: Government of Kenya (2007a).

Using consumption standards, the report then defines four separate poverty lines. One line is the "food poverty line." This attempts to measure how much money it takes for Kenyans to purchase a minimally adequate level of food, defined as equal to 2250 kilocalories per day. The report then defines an "overall poverty line," which includes the costs of purchasing a minimal level of consumption goods other than food. The costs of purchasing both food and non-food products varies substantially between the urban and rural regions of Kenya. Because of this, the report also establishes separate poverty lines for the country's urban and rural regions. In Table 2.5, we present the figures for the four official consumption poverty lines. As we see, the overall poverty lines are Ksh 1,562 per month for rural areas and Ksh 2,913 per month for urban areas.

We can now use these threshold figures to provide perspective on the median earnings of informal and formal sector workers that we presented in Table 2.4. We must proceed with caution in making these comparisons, keeping in mind that we are comparing data on earnings from employment with consumption-based poverty lines. This means that the working people whose earnings are below the poverty line do not necessarily live in poverty, as measured by a consumption-based poverty line. Those with low earnings may be experiencing only a one-time drop-off in their income. They may also be living in families where other members bring home sufficient income to maintain the family above a poverty standard. They may also be growing their own food or receiving other types of in-kind income to supplement their earnings from employment.

Considering all these important qualifications, it will still be useful to consider the relationship between workers' earnings and the official government poverty lines. To begin with, the urban poverty line of Ksh 2,913 per month is about 25 percent below the Ksh 4,000 in median monthly earnings of both paid employees and self-employed own-account workers in the urban informal sector. Paid employees in the formal sector earn about three times the level of the Ksh 2,913 urban poverty line.

Now, of course, a high proportion of income earners have to support not only themselves with their earnings, but other family members as well. Let us assume for illustrative purposes that, for example, the average working person in Kenya supports one other person through his/her earnings, and consider the implications. First, for urban informal paid employees, dividing their Ksh 4,000 monthly earnings among two people means that each person lives on Ksh 2,000 per month. This is about one-third below the urban poverty line of Ksh 2,913. Even with urban formal paid employees, dividing Ksh 9,000 per month among two people means that both people are living on Ksh 4,500 per month. This amount is only slightly more than 50 percent above the urban poverty line. The story is similar in comparing the incomes of rural workers with the Ksh 1,562 rural poverty line.

Among all the categories of working people in Kenya for whom we have data, the only groupings that, on average, clearly earn incomes above the poverty line, are those employed in the public and semi-public sectors. In short, we see from these figures that being employed in Kenya does not ensure that one will be living out of poverty.

SOURCES OF POVERTY-LEVEL EMPLOYMENT: LOW HOURS AND LOW EARNINGS

To gain further perspective on this question, in Table 2.6 we report figures on employed people in Kenya whose household income levels place them below the overall consumption poverty lines—based on either the urban or rural consumption poverty lines, depending on where the households are located.

Since we do not have income data for self-employed agricultural workers, we are able to compile family income levels only for those families that include no self-employed agricultural workers. So again, due to this gap in the available data, we have to exclude about 53 percent of Kenyan households in exploring this question. Nevertheless, we are still able to observe the levels of income from employment for a total of 4.3 million Kenyans. These workers are drawn from about one-third of all rural households and over 90 percent of urban households.

Table 2.6a shows the proportion of labor force participants who live in poor households, defining poverty according to the overall consumption line for both rural and urban areas. As we see in Table 2.6a, of all Kenyans who are participating in the labor force but are unemployed, roughly 65 percent live in poverty. But as the table also shows, the proportions living in poverty are basically the same if a Kenyan is employed and working up to 39 hours per week. Specifically, for those working 1-27 hours per week, nearly 70 percent live in poverty. Among those working 28–39 hours per week, about 66 percent live in poverty.

In other words, excluding those in the agricultural self-employed category, we see that being employed in Kenya up to 39 hours per week itself provides no clear benefit to a working person as a means of living above the poverty line. It is

Table 2.6 Sources of Poverty for Labor Force Participants: Insufficient Hours of Employment versus Low Earnings

A. Proportion of Labor Force Participants Living in Poverty

Unemployed	65.9%
1–27 hours/week	69.8%
28–39 hours/week	65.6%
40 or more hours/week	46.1%

B. Breakdown of All Labor Force Participants, According to Hours Worked per Week

	Number of labor force participants in category	Percentage of labor force participants in category
Unemployed	628,409	14.6%
1–27 hours/week	492,773	11.4%
28–39 hours/week	404,722	9.4%
40 or more hours/week	2.8 million	64.6%
TOTAL	4.3 million	100.0%

C. Breakdown of Labor Force Participants in Poverty, According to Hours Worked per Week

Number of hours worked/week	Percentage of poor workers in category
Unemployed	18.0%
1–27 hours/week	15.0%
28–40 hours/week	11.5%
Over 40 hours/week	55.5%

Note: Figures do not include labor force participants in households with a worker in agricultural self-employment.
Source: 2005–06 KIHBS.

true that among the labor force participants working 40 hours or more per week, the percentage living in poverty does go down, to 46.1 percent. Still, this percentage remains very high. It means that, even among workers employed 40 hours or more per week, nearly 50 percent live in poverty, based on the official consumption poverty line.

This poverty figure for those working 40 hours or more per week is especially important since a large majority of Kenyans do work 40 hours or more per week. More specifically, as we see in Table 2.6b, of the almost 4.3 million labor force participants with no agricultural self-employed workers in the household, 2.8 million, or roughly 65 percent, are working 40 hours or more per week.

This means, in turn, that even though the chances of living in poverty in Kenya do go down somewhat if one works 40 hours or more per week, it is still the case that the overwhelming proportion of labor force participants in Kenya who live in poverty are also working 40 hours or more per week. In fact, as we see from Table 2.6c, 55 percent of all labor force participants who live in poverty are also working over 40 hours per week. Only 18 percent of labor force participants living in poverty are actually unemployed.

Considering these data overall, a key message emerges, both for our study and for economic policy discussions in Kenya more generally. It is that the most serious problem facing Kenyans in the labor market today is not unemployment per se or even low hours per se. It is that, even among those Kenyans (apart from the agricultural self-employed) who are working long hours—i.e. 40 hours or more—the chances are very high that one will be living in poverty. This conclusion applies to working people in both rural and urban areas.

Of course, policies for fighting open unemployment per se in Kenya need to be advanced. But these data show clearly that it is even more critical to raise earnings levels substantially for the overwhelming majority of Kenyans participating in the labor force who are employed but, despite the fact that they are employed, are still living in poverty.

NOTES

1. To clarify the distinctions between wage employees in the informal and formal sectors, the information on type of employer contained within the KIHBS is utilized. Formal employers are those that workers identify as one of the following: private sector company, government agency, state-owned company, company that is majority-owned by the Kenya government, international organization, or non-governmental organization. Informal employers are those that fall outside all of those categories, such as an individual.
2. The definition of openly unemployed in the labor force survey refers to people who, during the reference period, "were without work but currently available for work and actively seeking work, or were without work because of layoff or off-season but currently available for work."
3. The *Labour Force Analytical Report* by the Kenya National Bureau of Statistics provides evidence on workers who involuntarily work less than 28 hours per week (Government of Kenya 2007b). This is useful information. But it is not a full indicator of employed people experiencing labor market difficulties, since it does not consider the situation for those earning poverty-level incomes even if they are working more than 28 hours.
4. The last category, "other," includes workers who do not provide information about their employment status within the informal sector.

3. Profile of Non-agricultural Household Enterprises

Non-agricultural household enterprises are a basic foundation of the Kenyan economy. Any strategy for expanding decent employment and reducing poverty in Kenya will have to focus on the non-agricultural household sector—to expand opportunities for people working in the sector, either by improving conditions within the sector itself or by creating more opportunities for decent employment outside this sector.

The 2005–06 KIHBS provides access to an unprecedented statistical portrait of this sector—its size, employment patterns, costs, sources of funds for financing expansion, and earnings. In this chapter, we present some of the most important statistical evidence that is now available.[1]

The KIHBS defines non-agricultural household enterprises as follows: they are unincorporated income-generating establishments operated by one or more members of the household and not directly engaged in agricultural production. Household enterprises do not need to be physically located in the household. Based on this definition, a household enterprise can either be informal or formal.

As we see in Table 3.1, there are about 2.1 million non-agricultural household enterprises in Kenya.[2] Roughly 90 percent are informal enterprises and 10 percent are formal.[3] In terms of employment, about 5.2 million people total are working in non-agricultural household enterprises, including contributing family workers. Of the 5.2 million employed in non-agricultural household enterprises, 4.1 million, or 79 percent are working in informal enterprises, and 1.1 million, or 21 percent, in formal enterprises.

The domestic market within Kenya itself is by far the most important source of sales for Kenyan household enterprises, both informal and formal. Almost no Kenyan household enterprises—less than one tenth of 1 percent of the more than two million firms—sell a significant fraction of their goods and services on export markets.

With respect to the domestic market itself, roughly 90 percent of non-agricultural household enterprises sell directly to consumers. Most of the remaining 10 percent of these firms sell to private businesses within Kenya. Almost no household enterprises sell their products to the public sector.

Table 3.1 Overview on Kenyan Household Enterprises

Total number of non-agricultural household enterprises: 2,058,953
- 1,867,312 Informal enterprises (90% of total)
- 191,281 Formal enterprises (10% of total)

Total employment in non-agricultural household enterprises: 5.2 million
- 4.1 million in informal enterprises (79% of total)
- 1.1 million in formal enterprises (21% of total)

Source: Authors' calculations from 2005–06 KIHBS.

We will focus in later chapters of this study on detailed measures to expand opportunities for household enterprises. But for now, one simple point is clear: any economic strategy for raising the overall level of demand and spending within Kenya's domestic market will necessarily benefit the country's non-agricultural household enterprises.

HOUSEHOLD ENTERPRISES BY INDUSTRIAL SECTORS

As we see from Table 3.2, the overwhelming majority of non-agricultural household enterprises—82 percent of the total number of firms—are in the business of providing some sort of service. Of all non-agricultural household enterprises, 73.8 percent are informal and 8.2 percent are formal. Most of the remaining household enterprises are in manufacturing. As the table shows, manufacturing firms account for roughly 10 percent of all household enterprises. And the overwhelming majority of manufacturing household enterprises are informal, just as with the service-providing firms. When adding together services and manufacturing household enterprises, we account for approximately 92 percent of all household enterprises. Of the remaining 8 percent of all household enterprises, 5.2 percent are in agriculture and 3 percent are undefined ("other").

Service Sector

Because of the importance of the service sector among household enterprises, it will be useful to consider the types of firms operating within this sector in more detail. We present data on this in Table 3.3.

As the upper panel of the table shows, the overwhelming majority of service sector household enterprises are in retail trade. Retail trade itself accounts for a total of about 63 percent of all non-agricultural household enterprises. Again, most of these firms are also informal. Other than retail, the areas that have some

Table 3.2 Non-agricultural Household Enterprises by Broad Industrial Sectors

	All enterprises	Informal	Formal
TOTAL	100.0%	90.3%	9.7%
Services	82.0%	73.8%	8.2%
Manufacturing	9.7%	8.6%	1.1%
Agriculture, forest, fisheries*	5.2%	5.1%	0.1%
Other	3.0%	2.9%	0.1%

Note: * Non-agricultural enterprises may operate in agriculture-related activities, even if they are not directly engaged in agricultural production.
Source: Authors' calculations from 2005–06 KIHBS.

Table 3.3 Service Sector Enterprises by Sub-sectors

	All service-industry firms	Informal firms	Formal firms
TOTAL	82.0%	73.8%	8.2%
Retail trade	62.8%	58.0%	4.8%
Other trade	6.0%	5.1%	0.9%
Personal services	3.7%	3.2%	0.5%
Repair services	3.0%	2.6%	0.4%
Transport services	2.5%	2.1%	0.4%
Business services and finance	1.6%	1.0%	0.6%
Other	2.5%	1.8%	0.7%

RETAIL TRADE SUB-SECTOR BY CATEGORY

	All retailers	Informal firms	Formal firms
RETAIL TOTAL	62.8%	58.0%	4.8%
General retail/other	40.8%	36.9%	3.8%
Food retailing	17.8%	17.3%	0.4%
Restaurants	3.7%	3.2%	0.5%
Accommodation	0.6%	0.4%	0.1%

Source: Authors' calculations from 2005–06 KIHBS.

Table 3.4 Household Enterprises in Manufacturing, by Sub-sectors

	All manufacturing-industry firms	Informal firms	Formal firms
TOTAL	9.7%	8.6%	1.1%
Textiles, clothing and garments	3.9%	3.5%	0.4%
Food processing	2.3%	1.8%	0.5%
Furniture and wood products	2.2%	2.1%	0.1%
Other	1.3%	1.2%	0.1%

Source: Authors' calculations from 2005-06 KIHBS.

significant representation are in personal services (such as beauticians, laundries, and photographers), repair services and transport services.

In the lower panel of Table 3.3, we provide further detail on the retail trade. Here we see that the overwhelming majority of retail household enterprises are considered "general retail." General retailers account for 41 percent of all household enterprises. Their activities obviously vary widely. They include mostly street traders selling clothing, cookware, and other small household items. The next two largest categories of household enterprise retailers are food retailers and restaurants. These two categories together account for 22 percent of all household enterprises.

In Table 3.4, we provide a more detailed breakdown of the roughly 10 percent of non-agricultural household enterprises that are engaged in manufacturing. As we see, the largest category here, about 4 percent of all non-agricultural household enterprises, are producing textiles and clothing. The other two relatively large categories of household enterprises in manufacturing are food processors (2.3 percent of all non-agricultural household enterprises) and producers of food and wood products (2.2 percent of all non-agricultural household enterprises).

PROFILE OF EMPLOYMENT IN HOUSEHOLD ENTERPRISES

We now consider the data on employment in Kenya's non-agricultural household enterprises.[4] In Table 3.5a we see the breakdown in employment according to sectors. Similar to what we have seen already in terms of number of firms, with employment, the overwhelming majority of household enterprise employment is in services and the informal sector. Thus, about 70 percent of all household enterprise employment is in services, with 13.8 percent in manufacturing and 4.4 percent in agriculture.

Table 3.5 Distribution of Employment in Non-agricultural Household Enterprises

	Total	Informal	Formal
A. SECTORAL DISTRIBUTION OF EMPLOYMENT			
Services	69.9%	55.0%	14.9%
Manufacturing	13.8%	7.3%	6.5%
Agricultural*	4.4%	3.9%	0.5%
Construction	1.0%	0.8%	0.3%
Mining/quarrying	0.9%	0.8%	0.1%
Other/unknown	9.9%	9.9%	0.0%
B. CATEGORIES OF EMPLOYMENT IN HOUSEHOLD ENTERPRISES			
Unpaid family members	37.2%	28.4%	8.8%
Own-account workers	34.1%	31.6%	2.6%
Employees	19.5%	10.0%	9.5%
Employers	3.0%	2.3%	0.7%
Other/unknown	6.1%	5.5%	0.7%

Note: * Non-agricultural enterprises may operate in agriculture-related activities, even if they are not directly engaged in agricultural production.
Source: Authors' calculations from 2005–06 KIHBS.

In Table 3.5b, we show the distribution of employment in household enterprises according to categories of employment, including own-account workers, employees, employers, and unpaid family members. As we see, the largest category of employment is unpaid family members, accounting by itself for 37 percent of all household enterprise employment. Own-account workers—people working alone for themselves—represent another 34 percent of all household enterprise employment. Thus, own-account workers and unpaid family members together account for more than 70 percent of all employment in household enterprises. The next largest category, 19.5 percent of all household enterprise workers, consists of employees working for someone else. Employers, those who are running household enterprises that include paid employees, represent only 3 percent of household enterprise employment.

COSTS OF OPERATING HOUSEHOLD ENTERPRISES

In Table 3.6, we report figures showing the costs experienced by non-agricultural household enterprises in running their businesses. As the table shows, the two largest categories of costs are the purchasing of goods that are resold in

Table 3.6 Breakdown of Costs for Non-agricultural Household Enterprises

	Percentage of total costs for firms				
	All household enterprises	Services firms	Manufacturing firms	Informal firms	Formal firms
Cost of goods resold (inventories)	53.6%	59.5%	19.9%	54.7%	43.8%
Raw materials	17.5%	15.0%	49.5%	17.8%	14.4%
Transportation	7.3%	7.2%	6.1%	7.5%	5.5%
Wages/salaries	5.7%	3.8%	8.0%	4.8%	13.9%
Rent	5.0%	4.7%	4.2%	4.7%	7.5%
Licenses and taxes	4.3%	3.8%	5.5%	3.8%	8.5%
Utilities	1.5%	1.5%	2.2%	1.5%	1.3%
Other	4.5%	4.0%	4.1%	4.6%	3.9%

Source: Authors' calculations from 2005–06 KIHBS.

retail markets—i.e. inventory purchases—and raw materials. Not surprisingly, there is a large difference between service and manufacturing firms in terms of the relative cost burdens of purchasing inventories as opposed to raw materials. For service firms, inventories account for nearly 60 percent of all costs and raw materials account for only 15 percent. With manufacturing firms, raw materials account for 49.5 percent of all costs and inventories account for 19.9 percent.

Across sectors, wages and salaries are not nearly as large a cost element as are inventories and raw materials, accounting, on average, for only 5.7 percent of total costs. This is not surprising, given that, as we have seen, the overwhelming majority of household enterprise employment consists of own-account workers and unpaid family members. At the same time, it is also not surprising that there are large disparities in the relative size of the wage/salary bill when we move from considering informal to formal enterprises. With informal enterprises, wages and salaries account for only 4.8 percent of total costs, while, with formal household enterprises, wages and salaries rise to almost 14 percent of total costs.

One other important set of figures that arises with these cost figures is the disparity between informal and formal enterprises in terms of the proportions they pay for licenses and taxes. We see these figures in Table 3.6. As the table shows, informal firms are paying an average of 3.8 percent of their total costs in licenses and taxes, while formal enterprises pay 8.5 percent. Thus, informal firms would have to increase their licenses and tax obligations quite significantly in order to operate as formal enterprises and receive the benefits from being a

Table 3.7 Sources of Start-up Credit for Non-agricultural Household Enterprises

| | Percentage of credit by source | | |
	All enterprises	Informal enterprises	Formal enterprises
Own savings	52.3%	51.9%	56.6%
Family gift or loan	21.8%	21.8%	22.2%
Sale of existing asset	6.1%	6.1%	6.8%
SACCO	3.2%	3.0%	5.0%
Bank, financial institution	0.7%	0.6%	1.3%
Money lender	0.4%	0.4%	1.1%
Other source*	20.6%	20.9%	17.6%

CREDIT SOURCES ACCORDING TO NUMBER OF EMPLOYEES

| | Number of employees | | | | |
	0	1-4	5-9	10-19	20 and over
Own savings	51.5%	57.2%	37.1%	67.4%	53.8%
Family gift or loan	22.1%	20.2%	20.4%	19.6%	24.8%
Sale of existing asset	6.2%	5.8%	9.6%	3.7%	2.8%
SACCO	2.4%	6.9%	21.0%	5.5%	5.4%
Bank, financial institution	0.5%	1.4%	1.1%	0.0%	12.5%
Money lender	0.3%	0.6%	9.6%	0.9%	0.0%
Other source*	21.2%	17.6%	12.4%	17.2%	15.4%

Note: * No information in survey on these sources.
Note: Percentages do not sum to 100% because categories are not mutually exclusive.
Source: Authors' calculations from 2005–06 KIHBS.

formal sector firm. Observing this large cost differential between informal and formal enterprises raises an obvious policy-related point: what are the benefits that would accrue to informal firms from joining the formal sector? Unless there are clear and significant benefits for firms in the formal sector, it will be to their obvious advantage to remain informal and face significantly lower costs in terms of licensing and taxes.

SOURCES OF START-UP CREDIT

How do household enterprises obtain funds to create their businesses? We present data on this in Table 3.7. The figures in Table 3.7 show that the great majority of non-agricultural household enterprises rely on either their own savings or funds from family members to provide the initial financing for their businesses. Moreover, the differences between informal and formal enterprises are not large in this case. As the table shows, 52.3 percent of all household enterprises rely on their own savings, and another 21.8 percent rely on family gifts or loans—in total these two categories account for 74 percent of all household enterprises. What is also notable is the small contributions here by SACCOs, which provide start up funds to only 3.2 percent of household enterprises. The formal commercial banks appear to play almost no role whatsoever in helping household enterprises to begin operations.

In the lower panel of Table 3.7b, we break down these results by the size of household enterprises, specifically according to the number of workers that firms employ. Here as well, there are no dramatic departures from the overall pattern, which is that most household enterprises rely on their own savings or support from their families. But there are still some notable differences to consider as one moves from firms with no employees to those with relatively large numbers of employees. Specifically, SACCOs and even commercial banks start to play a more prominent role as sources of financing as firms grow larger. In the case of household enterprises with five to nine employees, 21 percent have received financing from SACCOs. This number does fall as the household enterprises get larger—with only 5.4 percent of household enterprises that employ 20 or more workers receiving support from SACCOs. At the same time, 12.5 percent of household enterprises with 20 or more employees are receiving start-up financing from commercial banks. Still again, other than these largest of household enterprises, firms are essentially getting no support from the formal banking sector.

It is true that there is some significant uncertainty associated with these findings, given that the unspecified "other source" is large, accounting for more than 20 percent of all start-up credit to household enterprises. Yet, though we are unable to identify what these credit sources are, it is clear from the survey results as to what they are not—that is, clearly the funds in this category are not coming from SACCOs or commercial banks, or they would have been identified as such. The main finding of this table remains firm—that Kenyans starting a new household enterprise receive almost no support from either the microfinance or commercial banking sectors.

EARNINGS FROM HOUSEHOLD ENTERPRISES

We have already reviewed earnings figures for individuals in the labor force in Chapter 2. We will now consider earnings from the perspective of the household enterprises as entities, as opposed to the people who are working in these enterprises, or other types of enterprises, in Kenya.

In the Chapter 2 discussion, we saw that the earnings received by a majority of working people placed them close to the official food consumption poverty line. As should not be surprising, we find basically the same result in considering the earnings data from the perspective of the non-agricultural household enterprises themselves. These figures are reported in Tables 3.8a–c.

As we see in Table 3.8a, the median level of monthly earnings for all non-agricultural household enterprises is Ksh 2,370. This figure is 50 percent above the official rural consumption poverty line, and is 19 percent below the official urban poverty line. What makes this low figure especially notable is that, as we saw, the largest single category of workers within household enterprises is "unpaid family members." This means that, in a significant number of household enterprises, the overall earnings in the range of Ksh 2,400 per month is meant to supply a livelihood for more than one person working at the enterprise.

Beyond these median earnings figures, there are also significant differences in earnings based on different factors. First, as we see in Table 3.8a, earnings for informal sector firms are consistently lower than those for formal sector firms. In services, the average informal sector firm earns about one-third less than the average formal sector firm. In manufacturing, informal sector firms earn, on average, a little more than one-tenth as much as formal sector firms.

As we see in Table 3.8b, there are also large disparities in the level of earnings within both the informal and formal sectors. In the informal service sector, for example, the earnings of the lowest 25 percent of firms average only about 14 percent as much as the best-earning 25 percent of informal enterprises. The differences are even sharper among manufacturing firms in the informal sector, and still more among all firm types in the formal sector. Thus, among manufacturing household enterprises in the formal sector, the lowest 25 percent of earners are receiving 4.4 percent of what the best-earning 25 percent of firms receive.

In Table 3.8c, we present figures on earnings based on the number of employees in firms. As we see there, average earnings do initially rise at a rate equivalent to the increase in the number of employees. Thus, firms with zero employees earn an average of Ksh 2,000 while those with one employee earn Ksh 4,310 and those with two paid employees earn about Ksh 8,100. Only when firms reach a size of more than 20 employees do we observe a growth in earnings beyond what would correspond to the increase in employees.

Table 3.8c also breaks down these earning figures according to informal and formal enterprises. As we see, for smaller firms, with zero employees, informal firms do earn less, but only about 13 percent less. However, as firm size grows to two employees or move, the differential between the earnings of informal and formal firms grows sharply. For example, with firms employing 5–9 workers, the informal firms are earning 5.7 percent of the earnings of formal firms.

The general point is this: As we have seen, most household enterprises in Kenya are informal and very small scale. The earnings that these firms receive,

Table 3.8 Monthly Earnings Figures for Non-agricultural Household Enterprises

A) ALL HOUSEHOLD ENTERPRISES—MEDIAN MONTHLY EARNINGS (in Ksh)

	All firms	Informal firm earnings	Formal firm earnings	Informal firm earnings as percent of formal firms
ALL SECTORS	2,370	2,200	6,000	
Services (82.0% of household enterprises)	2,450	2,300	6,000	38.3%
Manufacturing (9.7% of household enterprises)	1,667	1,200	9,540	12.6%
Agriculture, forest, fisheries (5.2% of household enterprises)*	2,000	1,900	3,000	63.3%

B) MONTHLY EARNINGS BY INFORMAL/FORMAL SECTORS (in Ksh)

	Median earnings	Earnings of lowest 25% of firms	Earnings of highest 25% of firms	Earnings of lowest 25% of firms as percent of highest 25%
Informal sector				
Services (74% of household enterprises)	2,300	750	5,500	13.6%
Manufacturing (8.5% of household enterprises)	1,200	438	4,000	11.0%
Agriculture, forest, fisheries (5.1 of household enterprises)*	1,900	900	3,500	25.7%
Formal sector				
Services (8.2% of household enterprises)	6,000	1,340	20,750	6.5%
Manufacturing (1.1% of household enterprises)	9,540	2,037	46,160	4.4%
Agriculture, forest, fisheries (0.1 of household enterprises)	3000	1,000	12,000	8.3%

C) Enterprise Earnings by Number of Employees (in Ksh)

	Median of all household enterprise earnings	Median informal firm earnings	Median formal firm earnings	Informal firm earnings as percent of formal firm earnings
0 paid employees	2,000	2,000	2,300	87.0%
1 paid employee	4,310	3,400	7,244	46.9%
2 paid employees	8,100	6,800	14,951	45.5%
3-4 paid employees	6,710	5,833	22,300	26.2%
5-9 paid employees	10,000	4,167	73,200	5.7%
10-19 paid employees	9,700	9,000	68,750	13.1%
Over 20 paid employees	70,000	n/a	666,667	n/a

Note: * Non-agricultural enterprises may operate in agriculture-related activities, even if they are not directly engaged in agricultural production.
Source: Authors' calculations from 2005–06 KIHBS.

on average, are very low—not sufficient, on average, to maintain the people working in them above the consumption poverty line. If household enterprises are formal and relatively large in size, their earnings are dramatically higher.

However, it is obviously a great challenge for household enterprises to grow beyond operating as a small-scale firm. As we have seen, these firms have almost no access to credit. Moreover, the very large number of household enterprises in operations means that competition among them is necessarily strong. These are issues that we will want to consider seriously in discussions on economic policy.

FACTORS INFLUENCING HOUSEHOLD ENTERPRISE EARNINGS

As part of our use of the 2005–06 KIHBS data set, we have conducted a formal statistical analysis of the factors that influence the levels of earnings for non-agricultural household enterprises. This means that we can answer to a significant extent why we see the large variations in the patterns of earnings that emerge in Table 3.8a–c. In Appendix 1, we present the results of the model in full. Here we want to highlight the main findings of the model. These key findings are as follows:

1. As noted at the outset of this chapter, household enterprises in Kenya sell almost exclusively within the domestic Kenyan market. But, within this

framework, the enterprises that are able to sell to businesses within Kenya have higher earnings than the enterprises that are able to sell only to other households or to individuals on the streets. Therefore, forming linkages among household enterprises and other domestic businesses in Kenya should raise average earnings of household enterprises. At present, almost no household enterprises are selling to public sector entities.

2. If an enterprise obtains start-up capital from a SACCO, this has a large and significant positive impact on earnings. This could be due both to the access to credit that is provided through the link with the SACCO, and also possibly to the network of support that the SACCO can provide. This finding is especially important, given that, as we have observed above, less than four percent of household enterprises are currently receiving start-up credit from SACCOs, and almost no household enterprises receive start-up credit from commercial banks.

3. If a household enterprise is involved in contingent or seasonal activities—that is, it operates for only a fraction of the year—this has a significant negative impact on the enterprise's average monthly earnings. As household enterprises increase their activity level to year-round operations, earnings increase substantially.

4. The educational level attained by the manager/owner of a household enterprise will have a significant positive impact on earnings. The higher the manager's level of educational attainment, the higher will be the firm's level of earnings, holding all other influences on earnings constant.

5. As the number of paid employees increases, so do the earnings of household enterprises. There is some evidence that earnings may also increase as the number of unpaid family workers employed in the enterprise increases. But the evidence on the positive effects on earnings of unpaid family members is not definitive (i.e. not statistically significant).

6. Household enterprises in manufacturing activities have lower earnings than other enterprises. This finding, which comes out of our formal statistical model is also evident from the descriptive data that we presented in Table 3.8.

7. The longevity of the household enterprise—i.e. the number of months it has been in operation—has no impact on earnings. Newer operations earn at roughly the same levels as older ones.

8. Women operating household enterprises on their own earn less than men in equivalent situations. This suggests that gender biases exist in the operations of household enterprises. Women, for example, may experience more difficulties dealing with suppliers, and getting access to markets.

CONSIDERATIONS FOR POLICY PROPOSALS

It is clear from the foregoing presentation of data that improving employment opportunities and living standards in Kenya must be linked closely with successful efforts to raise earnings opportunities for the country's household enterprise sector. Three separate factors would seem crucial as considerations for policy:

1. Raising productivity and expanding the domestic market in general, but also shaping policies so that household enterprises specifically will benefit from these overall economic gains.
2. Improving access to credit for household enterprises. From the evidence we have presented, the level of involvement by the SACCOs, to say nothing of commercial banks, can be improved by a great amount.
3. Reducing the overall number of household enterprises, so as to reduce competition among them. To do this will also mean increasing opportunities for formal sector employment.

These are all issues that we will take up in the chapters ahead on developing specific policies that will be effective in expanding employment opportunities and reducing poverty.

NOTES

1. The most extensive set of evidence on informal manufacturing firms prior to that supplied by the 2005–06 government survey is that presented in Bigsten, Kimuyu, and Lundvall (2004). Bigsten et al. conducted their own more limited survey of small manufacturing informal firms, and also compared their data on these informal firms with the formal enterprises that they also surveyed themselves. We consider the policy recommendations in this paper in later chapters.
2. Note that it is possible for households to be operating more than one non-agricultural enterprise.
3. Informal enterprises are not officially registered with the Registrar of Companies. Formal enterprises are registered.
4. It is important to recognize that we cannot reliably make direct comparisons between the overall employment data reported in Chapter 2 and the employment figures for the non-agricultural household enterprises presented here (that is, in particular, directly comparing the 5.2 million employment figure for non-agricultural household enterprises reported here with the overall employment figure of 12 million reported in Chapter 2). This is because the data from the two chapters come from different sets of questions within the overall 2005–06 KIHBS. For the Chapter 2 data, the reference period for defining the number of people employed is the past seven days relative to when the survey questions were being answered. With these Chapter 3 figures, the reference period was the past month relative to the date of answering the survey questions.

4. Labor Costs, Labor Market Institutions and Employment Expansion

As we have seen from our brief review of data, Kenya has severe problems in terms of creating decent employment opportunities for its citizens. An explanation that economists frequently make as a cause of inadequate employment growth is that excessive labor costs are discouraging businesses from hiring more workers. By definition, excessive labor costs would result when total compensation for workers is out of line with the productive contributions that these workers are capable of making to firms that would consider hiring them. To break this problem down, high labor costs can be seen as resulting from some combination of: 1) overall compensation of workers, including wages and benefits, being excessively high; 2) productivity being excessively low; or 3) rigidities in the legal and institutional environment which prevent compensation and productivity from matching up more closely.

Variations on this argument have been made in a range of regional settings to explain the persistence of high unemployment. Perhaps most prominently, arguments about excessive wages and benefits and inflexible labor markets have been frequently cited to explain the problems of mass unemployment in Western Europe since the 1970s. Comparable arguments have been used in sub-Saharan Africa as well, perhaps most notably in South Africa, where the official unemployment rate still hovers at around 26 percent.[1]

Some analysts have begun to examine the extent to which such arguments may also apply to the Kenyan situation, after adjusting, of course, to the specifics of Kenya's economy. Some notable recent studies that focus on this question have been sponsored by the World Bank, including "Labor Institutions, Labor-Management Relations, and Social Dialogue in Africa" by Alby, Azam, and Rospabé (2005); and the preliminary Concept Note by the World Bank titled "Jobs in Kenya" (World Bank 2005a). As the authors of the 2005 Concept Note make clear, this document is very much a preliminary report on a longer-term work in progress. These preliminary reports are designed to provide background material for a full-scale World Bank study on employment issues in Kenya. But as of this writing, the full-scale study is not yet available publicly. We will therefore draw on these currently available World Bank studies to inform our own discussion.

The World Bank's concern over excessive labor costs and rigidities in the formal labor market come out clearly in the Concept Note. For example, the Concept Note states that:

> With flexibility of the labor market a major policy concern, the question arises whether government prescribed labor mechanisms are a significant reason for wage rigidity, if any, in specific production sectors or the constrained labor mobility of Kenya? (p. 10).

The concerns of the World Bank are also clearly shared by the International Monetary Fund (IMF). Thus, the Concept Note explains the IMF position as follows:

> The main concern of the IMF …is the escalating wage cost in the public and private sector in Kenya. In its forward looking program the IMF will work with the government to make the wage management more tractable and to address the escalating wages. The [joint World Bank/IMF project]… will consider the minimum wages and other wage guidelines and help the government put in place and operationalize systems to support this (p. 14).

These concerns of both the World Bank and IMF stem from some basic facts about the Kenyan labor market, which we have already reviewed. The most important is that, as of the most recent 2005–06 estimates, only 14 percent of employed Kenyans are working in the formal sector, with 36 percent in informal employment of some sort and fully 50 percent in agricultural self-employment.

The data showing trends in the growth of the various sectors have been unreliable in the recent past.[2] Nevertheless, we believe it is safe to acknowledge that, over the past decade, employment growth in Kenya's formal sector has been substantially weaker than in the informal sector. If we can accept this as a general trend, this would suggest that, as population in Kenya grows, new labor market entrants are primarily moving from the rural areas into the urban informal sector.

The basic reason this overall pattern is of concern is that employment opportunities are clearly far superior in the formal sector. As we have seen from the 2005–06 survey data in Chapter 2, the median monthly wage for workers in the formal sector range between Ksh 6,160 in private firms and Ksh 15,375 in public employment. These wage levels are dramatically higher than the median wage of Ksh 2,880 for informal sector workers who are paid in wages. And even this wage differential does not adequately capture the relative advantages of working in the formal sector, given that a very high proportion of informal sector workers are either own-account workers or unpaid family members, generally earning less than average wage earnings in the sector, or nothing at all.

In short, it is clear that the most desirable development path for Kenya would be through the expansion of decent employment opportunities in its formal economy. The issue is how best to achieve this most desirable outcome.

To some analysts, the fact that the formal sector in Kenya is experiencing stagnating employment suggests, in itself, both an explanation for the problem and a solution. The explanation is straightforward: businesses will not hire more workers because they are convinced that the costs of doing so will exceed the benefits. Businesses therefore choose either to 1) maintain their operations at a lower level than they would if the benefits of hiring more workers exceeded the costs; or 2) increase the use of machines in their operations as a substitute for employing workers as their preferred means of expanding their operations. Seen from this perspective, the solution to the problem of unemployment is also straightforward: to lower the costs businesses face in hiring more workers.

There are four possible ways in which the costs to businesses of hiring workers could fall:

1.   Workers receive lower overall compensation, including wages and benefits;
2.   The industrial relations system and labor market regulations—including laws and regulations regarding workers' rights to organize, conflict resolution, and hiring and firing—operates with more flexibility for business;
3.   Workers perform their workplace operations at a higher level of productivity; or
4.   The government absorbs some portion of the costs of hiring workers.

From the perspectives of both the World Bank and the IMF, at least as expressed in the Concept Note, the preliminary focus appears to be on the first two ways to reduce business costs, i.e. to lower wages and benefits for workers and to increase the flexibility of the Kenyan formal labor market. We will focus on these two considerations in this section of our study. But we also provide some brief discussion in this section on raising productivity and government employment subsidies—i.e. using government subsidies as a way of reducing labor costs for business. We then also take up these latter two concerns in more depth later in the study.

LOWERING FORMAL SECTOR WAGES TO INCREASE EMPLOYMENT

To evaluate the net welfare effects of reducing wages in Kenya's formal economy, we need to begin by estimating how many new formal sector jobs are likely to be created through reducing wages. Once we have such an estimate, we can then assess the net benefits of such wage cuts. Let us assume for the purposes of this exercise that our aim is to increase the number of formal private sector wage earners by 25 percent. From the 2005–06 survey data, this would mean increasing employment in this sector by about 190,000 jobs, from the 2005/2006 level of about 770,000 to 960,000.

Economists estimate the relationship between relative changes in wage rates and employment levels through calculating a "wage elasticity of employment." Wage elasticities measure by how much we would expect employment to rise as a result of wage levels going down.

We do not know of any recent studies that have estimated wage elasticities for Kenya's formal sector. However, to establish at least a rough approximation of an elasticity, we can extrapolate from elasticity estimates that have recently been generated for South Africa and Ghana. The elasticity figure for black formal sector workers in South Africa that has been frequently used, by World Bank researchers among others, is -0.71 (Lewis 2001). That is, if wages for black formal sector workers in South Africa were to fall by 10 percent, this elasticity figure suggests that employment would rise by about 7 percent. In the Ghana case, a 2000 paper by Francis Teal finds that the employment elasticity in manufacturing is around -0.5. That is, for the manufacturing sector in Ghana, a cut in wages of 10 percent would generate a 5 percent increase in employment.

Assuming these estimates for South Africa and Ghana are broadly accurate, it is reasonable to assume as a rough approximation that the elasticity in Kenya for formal paid employment is likely to be in the range of -0.6. This means that to generate an additional 190,000 private sector formal economy jobs strictly through a strategy of wage-cutting, wages in the private formal sector would have to fall by about 42 percent.

According to the data we reported in Table 2.4, the median monthly wage level in the formal private sector as of 2005–06 was roughly Ksh 6,160. The breakdown between the urban and rural regions is an urban average of Ksh 9,000 per month, and a rural average of Ksh 4,800 per month. In Table 4.1, we work through step by step the scenarios of cutting these wage levels sufficiently to generate, on their own, an employment expansion of 25 percent, divided equally between the urban and rural formal private sectors.

As Table 4.1a shows, for the urban sector, the median monthly wage will have to fall to Ksh 5,220. This would bring the level of urban private formal employment to 523,550. For the rural formal private sector, the median monthly wage would have to fall to Ksh 2,784. This wage cut would increase employment in this sector to 440,296.

How significant would this wage cut be for the living standards of workers and their families? We provide a rough sense of this in Table 4.1b. The average formal private sector worker now supports one other person if they live in an urban area, and 1.3 other people if they live in a rural area. As such, as the table shows, for the urban worker and his/her one dependent, the one wage on which these two people live prior to the wage cut puts them at 50

*Table 4.1 Scenarios for Expanding Formal Private Employment by 25%
Through Wage-cutting (assume wage elasticity of demand for formal private
employment at -0.60)*

A) Wage Levels Necessary for 25% Employment Expansion

	Urban private employment	Rural private employment
Total employment in 2005–06	418,840 (3.5% of total employment)	352,237 (2.9% of total employment)
Actual median monthly real wage	9,000	4,800
Monthly wage level needed to increase employment by 25% (42% wage cut)	5,220	2,784
New employment level resulting from 42% wage cut	523,550	440,296

B) New Wage Levels and Poverty Thresholds

	Urban private employment	Rural private employment
Average number of people supported by one wage earner	2.0	2.3
Actual income level relative to regional poverty threshold *urban threshold=Ksh 2,913 rural threshold=Ksh 1,562*	50% above poverty threshold *(Ksh 9,000/2 people)/ Ksh 2,913*	34% above poverty threshold *(Ksh 4,800/ 2.3 people)/Ksh 1,562*
Income level after wage cut relative to overall poverty threshold	10% below poverty threshold *(Ksh 5,220/2 people)/ Ksh 2,913*	23% below poverty threshold *(Ksh 2,784/ 2.3 people)/Ksh 1,562*

Note: Hypothetical scenarios derived from data in Chapter 2 tables.

percent above the regional poverty line. After the wage cut, these two urban residents would now be living at 10 percent below the poverty line. The comparable situation would be more difficult still for a rural worker and the 1.3 other people depending on that worker's monthly income. Before the wage cut, these 2.3 people would be living 34 percent above the rural poverty line. After the wage cut, their reduced income level would place them 23 percent below the rural poverty line.

Now, of course, though the wages of roughly 770,000 workers would decline sharply through such a scenario, the average living standard of workers would not fall correspondingly. This is because the wage-cutting scenario would also generate about 190,000 people newly employed workers in the private formal sector. Most of these people would likely have migrated out of the informal labor market into these newly-created formal sector jobs. The wages for those coming from the informal sector to these newly-created formal sector jobs would be around 60 percent higher than what they had been earning in informal employment. This would be the key benefit from the wage-cutting scenario that we have worked through here.

In sum, the net effect of the wage-cutting scenario—including all the workers receiving either wage cuts or wage increases and the additional people who live off of these workers' incomes—would be as follows:

1. Nearly 1.7 million Kenyans would see their living standard fall sharply. This would include both the 770,000 workers and the roughly 900,000 additional people who live off of the wages of these workers.[3] These 1.7 million people would see their income levels fall, on average, to between 10 percent and 23 percent below their respective urban or regional poverty lines; and

2. About 400,000 Kenyans would experience a large increase in income. As above, this would include both the 190,000 workers newly hired into higher-paying formal sector jobs and the roughly 210,000 people who live off of the income of these workers.[4] Despite these people enjoying rising incomes, they would, on average, also still be living between 10 and 23 percent below their respective urban or regional poverty lines.

There is another consideration here in terms of net welfare effects. The fact that somewhere in the range of 1.7 million Kenyans will have to see a sharp decline in their living standards will of course generate social unrest. This, in turn will create an unstable atmosphere for private investors. The decline in private investment will in turn lead to a job contraction. In short, the positive employment effects that might result from a decrease in wages and living standards will be undermined by the destabilizing effects of cutting living standards.

Note, finally, that even if private formal employment could be expanded by 25 percent through wage cuts of over 40 percent, the total level of private formal employment would remain less than one million people. That is, at the current size of the Kenyan labor force, this large a wage cut in the private formal sector would still, by itself, mean that private formal employment would remain at less than 7 percent of the total Kenyan work force. Wage cuts would have to be substantially larger still for the private formal sector to grow to employing more than 10 percent of the total Kenyan workforce.

INDUSTRIAL RELATIONS AND LABOR MARKET RIGIDITIES

To what extent has the expansion of decent employment opportunities in Kenya possibly been hindered by the country's system of industrial relations, including regulations concerning hiring, hours, and firing; the extent and strength of union power in labor markets; and minimum wage standards? The World Bank's Concept Note (2005a) suggests that these factors may be playing an important role in holding back employment growth in the private formal sector. Yet the evidence informing these policy concerns is mixed, including data from the World Bank's own studies.

The most extensive set of evidence that relates to these issues comes from the World Bank's 2005 study "Labor Institutions, Labor-Management Relations, and Social Dialogue in Africa," by Alby et al.[5] This study presents results from surveys of businesses throughout Africa, and also offers comparative statistics from other regions of the world. In Table 4.2 we present some of the most important data from that study.

As an initial methodological point, we should note that most of the evidence in the Alby et al. study is derived from surveying the owners and managers of businesses in Kenya and elsewhere. It is of course appropriate for researchers to obtain the views of business owners and managers in establishing the extent of rigidities in labor markets, and it is a common practice to do so. At the same time, we should recognize that, in general, business owners and managers are not disinterested observers on such questions. All else equal, they operate with a vested interest in promoting reductions in the regulations that limit their freedom to operate and potentially raise their costs. As such, the findings from survey questions on these matters will tend to have some upward bias— that is, overstating the impact of regulations in affecting their business operations. This does not mean that the findings cannot be valid or informative. But we do need to interpret the findings in light of this inherent upward bias.

Table 4.2a gives evidence from surveys of business firm owners and managers on the difficulties and costs associated with hiring, managing working hours, and firing. The first three columns are index numbers on "difficulty of hiring," "rigidity of hours," and "difficulty of firing," with scores ranging between 0 and 100, with 100 representing the highest level of regulation. The fourth column, "rigidity of employment index," is an average of the first three index numbers.

From these four columns of figures, it is clear that Kenya ranks very low in terms of the rigidity of employment conditions, at least as perceived by the country's business owners and managers. Considering the overall "rigidity of employment index," Kenya's index number of 24 places it substantially below the averages both for sub-Saharan Africa, at 56, and Latin America and the

Table 4.2 Industrial Relations and Labor Market Rigidities in Kenya: Summary of World Bank Survey Evidence

A) RIGIDITY OF EMPLOYMENT INDEX

	Difficulty of hiring index	Rigidity of hours index	Difficulty of firing index	Rigidity of employment index	Firing costs (weeks)
Kenya	22	20	30	24	47
Sub-Saharan Africa	53	64	50	56	59
Latin America and the Caribbean	44	53	34	44	70

Note: Index components are scored between 0 and 100, with 100 representing the highest level of regulation. The "Rigidity of Employment Index" is the average of the first three indices.

B) HIRING AND FIRING PROCEDURES:
PERCENTAGE OF FIRMS CITING ITEM AS SIGNIFICANT OBSTACLE

	Hiring	Layoff
Kenya	5.2%	20.9%
Ethiopia	0.5%	9.8%
Nigeria	4.8%	10.6%
Uganda	4.1%	8.3%
Zambia	1.0%	26.7%

C) PERCENTAGE OF BUSINESS FIRMS CITING LABOR REGULATIONS
AS SIGNIFICANT OBSTACLE TO DEVELOPMENT

Kenya	22.5%
Ethiopia	4.6%
Tanzania	12.1%
Uganda	10.8%
Zambia	16.9%

Source for Panels A–C: Alby et al. (2005).

Caribbean, at 44. As we see in the last column of Table 4.2a, Kenya is also well below the averages for these two regions in terms of firing costs.

This clear finding from Table 4.2a—that Kenya has less rigid labor market conditions than the averages for sub-Saharan Africa and Latin America—becomes less evident in considering the findings from Table 4.2b–c. Here we see that, compared with other sub-Saharan African countries, Kenya ranks relatively high in terms of hiring and firing procedures as significant obstacles to conducting business and "development" more generally. In other words, these findings seem to conflict with the figures in Table 4.2a, even though both sets of figures are taken from the same World Bank research paper by Alby et al. (2005).

It is not clear from the Alby et al. paper itself whether the data provided in Table 4.2a–c all come from the same survey of business owners and managers. If they are in fact coming from different surveys, this could explain at least part of the discrepancy in the rankings on Kenya relative to other countries. But even if all these data come from the same survey, it is possible that the disparities in responses result from differences in how particular questions were worded.

In any case, if we focus only on the results we report in Table 4.2b–c, the findings still do not support a conclusion that labor market rigidities in Kenya operate as significant barriers to employment expansion. Thus, even the figures where Kenya comes out least favorably—that is, in the findings on number of firms citing layoffs and labor market regulations as significant obstacles—we still see only 21–22 percent of business owners citing this as a problem. This means that close to 80 percent of firm owners/managers do not see labor market regulations as a significant problem. In the case of hiring procedures, as we see in Table 4.2b, again more business owners/managers in Kenya see this as a problem than their counterparts in other sub-Saharan African countries. But still, only about 5 percent see the hiring procedures as a problem—in other words, about 95 percent of owners and managers do not see hiring procedures as a problem.

Considering the overall weight of evidence presented by the Alby et al. study, and evaluating these findings in light of the propensity for some upward bias that is inherent in surveying business owners and managers on these questions, it is reasonable to conclude that most business representatives in Kenya consider labor market regulations around hiring, firing, and hours to be relatively minor barriers to expansion, if they are barriers at all. There is clearly a subset of managers that consider these regulations to be a significant problem. But those business owners who feel that way represent a small minority of all business owners/managers operating in Kenya's formal sector.

The Impact of Labor Unions

The World Bank's Concept Note (2005a) suggests that labor unions may be operating as a significant source of labor market rigidities in Kenya. But the evidence suggests that, as with the regulations on hiring, firing, and hours, this is unlikely to be a significant barrier to the expansion of decent employment. If for no other reason, this is because unions represent a small and diminishing portion of Kenya's labor force. In Table 4.3, we report figures from the same 2005 World Bank study by Alby et al. (2005). As we see there, union membership in Kenya fell from 700,000 in 1985 to 436,036 in 2000, a decline of 38 percent. As we also see in the table, the

Table 4.3 Recent Union Membership in Selected Sub-Saharan Countries

	First available year	Last available year	Change in membership 1985 - 2000
Kenya	700,000 (1985)	436,036 (2000)	-37.7%
Tanzania	470,000 (1995)	311,096 (2001)	- 33.8%
Uganda	102,000 (1989)	63,000 (1995)	-38.2%
Zambia	320,000 (1985)	242,752 (2001)	-24.1%
Ghana	700,000 (1990)	572,598 (1998)	-18.2%

Source: Alby, Azam, and Rospabé (2005).

decline in union membership in Kenya corresponds with a pattern for other sub-Saharan African countries over roughly the same period.

In terms of providing more recent figures on unionization in Kenya, the 2005–06 KIHBS does include a question on whether people were members of a "trade union or welfare association." These results can be broken down according to whether people are employed in agricultural self-employment or the formal or informal sectors. From these survey data, there is no way of separating out union membership from membership in "welfare associations." Nevertheless, the results from the survey convey some broad patterns:

1. Membership in unions and welfare associations are concentrated in Kenya's formal public sector;
2. It is likely that about 70 percent of public sector employees are unionized, with the largest grouping being teachers and civil servants below the senior level; and
3. Union membership in the private formal sector is probably around 20 percent of total employment in that sector.

Overall then, the evidence suggests that, as of 2005–06, about 25–30 percent of Kenya's formal sector wage workers are unionized. This would mean that about 4 percent of Kenya's total workforce—including those in the informal sector and agricultural self-employment—are unionized. At the same time, the Alby et al. study (2005) reports that 58.5 percent of Kenyan firms state that non-unionized workers also benefit from union-negotiated contracts (p. 25). Thus, the scope of union influence may extend beyond its small base of members in the private formal sector.

Still, other evidence suggests that the scope of union power remains modest. Among other factors, the decline in union membership since the mid-1980s suggests that, to the extent that unions may have the capacity to operate as a rigidity in Kenya's formal labor market, the disruptive force of this rigidity should clearly have diminished sharply, not increased, since the mid-1980s. Consistent with this, the Alby et al. study also reports that in 2003, 93.6 percent of firms surveyed in Kenya reported losing zero work days due to strikes and labor unrest (p. 40).

More generally, a careful 2005 econometric study by Manda, Bigsten, and Mwabu, observes as follows:

> The trade unions' main aim is to improve the welfare of its members by negotiating higher earnings for its members, better conditions of service, and increasing job tenure. To achieve these objectives, unions need a strong financial base and bargaining power. However, in Kenya, unions are generally financially weak and are occasionally faced with internal leadership struggles. Their main source of finance is membership fees, which are not high enough to sustain drawn-out strikes. Also, their ability to strike is limited by control of union activities by the government through legislation, and by threat of de-registration ... Unions can still influence the level of earnings and working conditions of their members through collective bargaining, although the unions sometimes lack resources to hire negotiators with skills and abilities to match the full-time negotiators of the employers (2005, p. 1693).

Manda et al. conclude from their econometric analysis that unions in Kenya do help formal sector workers obtain a wage premium in addition to getting protection from excessively long hours of work and from arbitrary job loss. At the same time, they find that elite-level workers in Kenya do not join unions, and thus, the gains generated by unions are received primarily by less-skilled production level workers.

We should also add that, as a general matter, it is not necessarily the case that relatively high rates of unionization should necessarily serve as a barrier to expanding decent employment opportunities in Kenya or, more generally, to promoting the country's overall economic progress. Indeed, in 1995, the World Bank's own *World Development Report* (noted that it is "possible to identify the conditions and policies under which free trade unions can advance rather than impede development." Following up on this, a more recent World Bank publication of 2003, *Unions and Collective Bargaining*, recognized that "high unionization rates lead to lower inequality of earnings and can improve economic performance in the form of lower unemployment and inflation, higher productivity and speedier adjustment to shocks"[6] (quoted in Freeman 2005, p. 134).

Minimum Wage Laws

Kenya currently operates with a wide array of minimum wage orders that apply to different sectors, regions of the country, and job categories. In all, there are 45 separate minimum wage standards. The figure doubles to 90 if we also count the fact that there are separate rates depending on whether a housing allowance is included. In Table 4.4, we present the range of minimum wage rates in Kenya for 2005.

Table 4.4 *Minimum Wage Standards in Kenya, 2005 (in Ksh)*

Occupation	Nairobi, Mombasa, & Kisumu			All other municipalities & Mavoko, Ruiru, and Limuru			All other areas		
	Monthly	Daily	Hourly	Monthly	Daily	Hourly	Monthly	Daily	Hourly
1. General labourer, cleaner, sweeper, gardener, ayah house servant, day watchman, messenger	4,638	223.1	41.4	4,279	205.1	37.9	2,474	125.4	23.2
2. Miner, stone cutter, turnboy, waiter, cook, logger, line cutter	5,010	252.7	48.5	4,892	236.6	42.9	3,965	191.5	35.6
3. Night watchman	5,175	248.35	46.65	4,797	231.3	42.5	2,952	142.4	27.2
4. Machine attendant, sawmill sawyer, machine asst., mass production machinist, shoe cutter, bakery worker, bakery asst., tailor's asst.	5,257	252.7	48.5	4,892	236.6	42.9	3,965	191.5	35.6
5. Machinist (made to measure), shoe upper repairer chaplis maker, vehicle service worker (petrol & service stations), bakery plant hand, laundry operator, jnr. clerk, wheel tractor driver (light)	6,001	289.2	53.8	5,614	270.3	50.5	4,590	222	41.4
6. Printing machine operator, bakery machine operator, plywood machine operator, sawmill dresser, shop asst., machine tool operator, doughmaker, table hand baker or confectioner, copy typist, driver (cars and light vans)	6,261	301.1	56.3	5,778	277.7	51.4	4,776	229.5	42.5
7. Pattern designer (draughtsman), garment and dress cutter, single-hand oven man, charge-hand baker, general clerk, telephone operator, receptionist, storekeeper	7,145	343.5	64.4	6,531	314.15	57.9	5,569	267	49.9

(cont.)

94

Table 4.4 (cont.) *Minimum Wage Standards in Kenya, 2005 (in Ksh)*

Occupation	Nairobi, Mombasa, & Kisumu			All other municipalities & Mavoko, Ruiru, and Limuru			All other areas		
	Monthly	Daily	Hourly	Monthly	Daily	Hourly	Monthly	Daily	Hourly
8. Tailor, driver (medium-sized vehicle)	7,873	378.9	70.1	7,237	348.6	64.5	6,452	315.1	57.9
9. Dyer, crawler tractor driver, salesman	8,692	416.9	78.1	8,110	390.3	72.65	7,320	351.3	64.6
10. Saw doctor, caretaker (buildings)	9,620	463.2	86.6	8,982	432.5	80.6	8,367	402.2	74.8
11. Cashier, driver (heavy commercial vehicle), salesman driver	10,467	503.9	94.3	9,849	474.1	89	9,235	443.9	83
12. Ungraded artisan	6,261	301.1	56.3	5,778	277.7	51.4	4,776	229.5	42.5
Artisan grade i	10,467	503.9	94.3	9,849	474.1	89	9,235	443.9	83
Artisan grade ii	8,692	416.9	78.1	8,110	390.3	72.65	7,320	351.3	64.6
Artisan grade iii	7,873	378.9	70.1	7,237	348.6	64.5	6,452	315.1	57.9
Average	7,295.47	351.62	65.83	6,795.67	327.20	60.69	5,829.87	281.44	52.25

Note: Daily and hourly rates are inclusive of housing allowances. Monthly rates are exclusive of housing allowances.
Source: Government of Kenya, Agricultural Industrial Order (2005).

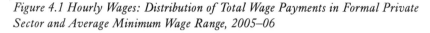

Figure 4.1 Hourly Wages: Distribution of Total Wage Payments in Formal Private Sector and Average Minimum Wage Range, 2005–06

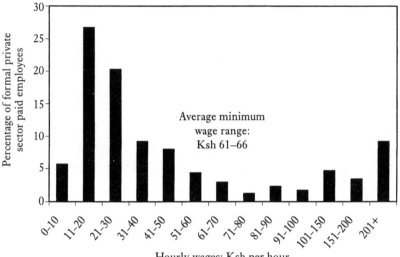

Hourly wages: Ksh per hour

Note: Wage payments include basic salary and allowances.
Source: 2005–06 KIHBS.

In August 2007, the Minister of Labour, Dr. Newton Kulundu, announced that the government was planning to eliminate minimum wage standards.[7] Instead, Kulundu said that the Productivity Centre of Kenya established by the Ministry of Labour would aim to set wage standards based on productivity levels. It is not yet clear how the Productivity Centre would establish productivity levels and the appropriate wage levels corresponding to productivity. The minimum wage laws are likely to remain in force until such issues are settled. In any case, the role of minimum wages is clearly being scrutinized carefully as our study is being published.

It is thus an appropriate time to evaluate what the impact of minimum wage standards has been on the actual wages paid to workers in Kenya. In considering this question, we again focus on conditions for paid workers in the formal private sector. As we saw in Table 2.1 above, there were in 2005–06 about 10.3 million Kenyans earning income either through agricultural self-employment or in the informal sector. However, we know that, at least with respect to those employed in informal arrangements in both agricultural and non-agricultural settings, labor market regulations would be enforced in rare exceptions only. Indeed, the lack of regulatory standards is one of the main defining features of

Figure 4.2 Monthly Wages: Distribution of Total Wage Payments in Formal Private Sector and Average Minimum Wage Range, 2005–06

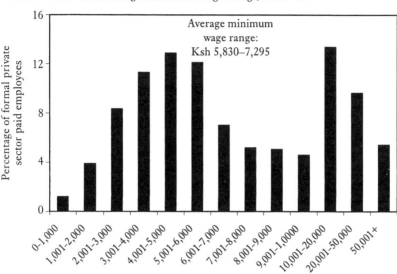

Note: Wage payments include basic salary and allowances.
Source: 2005–06 KIHBS.

an economy's informal sector. There were also another roughly 650,000 paid employees in Kenya's public and semi-public sectors in 2005–06. However, with public sector employees, their wage rates are not set directly by market forces but rather by government standards. The situation is similar for semi-public sector employees. Hence, in asking to what extent the country's minimum wage standards might be affecting the operation of labor markets, the most relevant context in which to consider the question is within the formal private sector, accounting for about 770,000 workers in 2005–06.

What has been the impact of minimum wage standards on the actual wage levels paid in the formal private sector? We can obtain a sense of this by examining Figures 4.1–3, which show the actual distribution of wage rates in the formal private sector during the 2005–06 labor force survey along with the range of average minimum wages for 2005. We present the wage rate figures in monthly, daily, and hourly terms, to match the time-frames in which the Kenyan government sets minimum wage standards.

Beginning with the data on hourly wages in Figure 4.1, we see that there is little correspondence between the range of average minimum wage rates and

Figure 4.3 Daily Wages: Distribution of Total Wage Payments in Formal Private Sector and Average Minimum Wage Range, 2005–06

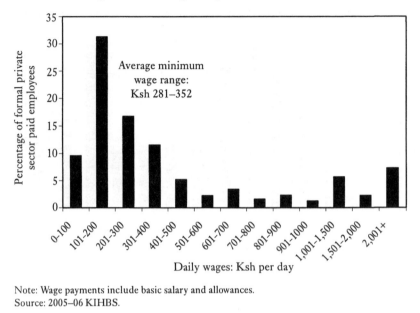

Note: Wage payments include basic salary and allowances.
Source: 2005–06 KIHBS.

the actual level of hourly wages that workers received in 2005–06. In particular, we see that about 73 percent of hourly workers in the private formal sector are paid below the lowest average figure for the statutory minimum wage. From this figure, it appears that the minimum wage mandate has little, if any, influence on where actual wages are set in the formal private sector.

However, most workers in Kenya's formal private sector are paid on a daily or monthly basis, not on an hourly basis. It is therefore important to see how the daily and monthly wages that are paid match up against the minimum wage standards for these pay periods. We observe these relationships in Figures 4.2 and 4.3. As we can see from these two figures, there is greater correspondence between the actual market wages paid and the range of average minimum wages applied to the daily and monthly pay periods. Still, even with these two figures, between 43–50 percent of private formal sector workers are earning wages below the lower-range average for the statutory minimum wage. These findings suggest that, as of 2005–06, the minimum wage laws are exerting little influence in actual wage-setting within the formal private sector.

Are the minimum wage laws in Kenya acting as a rigidity, impeding the expansion of decent employment opportunities in the country? If somewhere

between 40–70 percent of private formal sector workers are paid below the average minimum standards, it is difficult to see how these standards are serving as a
significant barrier to employment expansion. Of course, we have seen in Chapter 2 that wages in the formal sector are maintained at a substantially higher
level than the informal sector. However, the evidence we present here makes
clear that this differential is not due to formal sector businesses being required
to uphold minimum wage laws. Private formal sector businesses are consistently
violating the minimum wage laws. The higher wages in the private formal sector
are rather the result of significantly higher levels of productivity, sales, and profitability in the formal sector.

Given their current ineffectiveness in setting actual wage floors, should the
minimum wage laws be repealed, as is currently being proposed by the Labour
Minister? In fact, the 2005 levels for the minimum wage were serving a useful
function in establishing a decent standard that would enable working people
and their families to live above the poverty line. Consider the 2005 average
monthly minimum wage for Nairobi, which was Ksh 7,296. If we allow that, on
average, this monthly wage payment was used to support one person in addition
to the wage-earner herself, that would mean that these two people would each
live on Ksh 3,648 per month (i.e. Ksh 7,296/2). A monthly income level of Ksh
3,648 would place a resident of Nairobi at an income level about 25 percent
above the overall urban poverty line of Ksh 2,913.

Given these figures, to conclude that the minimum wage should be eliminated or significantly reduced from its current levels is to therefore also conclude that the Kenyan economy is unable to pay even those workers with jobs in
the formal private sector a wage that will keep them and their families out of
poverty. Rather than seek to eliminate or weaken a minimally decent wage standard in an effort to promote employment growth, it would seem preferable, at
least as an initial endeavor, to pursue alternative policy approaches for expanding decent employment, including raising productivity, increasing access to
credit, improving marketing capacity, and maintaining a more competitive exchange rate. At the same time, the degree of detail involved in setting minimum
wages according to job categories and regions is excessive. The beneficial effects
of minimum wages would be strengthened by a more simplified system.[8]

We should note finally on this issue some general findings from the recent
professional literature concerning the effects of minimum wage standards on
employment and poverty in developing countries.[9] A summary of this recent
literature have found the following two major conclusions:

1. There is no statistically robust effect on employment levels of higher mini-
    mum wages, assuming the minimum wage mandates are set at a level con-
    sistent with a country's level of productivity and overall development. This
    does not mean that higher minimum wages in developing countries posi-

tively promote higher employment. The findings rather suggest that any negative employment effects appear weak. This is especially true after one also factors in other forces contributing to a country's formal sector employment levels, such as the level of investment and aggregate demand. Moreover, a higher minimum wage may itself contribute both to stronger investment and aggregate demand. One possible channel for this effect is that a higher minimum wage will promote more cooperation between employers and workers, which, in turn, will encourage higher productivity and a more stable investment climate.

2. Because higher minimum wage rates (consistent with a country's overall level of productivity and development) will bring more income to low-wage workers and their families, without necessarily reducing the total number of low-wage jobs available, it follows that a higher minimum wage can be an effective tool for reducing poverty. The chain-of-effects is straightforward: a decent minimum wage standard can bring more money to low-wage workers and their families without reducing the overall number of jobs available to them. This was the main conclusion of an important study by Lustig and McLeod (1997). Their main conclusion has been affirmed by many subsequent studies.

UNIT LABOR COSTS, PRODUCTIVITY, AND GOVERNMENT SUBSIDIES

Our discussion thus far does not support the general approach of Kenyan policymakers attempting to push down the country's wage levels or reducing the role of unions or minimum wage standards as measures to reduce average unit labor costs faced by the country's businesses. But this does not mean that Kenya should neglect measures that could reduce unit labor costs. It rather suggests that the preferred ways of reducing unit labor costs for businesses are by raising productivity or through providing subsidies to businesses that are aggressively hiring workers into formal sector jobs. We briefly consider both the issues of productivity and employment subsidies in this section. We discuss them in greater depth in later sections of this study—on productivity growth through infrastructure investments and on the financial system and a large-scale subsidized credit program. Within this larger perspective, it should also be clear that, in our view, reducing unit labor costs per se cannot serve Kenya as an effective engine of decent employment expansion. As we will explain at length in subsequent chapters, our own policy approach for employment expansion focuses rather on raising productivity within a framework of increased public infrastructure investments, expanding support for private businesses, and a growing domestic market.

Productivity and Global Competitiveness

Concerns have emerged in Kenya that relatively high unit labor costs are becoming an impediment to continued export success in the tea and cut flower industries.[10] Competitors such as Malawi and Ethiopia are noted for having lower wage rates and thus likely to become increasingly competitive against Kenyan producers of tea and cut flowers. However, what is not sufficiently recognized in such discussions is the fact that productivity—including land and labor productivity—is higher in Kenya, even after allowing for fall-offs in productivity in Kenya since the 1980s. Thus, labor productivity in Kenya is at least 15 percent higher than in Malawi and overall productivity is about 20 percent higher than in Ethiopia (World Bank 2005b.)

These recent observations, moreover, are consistent with the extensive earlier findings of Odhiambo, Kristanson, and Kashangaki (1996), which examined overall costs and profitability in Kenya, Uganda, and Tanzania for three crops: coffee, maize, and beans. In each of the cases, the authors found that labor is more expensive in Kenya but overall productivity is substantially higher. For example in coffee, in 1993 Kenya had fixed costs that were approximately 87 percent higher than Uganda and Tanzania and labor costs that were 7 percent higher than Tanzania and 26 percent higher than Uganda. However, yields in Kenya were 181 percent above those in Tanzania and 32 percent higher than Uganda. As such, the costs per kg of coffee in Kenya were 178 percent lower than Tanzania and 26 percent lower than Uganda. In addition, the Kenyan coffee was of higher quality and enjoyed a premium in price. This maintained profitability at a higher level in Kenya. Odhiambo et al. tell a similar story with maize and beans. Despite higher costs in Kenya, profitability in Kenya was still consistently higher than in both Uganda and Tanzania. In short, the focus here is to understand the sources of productivity growth, and to pursue the most effective means of improving productivity on a sustainable basis. This is a theme that we will explore in some depth in later sections of the study.

We would finally also note that improving competitiveness is not simply a matter of keeping labor costs down, either through lower wages or higher productivity. Exchange rate policy and marketing infrastructure are also crucial here. These are also topics we consider in later sections.

Government Subsidies for Employment Creation

In principle, there are significant advantages to this method of lowering unit labor costs. The key advantage is that workers are not being asked to experience pay cuts in order to encourage businesses to hire more of them. In general, we share the favorable evaluation of employment subsidies expressed by Jeffrey Lewis of the World Bank (2001), in his research on the employment situation in

South Africa. Lewis concluded with respect to South Africa, but also more generally, that "employment subsidies can be used as a strategy for increasing employment without producing negative consequences for productivity and competitiveness." [11] Lewis makes clear that employment subsidies are a distinctively supply-side approach to expanding job growth through promoting more labor-intensive production methods. At the same time, Lewis holds that "employment subsidies and demand-side job creation policies are not mutually exclusive."

However, there are serious issues to address in attempting to implement an effective employment subsidy program. The two broad forms that these measures can take are either as a general or a marginal employment subsidy. A general employment subsidy would apply to all workers, both new and already employed—businesses would receive government support, either through direct grants or tax benefits, based on the total number of workers on their payroll. A marginal subsidy would apply only when new workers are hired from a previously established base of employees. A general subsidy program would obviously be much larger in scope, and correspondingly much more expensive, than a marginal subsidy program. It would also reward businesses simply on the basis of their existing employment levels. But a marginal subsidy program, which does not face these problems, would also be much more difficult to administer. Such programs require that there be some measurement of what employment would have been without the subsidy program. As such, they create incentives for firms to under-report employment. They therefore also would place large administrative demands on the government.

Given these and related concerns, we present in our discussion of Kenya's financial system a kind of hybrid employment subsidy program. More specifically, the measure we propose is actually a credit subsidy program. But the organizing principle of this program is that commercial banks would connect with the country's microfinance institutions, to promote growth in small- and medium-sized businesses, as well as rural smallholders. These smaller enterprises will tend to hire a relatively high proportion of new workers as their level of business operations grows. This is how a credit subsidy program can also be regarded as a means of subsidizing employment. Relative to more standard general and marginal employment subsidy measures, our proposal has these advantages: 1) it has features of both a general and a marginal employment subsidy program; 2) as we will see later, it is capable of operating on a large-scale basis in Kenya without requiring correspondingly large direct government expenditures; and 3) it can serve both to stimulate aggregate business investment on the demand side of the economy, while also promoting more labor intensive production methods on the supply-side.

NOTES

1. On European unemployment, see, for example, Layard, Nickell, and Jackman (2005), Howell, Baker, Glyn and Schmitt (2007), and Heckman's comment on Howell et al. (2007). The debate on South Africa is reviewed in Pollin et al. (2006).
2. For example, the most recent previous labor market survey for Kenya, in 1998–99, reported the employment breakdown between the three main sectors as being 39 percent agricultural self-employment, 34 percent informal and 27 percent formal. It is most unlikely that, between the 1998–99 and 2005–06 surveys, the share of agricultural self-employment would have risen from 39 to 50 percent. This fact calls into question all other evidence on recent labor market trends in Kenya.
3. We estimate the 900,000 figure for people living off of the wages of the 770,000 formal private sector workers as follows. We have reported that, on average, each urban private formal sector worker supports one additional person, and each rural private formal sector worker supports 1.3 other people. Total private formal employment is divided roughly equally between Kenya's urban and rural regions. We therefore assume roughly that all private formal sector workers support 1.15 additional people, and thereby multiply 770,000 by 1.15 to generate the figure of 900,000.
4. The calculations for generating this estimate are identical to those described in the previous note.
5. The full-length version of this study is summarized in a November 2006 World Bank policy note of the same title.
6. The references to these World Bank studies can be found in Freeman (2005).
7. Mangoa Mosota, "Government to Discard Minimum Wages Policy," *The Standard*, August 14, 2007.
8. This is the key conclusion of the 2004 IPAR Discussion Paper by Omolo and Omati, "Is Minimum Wage Policy Effective in Kenya?"
9. Some of the key recent research studies include Alatas and Cameron (2003), Cukierman, Rama and van Ours (2001), Forteza and Rama (2006), Infante, Marinakis, and Velasco (2003), Islam and Nazara (2000), Lustig and McLeod (1997), Rama (2001), and Saget (2001).
10. Interview on March 13, 2006 with Mr. L. Tiampati, Managing Director of KTDA and Mr. D. Kimani, Finance Director, during a visit to KTDA headquarters.
11. Lewis (2001), p. 35. Lewis's overall discussion of this issue is on pp. 34–39 of his study.

5. The Rural Sector: Institutional Reform for Development

Any attempt at significantly improving employment opportunities and reducing poverty in Kenya cannot help but focus on the role of the rural population and the agricultural sector. Agriculture is, of course, a foundation of the Kenyan economy. Beyond this most obvious factor, there are at least five other important reasons why agriculture needs to be central to our overall analysis. These include the following:

1. A majority of Kenya's population reside in the rural areas. According to the 2006–07 KIHBS, in 2005, 85 percent of this group participated directly in crop farming, livestock rearing or both. In addition, 13 percent of urban households participated in agricultural activities.
2. A majority of the poor live in the rural areas. This is a result both of the larger population living in the rural areas and that rural areas are poorer on average than urban areas.
3. Because any real attempt at increased growth needs to transform the economy to have an industrial and service base, the rural population would initially be a major source of demand for products from the service and the industrial sectors.
4. Because managing a process of transition to an industrial economy ultimately means managing urban growth, improvements in the rural sector will help slow down the rural–urban migration and make the process of urbanization more manageable.
5. The level of wages is important in determining household income and thus the level of poverty. Agricultural earnings set the "reservation wage" in the economy—that is, the lowest wage that workers in the urban sectors would be willing to accept, given that they can work in the rural economy at this given rate of pay. Improvements in agriculture thus would result in a general increase in earnings across the country as the reservation wage went up.

The agricultural sector has remained a foundation of the Kenyan economy since independence. This is the case both in terms of the proportion of the population employed in the sector as well as the gross output of the sector. On average, agriculture contributed approximately 30 percent of GDP between 1964 and 2004. This relative contribution has fallen sharply since the 1990s, with the 1996–2004 average being 24 percent (World Bank 2005b). In the last three years there seems to have been a clear upswing in agricultural production, accompanying the economy's general growth upswing. According to the government's 2006 *Economic Survey*, the overall economy grew at 5.4 percent in 2005 while agriculture grew at 6.7 percent (Government of Kenya 2006c). The last time the agricultural sector grew this rapidly was from 1981 to 1982. If agriculture can continue to expand at healthy rates, if not necessarily at such peak levels that were achieved in 2005, we would expect that agriculture would continue to contribute at least 20 percent of GDP over roughly the next decade.

Will the agricultural sector be able to sustain its relatively rapid growth of the past two years? We saw at the outset of the study that, at least according to the official aggregate data, Kenyan agriculture has experienced a long-term decline in agricultural productivity—that is, an *absolute decline* in the level of productivity, not merely a slowdown in the rate of productivity growth. In what follows, we first provide an overview of this situation. We then consider specific conditions that prevail with Kenya's major crops, including tea and coffee, horticulture, maize and wheat, millet and sorghum, sugarcane and rice. We also discuss the livestock sector.

These detailed discussions will then form the basis for our policy recommendations aimed at raising productivity and international competitiveness in the agricultural sector. The seven themes that we develop out of our discussions on the various agricultural sectors are these:

1. learning from successes;
2. adaptation rather than replication of past successes;
3. recognizing resources and capabilities of smallholders;
4. designing effective extension services for smallholders;
5. returns to scale and agricultural cooperatives;
6. infrastructure improvements; and
7. cost of capital and access to credit.

Beyond these seven key themes, we also recognize the centrality of one additional issue here, which is land redistribution. However, this is a large topic in its own right, and we are unable, in this study, to give it the careful consideration it deserves. Of course, we encourage both policymakers and independent researchers to build on the important work that already exists on this question.[1]

Figure 5.1 Trends in Agricultural Productivity

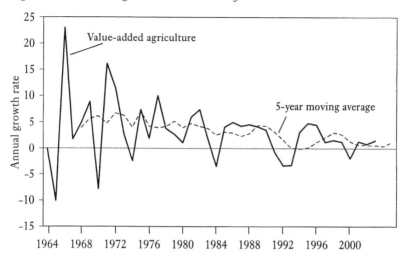

Source: World Bank (2005b).

OVERVIEW OF AGRICULTURE'S DEVELOPMENT AND DECLINE

Agriculture grew rapidly in the first decade of independence. It was, in fact, the principle engine of growth for Kenya's economy. However, in the last two decades, agriculture has fallen into a serious long decline. Figure 5.1 clearly illustrates the downward trend in the level of production. These data on levels of production fill out the picture that we initially conveyed in Figure 1.3, which we presented in Chapter 1 on the country's agricultural productivity trends. Unlike Figure 1.3 which shows value-added per worker, Figure 5.1 looks at the total value-added of the agricultural sector, regardless of how many people were required to produce that amount.

Agriculture in Kenya has remained predominantly rain fed, with less than 2 percent of the land being irrigated (World Bank 2005a) or about 6 percent of the total number of holdings (2006–07 KIHBS). As such, there are large year-to-year fluctuations that follow annual rainfall patterns. Thus, to illustrate the trend more clearly we have superimposed a five-year moving average on the line showing annual fluctuations. As Figure 5.1 shows, up to 1974 the five-year average output oscillated around the 5 percent mark. Crucially, this rate of growth in agricultural value-added was 1.4 percent faster than the country's rate of population growth. In other words, the agricultural sector was providing more than enough food to feed the country's growing population.

This rapid growth in agricultural production is attributable to several things, but two factors were the most important. The first was the high prices of primary commodities worldwide. The second was the opportunities for agricultural participation that were opened up for larger sections of the population with independence. Concurrent with this second factor was the more intensive and extensive use of land, as considerable amounts of land were transferred from large estate production to smallholders. In particular the expansion of African smallholders in tea and coffee contributed significantly to these historically high growth rates. We should note here that the success of agriculture, often seen as due to the pragmatic considerations of the government (see Lofchie 1993, for example), was not undergirded by a growth in land productivity at the aggregate level. At best, what was maintained were existing levels of productivity with expansion of crops to new areas. This observation should give pause to those who consider this period to have been a golden era of Kenyan agriculture and a model that should be replicated in the present.

Post-1974, the growth rate of agricultural output began to fall. What were the main forces behind this reversal? Some of this fall can be attributed to the spikes in oil prices in 1973–74 and 1979. These energy supply shocks in turn affected overall input costs in Kenya. Thus, as we can see in Figure 5.2, fertilizer utilization falls off considerably from 1973 up to 1979 before recovering a sharp upward growth trajectory from the 1980s onward.

A second, less thoroughly explored, factor is that the output expansion that was possible in the first few years after independence was reaching its limits. This is because that initial expansion resulted primarily from growing participation in agriculture by heretofore excluded segments of Kenya's population, rather than improvements in agricultural productivity. Further expansion of agricultural output would require institutional and technological changes to raise productivity rather than simply just increasing output with more tillers on the land. But such productivity gains did not occur generally across the agricultural sector. Up to around 1988–1990, the growth rate of agricultural production fell to a level roughly equal to the population growth rate. But beyond 1991, agricultural growth collapsed. The years 1991–1993 were the first three-year period since independence when agricultural output was actually negative for the full three-year stretch.

Some analysts, such as Gerdin (2002), suggest that the culprit for the slowdown in agricultural output was a stagnant level of productivity, due to the lack of increase in complementary inputs, such as capital goods. We would argue that there is not a single cause of the decline in agricultural output. Given the differences in institutional structure, capital intensity, and market penetration within the various sectors, aggregate measures of productivity decline are likely to mask differences by sector. Further it is likely that the stagnant agricultural

Figure 5.2 Trends in Agricultural Input Use (indexed to 1964)

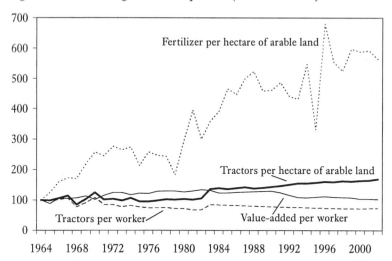

Source: World Bank (2005b).

productivity is partially an artifact of the measurement used rather than a real indicator of changes on the ground. The slowdown in the economy from around 1980 meant that there were fewer non-agricultural positions available. If people responded by staying in farming, this would mean that more workers per hectare are earning their keep through agriculture. Productivity per worker would therefore decline in this situation, even if farm output did not decline. This is clearly illustrated by the statistics on arable hectares of land per person. In 1964 there was 0.37 hectares per person. By 2002 this number had fallen to 0.15 hectares per person, a fall of just below 60 percent (World Bank 2005a).

Moreover, an examination of aggregate figures on labor productivity themselves do not tell a clear story. We can see this from Figure 5.2. As the figure shows, value-added per worker has remained nearly constant over the full period since independence. Between 1968 and 1980–82 there was a slight rise which flattened out. This was followed by a slow decline back to 1964 levels in the period 1982 to 2003. The changes in productivity cannot be explained simply by complementary inputs such as tractors per hectare which has remained roughly constant over the full period, or fertilizer application which, as the figure shows, has increased tremendously. In addition, both fertilizer and tractors are much more likely to be used in the cash crop sector and not the subsistence sector. For this reason alone, the story to this point is, at best, incomplete.

It is easy to dismiss the slowdown in the 1980s that continued into the early 2000s as simply a result of the mismanagement of the economy and political interference. Both were rampant, particularly in the late 1990s. And while it is true that political interference led to the deterioration of a number of sectors, it is also true that some sectors of Kenyan agriculture at least survived this period, and some even prospered. As such, it is important to see how different sectors of the agricultural economy succeeded under broadly adverse circumstances. Observing this will provide guidance as to the kinds of institutional arrangements that will be most conducive to success in the future.

COFFEE AND TEA SECTORS

Output and Productivity Trends

We begin by examining the cases of tea and coffee in particular because the contrasting experiences here will offer some useful findings on how to convert subsistence farmers into smallholding commercial farmers, and thereby increase income and employment and reduce poverty.

Tea and coffee have both been important cash crops over the period of Kenya's independence. Both have served at various points as the economy's leading earner of foreign exchange. In recent times, however, their performance has been remarkably different. Tea has done relatively well, with Kenya having become one of the top two black tea exporters in the world. Coffee, by contrast, has undergone a huge contraction. From a high of 128 thousand metric tons in 1988, coffee production has slumped to an average of around 50 thousand metric tons in the last five years.

The difference in the performance of the two crops can be observed in the data on per hectare productivity since independence. We show these data in Figure 5.3, a plot of the index of land productivity since independence (with 2005 as the base year for the index). The figure makes clear that the productivity of land in the tea sector has steadily increased. With coffee, productivity peaked in the 1980s and then began to decline. It is now at a level below where it was at independence.

In the case of coffee, some of its difficulties can be attributed to falling coffee prices internationally. This is clearly beyond the control of Kenyan policymakers. But a fair amount of the collapse is due to the failure of local institutions to adjust to falling prices. Mude (2006) offers a convincing argument that the fall in international prices is not the main cause of the fall in Kenyan coffee output. He shows this by comparing changes in output in different countries during the period that coffee prices fell. More specifically, he shows that prices for Kenyan coffee fell less than the group of five countries he uses for

Figure 5.3 Trends in Land Productivity for Tea and Coffee (indexed to 2005 levels)

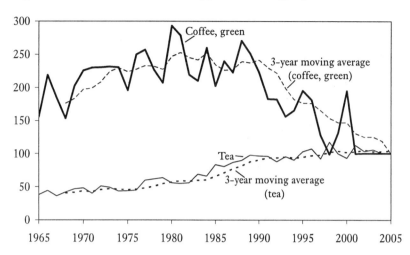

Source: Food and Agriculture Organization Statistics (FAOSTAT) (2006).

comparison. At the same time, he makes clear that coffee production fell substantially more in Kenya. In some cases, including Peru, Honduras, and Ethiopia, Mude shows that production actually increased, even in the face of price declines that were sharper than those in Kenya. In Peru and Ethiopia there was also an increase in yields per hectare. Mude attributes the experience in Kenya to the prevailing institutional arrangements in Kenya's coffee-growing sector.

The story in the tea sector is entirely different. Tea initially experienced slow productivity growth during the "golden" years of Kenyan growth. But tea productivity began to grow steadily in the late 1970s, and has continued its positive trend in productivity growth fairly steadily since. Between 1976 and 2005 the average growth in productivity was 3.5 percent per year while acreage expanded at the rate of 2.6 percent per year. During the 1980s, one of the slowest decades of growth for the Kenyan economy, productivity growth in the tea sector was 6.3 percent per year while acreage expanded at the rate of 2.8 percent per year.

Broadly speaking, the trend in coffee productivity mirrors that of agricultural productivity growth in Kenya more closely than does the productivity trend for tea. In many ways, early rapid expansion of coffee production was a major reference point for Kenyan agriculture generally having been initially regarded as a success story. As Figure 5.3 shows, from 1964 to 1980, productivity in the coffee sector grew tremendously. Overall productivity growth was 76 percent over these years. Over these same years, the area of land under cultivation growing coffee also expanded rapidly, rising from just above 81,000 hectares at independence to a high of 178,000 hectares by 1996. In the period 1979 to 1981, when coffee productivity peaked, the amount of area cultivated averaged just over 110,000 hectares. Land productivity in coffee then begins its sharp descent after 1980, falling by over 65 percent from its peak. As of 2005, land productivity in coffee was 39 percent below where it stood at independence.

What is it that explains the difference in the performance of tea and coffee? A decline in international prices is frequently invoked to explain declines in the output of primary commodities. However, as Deaton (1999) has shown, commodity price fluctuations cannot generally explain long-term trend declines in productivity.

For the experience with coffee in Kenya specifically, the decline in prices has been important. But it is not sufficient as an explanation for the productivity and output collapses unless one can show that the coffee industry is simply not cost effective in Kenya. The real question to resolve in the Kenyan case is why the coffee industry has been unable to manage the transition to a market in which falling unit prices have prevailed for roughly 30 years. Mude (2006) argues that this is due to the failure of local institutions to support the country's coffee industry. Moreover, we believe that Mude's argument is applicable more broadly to Kenyan agriculture. Kenya will be a price-taker on global markets with all primary commodities, either because its production is too small relative to world output to influence prices, as is true in coffee, or because the possibility exists for lower-price competitors to emerge, as is true with tea. We therefore now turn to a consideration of the contrasting institutional arrangements surrounding the production of coffee and tea in Kenya.

Contrasting Institutional Histories

Coffee and tea share similar early histories in Kenya. Both were introduced as cash crops mainly for European settlement farming, even though coffee is a native endemic plant of the East African highlands spanning from Ethiopia into Tanzania. In the 1920s, African farmers cultivated both crops successfully. However, colonial restrictions ensured that these crops were planted only by Europeans until close to independence and the Swynnerton agricultural reform. This reform was aimed at introducing modern farming techniques among the Africans. It also sought to create an African middle class that had a stake in the economy, and would therefore be supportive of the colonial government. On the European farms in the Kenyan highlands, coffee and tea were primarily grown in plantations. This situation still prevails in much of the world, due to the substantial capital required for the basic processing plants that must be on-farm or at least nearby. In Kenya, due to the activities of the cooperative movement in coffee and the Kenyan Tea Development Authority (KTDA) in tea, smallholders produce a substantial amount of the total output of these crops.

After independence, the Kenya government encouraged Africans to be cash crop farmers, especially in the tea and coffee sectors. This initiative deepened the reforms begun in the Swynnerton plan. As most of the African farmers were smallholders, new institutions were required to enable smallholders to grow the crops and get access to the processing plants. It was in the creation of these new institutions that significant differences arose in the trajectories of the coffee and tea sectors.

The crucial difference in organization between the sectors was the fact that, in the case of tea, the government created a parastatal to play the role of midwife to the smallholder tea producers. This was the KTDA. As of 2000, the KTDA was partially privatized, but this has not changed the services it provides to smallholders. The government defined the KTDA's role as including the provision of seedlings, fertilizer, and credit, training of farmers and supervision of cultivation, harvesting, transportation, and quality control of leaf, as well as assistance in marketing and processing of final products (Stern 1972).

In the coffee industry, no single organization was created to support smallholders. Instead, small coffee farmers were organized into local cooperatives that owned the local processing plant. With the exception of marketing, these cooperatives played the role that KTDA played in the tea sector. The Kenya Planters and Cooperative Union (KPCU) was formed in 1937. KPCU milled and marketed the coffee beans, and was responsible for remitting the revenues from sales back to the cooperatives. The cooperatives in turn paid the individual farmers. Crucially, however, unlike KTDA, KPCU represented both plantations and smallholders. It was not specifically designed to improve the lot of smallholder farmers.

These historical differences between the KTDA and KPCU are reflected in their current institutional arrangements. Thus, at present, coffee cooperatives cover small local areas below district level and include, on average, roughly 500 or so farmers as members (Government of Kenya 2003b). In 2002, there were 569 cooperatives which owned 994 factories. These societies ranged in the amount of coffee processed. Some processed as little as 17 metric tons a year, while larger ones processed up to 10,000 metric tons a year (European Commission 2004).

By contrast, with the smallholder tea sector, there are only 52 factories, each of which serves an average of 7,600 growers. In short, the tea sector enjoys tremendous advantages in scale at the processing level relative to the coffee cooperatives. But the advantages for tea smallholders extend beyond this single factor. While each coffee cooperative operates individually in terms of processing, management, and procurement of fertilizers, the tea sector is vertically integrated. Each tea factory is owned by the farmers themselves in the region, but they are run on contract with the KTDA. KTDA, in turn, is owned by all the factories. This arrangement allows KTDA to procure services and employ professionals at the national level while each cooperative operates in similar fashion at the local level. For example, KTDA purchases fertilizers for all the tea farmers together. It is thus able to source these inputs internationally at lower cost. KTDA imports around 65,000 tons of fertilizer a year. Because of this bulk import, KTDA is able to supply fertilizer to farmers at a discount. In 2005, for example, the cost to farmers was approximately 14 percent lower than what was available in the local market.

The situation is comparable in the provision of credit to smallholders. KTDA is able to borrow for capital expansion either in local or international markets. Moreover, the KTDA offers smallholders a centralized deposit system for disbursing loans to farmers. This allows the KTDA and the financial institutions providing the loans to extend production credit to farmers on an efficient basis. All payments are processed through a central system and thus payments of loans can be guaranteed at relatively low cost to the lender (Government of Kenya 2003b).

In addition, KTDA also reaps returns to scale in the provision of extension, transportation, accounting and management, insurance and engineering services. KTDA also benefits its members through information-sharing among its various member factories or production zones. Lastly, KTDA still plays a role in supporting start-up operations. It assists tea farmers in starting their production operations in new zones and also helps them in building processing plants.

Overall, the operations of the KTDA have promoted both the expansion of opportunities for smallholders and a rise in the productivity of tea farmers. This is despite the volatility of tea prices on the global market. In fact, between 1964 and 1988, KTDA was able to reduce real unit costs by 94 percent from over Ksh 4,000 to Ksh 226 in 1975 prices (Grosh 1991). Recent interviews with the KTDA Managing Director and Chief Financial Officer indicate that in the recent past the company has continued to reduce its operating cost per unit of production.[2]

The experiences of smallholding coffee farmers with respect to the KPCU stands in sharp contrast to the successes of the KTDA. From independence through the late 1980s smallholder cooperatives led the expansion of coffee production. But beginning in the early 1990s, there was a clear slowdown in the proportion of coffee produced by smallholders, as well as in the level of productivity achieved by smallholders relative to estate farms. We would argue that the size of individual estates allowed them to respond more effectively to the deteriorating price conditions that prevailed during this period. Without a level of institutional support comparable to that provided for smallholding tea farmers, the coffee smallholders suffered disproportionately in the face of declining world coffee prices.

Finally, coffee smallholders and the cooperative movement in coffee generally were damaged by the revision of the Cooperative Act in 1997. This change deregulated the farming cooperatives, giving farmers complete control over their cooperatives, free of government involvement. Mude (2006) shows how, in an unregulated environment, cooperatives are susceptible to capture by corrupt individuals. Among other problems created by the deregulation measure, the system of election by having members line up behind their favored candidate provided a highly effective enforcement mechanism for a corrupt candidate who is able to monitor exactly who lined up behind him or her.

In short, the dramatically divergent experiences of tea and coffee farming in Kenya, especially as experienced by smallholders, offer clear lessons for policy. The primary lesson is that smallholders in Kenya can earn a decent livelihood producing cash crops if they operate within a framework of effective institutional support, such as that provided to smallholding tea farmers by the KTDA. In the absence of such support, as has been the case for coffee smallholders, the chances for smallholders to succeed are small. Moreover, the possibilities for success diminish further in the face of an unfavorable external environment. Here we refer especially to low commodity prices on the global market. But low global prices alone will not engender failure, if the support system within a sector is operating effectively.

HORTICULTURE

Despite the general slowdown in agricultural output, in the last ten years the horticulture sector has grown rapidly in importance, driven mostly by the exporting of flowers (Figure 5.4). Flower exports now accounts for 2.5 percent of GDP, which means it accounts for between 10 and 13 percent of exports. In 2004, it was the second largest foreign exchange earner after tea (HCDA 2006).[3] Kenya is now the leading flower exporter to the European Union, with approximately 31 percent of the market. Kenya is also successfully exporting fruits and vegetables.

The sector began production for export in 1957 when it started exporting what were termed as "Asian vegetables" to the British market. By 1963–65, beans, peas, lentils, and cashews averaged about 3 percent of Kenya's total exports (Government of Kenya 1966). By 1995 the industry accounted for 11 percent of exports and by 2004 a quarter of all Kenyan exports were horticultural products, with a total value of Ksh 31.7 billion. During the period 1995 to 2005, growth was phenomenal, with an average real growth rate of just over 10 percent per year. This was while the rest of the economy grew, on average, at around 2 percent per year (Figure 5.5).[4]

As an export success story, the industry stands out from other agricultural sectors. The tea, coffee, and pyrethrum sectors were designed specifically for

Figure 5.4 Average Share of Value of Horticultural Exports, 1995–2005

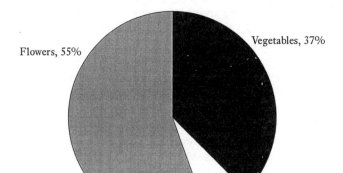

Sources: HCDA (various years); World Bank (2005b).

export, with over 95 percent of their product being exported. By contrast, the horticultural sector sells fully 96 percent of its product by volume within the domestic market, with only 4 percent being exported.

Of the exports over the last ten years, flowers (specifically an export sector) lead with a 57 percent value share. Fruits, on average, contribute 7 percent and vegetables are 37 percent. The majority of the fruits and vegetables produced (though not necessarily exported) are produced by smallholders. The Horticultural Crop Development Agency (HCDA) estimated that smallholders produce 80 percent of the total (HCDA 2006), although the number that are produced for export is very small (Bawdeen quoted in Muendo and Tschirley 2004). By contrast, the flower industry is made up of 50 or so farms cultivating a little over 2,000 hectares. Production is dominated by the ten largest farms which produce over 83 percent of flowers. This sector is highly capital intensive, with development of an acre of land being estimated to cost up to U.S. $1 million (Ngotho 2005).

What has made this sector successful? A number of factors have played a role. The most important include the following:

1.   Kenya's varied topography and climate. This creates amenable growing conditions for a wide variety of horticultural products. This is exemplified by the large variety of commodities exported. The HCDA keeps individual statistics for 51 types of flowers, 24 fruits and 74 vegetables.

Figure 5.5 GDP Growth Compared to Horticultural Sector Growth

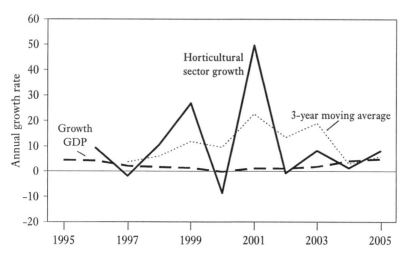

Sources: HCDA (various years); World Bank (2005b).

2. The sector's relatively long history of export experience, led by private-sector initiatives. Over time private networks of information have formed between Kenya and its main markets that give it some advantage over new producers.
3. The relatively good air connections between Europe and Kenya.[5]
4. The advantages offered to Kenyan agricultural exports through the Lomé/Cotonou conventions.
5. A well-regulated environment through HCDA. While the sector may have not received as much support as other sectors given HCDA's hands-off approach, it has benefited from a lack of political interference that has gone hand-in-hand with government support.

Even with these strengths and successes, horticulture in Kenya faces a number of major challenges. One is simply the reality of other African countries emulating Kenya's model, and that of Zimbabwe's earlier successes in this sector. Other African countries with similar climates and topography are now entering these export markets. For example, Ethiopia is aggressively pursuing foreign direct investment in flowers. There are reports that some flower farms have moved from Kenya to Ethiopia, even though, to date, there has not yet been a net decrease in the number of farms in Kenya.

More threatening is the plan by China to become the biggest exporter of roses by the year 2010. This plan aims at capitalizing on the low wages in the interior of Yunnan province. The Chinese government plans on making it possible via investments of up to U.S. $200 billion on infrastructure such as roads, rail, and new airports. Beyond the investment in public infrastructure the Chinese government is subsidizing farmers by providing them with free refrigerated trucks and other forms of support.[6] In terms of processed food products Kenyan producers face competition from South African producers. This is particularly the case for fruit juices sold in most of the major supermarkets. Lastly, there is a growing movement in the West to encourage consumers to purchase locally grown foods and to label imported products with food miles. This is in an attempt to reduce the amount of carbon emissions in food growing and marketing.

How can Kenya successfully meet these challenges? Like all other parts of the agricultural sector, horticultural exporters face the basic constraints of poor infrastructure, lack of credit, and poor extension services (Nyoro 2002, IEA 1998). In this regard the export part of the industry is probably more susceptible to the constraints imposed by poor infrastructure because of the need for rapid transportation of goods, refrigeration, and high health standards that must be maintained. These constraints partially explain why the export trade is dominated by larger farms that have access to credit and capital, enabling them to more easily overcome the constraints. For example, Oserian, the largest flower farm, overcame the lack of breeding and planting material after initially collaborating with the Kenya Agricultural Research Institute (KARI) by paying to make use of KARI scientists and facilities, and then, in 2005, by building its own facility. Oserian was also able to provide heating for its greenhouses via a geothermal facility in collaboration with Olkaria Geothermal Power Plant. This enabled them to bypass the weak national infrastructure for energy distribution.

While physical infrastructure is a constraint for all producers, beyond this, the lack of an informational infrastructure, especially with regard to information on how to obtain the best market prices, is a major hindrance to smallholders. Large farms can either gather their own information in both local and overseas markets or purchase such information as needed. By contrast, smallholders have little access to basic price information from even local urban markets and thus often sell their goods at prices well below what they may get if they paid the cost of transportation to local urban markets. In some cases, middlemen who profit by buying cheaply from smallholders in rural areas get together and bar the smallholders from access to urban markets (IEA 1998). At present the price of information is not affordable for the smallholder. For example, there is a private-sector initiative, the Kenya Agricultural Commodities Exchange (KACE) which provides daily and weekly agricultural prices. Membership to receive this information costs U.S. $125 per year. This is an amount well beyond the reach of most smallholders. HCDA has information on international prices but at present does not have the ability to distribute that information to smallholders (IEA 1998).

More recently, the flower industry has also suffered from the appreciation of the Kenyan shilling. The rise of the shilling is considered by some observers as the main contributor to a fall of 15 percent of earnings in the sector.[7] This sector, which relies heavily on exports to the European Union, faces some uncertainty as we draw closer to December 2007, when the present duty-free trading regime with the European Union ends. While negotiations are taking place and it is hoped that Kenya will end up with an even more advantageous trading regime, it is also possible that these negotiations may fail. The fallback position, which is the General Systems Parity System, would see some Kenyan products, especially in agriculture, face additional duties. This would put them at a disadvantage against North African countries and others that already have free trade agreements with the EU.[8]

Another challenge is to use this sector more effectively to promote poverty reduction, and not simply, more narrowly, export success. We can see the problem by considering some basic data on ownership concentration in agriculture and economic growth. The most recent report on economic growth in the country reports that agricultural value-added at constant prices grew at 6.9 percent or 19 billion Ksh in 2005 (Government of Kenya 2006c). Of this increase, 6.2 billion Ksh was due to the increase in exports. Of the total amount of value-added growth generated by exports, 78 percent came from the flower sector. This represents 25 percent of the value-added growth in agriculture.

Estimates report that the largest ten flower farms in Kenya control well over 75 percent of the market, with Oserian, the country's single largest flower farm, itself accounting for well over 50 percent of production (Ngotho 2005). Assuming these reports are broadly accurate, it means that approximately 20 percent of all agricultural growth is due to ten companies, with one company providing well above 10 percent itself. Put another way, if agricultural output accounts for roughly 30 percent of the economy, and contributed slightly more than its share to the country's economic growth in recent years, then 6 percent of the growth of the entire country was due to ten farms or less.

Related to these overall figures on concentration within the sector is the fact that farms owned by EU nationals that produce in Kenya receive more favorable treatment by regulators than those owned by Kenyans. Thus, in the case of flower exports, the EU firms have their flowers inspected in bulk at relatively low prices. Kenyan firms, however, are forced to have their flowers inspected by stem, driving up the costs of the inspections (Ngotho 2005).

The overall point here is not to suggest that the large flower farms should be hindered in their efforts. We rather underscore the obvious point that if the benefits of horticultural production are to be used to reduce poverty in Kenya, more resources need to be channeled to supporting Kenyan national firms, especially smallholders, so that they also may benefit from the export markets.

Given these challenges facing the horticultural sector, there are also crucial opportunities for Kenya within this sector. These opportunities emphasize the need for policies—including infrastructural improvements, and making credit and extension services accessible to smallholders—that support the growth of the sector generally, and smallholders in particular. Moreover, these opportunities do not apply simply to the flower exporting sector, but to the smallholder fresh produce sector as well. This is assuming the appropriate policy framework can be established.

The first such opportunity is that horticulture is one of the few high-value sectors in the country where there is also significant consumer demand within the country, rather than having demand come primarily from exports. This creates an incentive for investors to build processing capacity within the country. This is in contrast with the coffee and tea sectors, where demand for the products is almost entirely from exports. In these cases, processing facilities can just as easily be built in importing countries. If horticultural processing capacity could be expanded in Kenya, this, in turn, could serve as a platform for exporting processed horticultural goods. Processed goods could initially focus on African markets, where Kenyan processors are likely to be highly competitive. Success exporting processed goods within Africa could then serve as the basis for expansion into the world market.

The second opportunity is the range of products offered, with different market opportunities. Thus, in the case of flowers, demand both in domestic and export markets should grow as incomes rise. With standard fresh produce, markets should also expand with incomes, but will remain attractive as a basic product for lower-income countries, such as China and India, as their economies continue to grow. Demand for all horticultural products should generally expand, especially in the oil-rich Middle East, in addition to the traditional high-income countries. Along with the still unexploited markets, the increased demand for organic produce provides a labor-intensive opportunity for this industry, particularly for smallholders. In addition, the rapid turnaround between planting, export, and payment for products means that the sector is able to access funds for inputs on a fairly short-term basis. This reduces the risk for lenders and thus may make credit more readily available to the sector (Nyoro 2002). Finally, this sector produces basic wage goods that will experience rising demand as urban centers expand.

MAIZE AND WHEAT

Maize and wheat are the most important grains in the country. Both are produced exclusively for domestic consumption. The amount of cropland devoted to maize is ten times as large as the cropland devoted to the next most widely cultivated crop, which in 2005 was coffee, with 167 thousand hectares planted. Presently maize is cultivated on 1.7 million of the 4.6 million hectares (37 percent) of arable land in Kenya while wheat is cultivated on 150,000 hectares.

Since 1964 both have seen increases in the amount of land devoted to their production. Wheat has grown more slowly, but more steadily. From 1964 to 1969, wheat grew by 24 percent before falling by about the same margin during the period 1971 to 1980. After 1981, there was a rebound so that by 2004 the amount of land used for wheat had stabilized at about 33 percent above what was used in 1964. Maize production has experienced greater fluctuations, but also more growth. From 1964 to 1976, the cultivated areas grew by 59 percent. Between 1976 and 1985 there was a fallback to the same amount of land as at independence. After 1985 there was steady growth and by 2005 the amount of land under maize cultivation was 70 percent larger than what it was at independence.

Similarly, productivity in these two crops has fluctuated, with a more dramatic trend in the yield per hectare for maize. We can see the land productivity trends for both crops in Figure 5.6. With maize, productivity increased through 1990, with the decade of the 1980s experiencing the most rapid improvements. The level of maize production in 1990 was fully 65 percent above that at independence. Since 1990 there has been a fall in productivity in maize, such that, by 2005, the level of production had fallen fully back to the same level as 1965.

With wheat, productivity grew from independence through 1985, by 57 percent. Productivity then became stagnant until 1993, after which the growth path of productivity was renewed, and even accelerated. At present, wheat productivity is 111 percent above its 1964 level.

What explains these divergent productivity experiences, and in particular, the collapse of productivity for maize? The initial expansion in both these crops can be attributed early on to the increased emphasis by the post-independence government on giving African farmers an opportunity to participate in commercial output. This went along with increased extension and research particularly on dry land varieties of maize. The work at the Kathumani Dry Lands Centre in producing hardy hybrids particularly stands out.

In the 1980s, Kenya's agricultural extension services for maize and wheat suffered from lack of resources as the economy slowed down (IEA 1998). This certainly contributed to the productivity decline. With respect to maize, another potential factor was the diminishing availability of hybrids as the extension and research services became less effective.

The difference in productivity trends is also due to the different institutional setting associated with each crop. Both types of farming were institutionally dependant on the Kenya Farmers Association (KFA) and later the Kenya Grain Growers Cooperative Union (KGGCU). The dissolution of the KFA and replacement by the KGGCU in 1984 resulted in declining services to farmers which affected both sectors. KGGCU was renamed KFA in 1996, but was de-

Figure 5.6 Trends in Land Productivity for Maize and Wheat (indexed to 2005 levels)

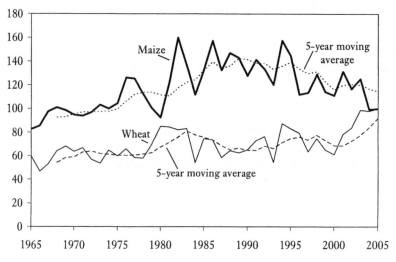

Source: Food and Agriculture Organization Statistics (FAOSTAT) (2006).

clared bankrupt in 2007. The scale of farming is very different in both sectors. Maize is farmed on small- and large-scale farms, while wheat is farmed almost exclusively on relatively large farms. We would argue that wheat farmers who were larger on average than maize farmers were able to respond to difficulties and opportunities in the economy by taking advantage of the returns to scale that existed. This promoted long-term productivity growth in wheat relative to maize.

Millet and Sorghum

Millet and sorghum are traditional grain crops that are consumed domestically. There is virtually no export market for these crops. Initially they were processed by small local millers, but more recently they have been processed by larger millers. They are now both available in packaged form in the major cities. Because neither of these crops is produced for export, there has been little government support for producers.

In terms of land use, there was a stable amount of land devoted to these crops from independence until around 1981. During this time the amount of area under millet rose slightly from 75,000 hectares to between 80,000 and 81,000 hectares from 1979 to 1981. There was a sharp fall-off in the early 1980s, though it is not clear whether this is due to statistical adjustments or actual changes in

Figure 5.7 Trends in Land Productivity for Millet and Sorghum (indexed to 2005 levels)

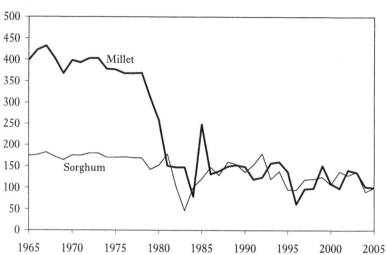

Source: Food and Agriculture Organization Statistics (FAOSTAT) (2006).

land usage. At its lowest point in 1984 millet occupied 29,000 hectares, roughly 38 percent of the area it covered at independence. Thereafter there was a gradual increase in the area harvested. In 2004 millet covered 115,000 hectares, an increase of 53 percent over the area covered at independence. Sorghum, on the other hand, was extensively planted at independence covering 201,000 hectares which rose to 210,000 hectares by 1980. This collapsed to 81,000 hectares in 1981 before slowly climbing to an average of approximately 130,000 hectares between 2002 and 2004, a fall of 35 percent below the level at independence.

We present in Figure 5.7 the patterns of land productivity for both millet and sorghum between 1964 and 2005. For both these crops, productivity per hectare drops off from their level at independence. Millet drops off by 75 percent while sorghum has a smaller but still substantial decline of 43 percent. Farmers growing these crops have never received significant extension support. This has resulted in the lack of planting materials for new farmers, and a corresponding reliance on existing farmers for continued production (IEA 1998). The situation with millet and sorghum has been replicated with other traditional food crops in Kenya, including cassava, yams, and sweet potatoes.

This lack of support for traditional food crops is consistent with a research and extension model that differentiated between food crops and cash crops, with cash crops being favored for support. This model was perhaps appropriate in the 1960s, when over 90 percent of the population engaged in some agriculture and practically everyone, including many urban workers, had access to land. Under these circumstances, the domestic market for food crops was thin.

With rapid migration from rural areas and a swelling of the urban population, the 1960s-style research and extension model is no longer appropriate. There is now a substantial domestic market for traditional food crops. This effectively transforms every crop into a cash crop, and every farmer into a cash-crop farmer, no matter how small their holdings. A further shortcoming of ignoring the traditional food crops is the fact that many of them are indigenous and are often hardier than other crops. Increased plantings of these crops should therefore help to ameliorate food shortages during dry spells.

Sugarcane and Rice

These two crops are produced in very different areas from the traditional major agricultural crops of Kenya. They are both produced in the lowlands of Nyanza and Western Provinces and also in the lowlands of Eastern and Coast Provinces. These crops are important because Nyanza, Eastern, and Western Provinces have exhibited among the highest poverty rates in the country at one time or other during the last ten years (UNDP 2001, Government of Kenya 2007a). As these are the major marketed crops in these areas, improvements in production of these crops could contribute substantially toward poverty reduction. Nyanza and Western Provinces are also regions identified as having the lowest improvements in land and labor productivity (Nyoro and Jayne 1999).

Land use for both has risen since independence. Initially, this was pushed by the desire for self-sufficiency. In both cases land use has increased by over 140 percent since independence. We see the patterns in terms of land productivity in Figure 5.8. As we see in the figure, with sugarcane, the increased use of land has been accompanied by an overall increase in productivity. Productivity in sugarcane peaked in 1982 at 220 percent of its independence level. It has since fallen substantially, but remains at 122 percent above the 1964 level. Productivity in rice farming has followed a different pattern, rising rapidly after independence, then falling steadily from the early 1980s onward. Land productivity in rice is now 30 below where it was in 1965, the year after independence.

The organizational structures of these two industries differ considerably. Most rice is produced by smallholders with relatively large-scale irrigation schemes. These smallholders sell their rice through the National Irrigation Board, which managed the arrangements. These arrangements suffered from the general collapse in the management of such institutions that was common in Kenya from the early 1980s through to about 2000. In addition, the high costs incurred by the National Irrigation Board resulted in lower producer prices for the farm-

Figure 5.8 Trends in Land Productivity for Sugarcane and Rice (indexed to 2005 levels)

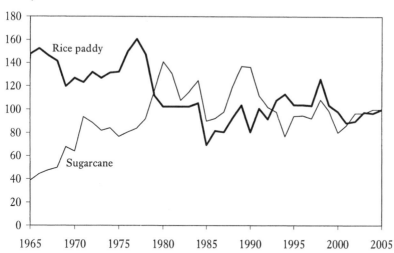

Source: Food and Agriculture Organization Statistics (FAOSTAT) (2006).

ers, causing a disincentive to produce (IEA 1998). Currently the government is in the process of revitalizing some of the smaller irrigation schemes and has so far rehabilitated 12 out of 28 non-functional schemes.[9]

By contrast, the sugarcane sector was centered around the seven sugar factories in three zones of South Nyanza, Nyanza, and Western Kenya. Presently only six of these factories are in operation—South Nyanza Sugar Factory in South Nyanza; Muhoroni, Chemelil, and West Kenya in Nyanza; and Mumias and Nzoia in Western Kenya (EPZ 2006). Miwani, which was founded in 1927 and was the oldest sugar factory in the country, was closed in 1999 due to lack of profitability. Similarly, Muhoroni, the second oldest factory, is currently under receivership.

While the sugar industry was liberalized in the early 1990s, a majority of the firms are still government owned or have a large government shareholding. Mumias, the largest factory, is the exception as a publicly listed firm. Each sugar factory has a catchment area from which it draws its raw sugarcane from smallholders. Over 90 percent of the sugarcane is produced by smallholders, with the remaining 10 percent coming from the small group of large factories (EPZ 2006). Given the high smallholder participation in this industry, improvements in productivity are likely to also bring significant reductions in poverty. Each factory provides services to the growers much in the same way that KTDA

Figure 5.9 Sugar Factory Capacity and Share of Total National Sugar Production, 2003 (indexed to 2005 levels)

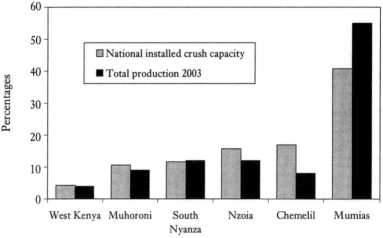

Sources: EPZ (2006) and USDA (2006).

does for tea. It provides input credits and fertilizers, land preparation, and planting. The farmer is then responsible for applying the fertilizer and for the general husbandry of the crop. The factory also harvests the crop. Note here that the factory provides more in services than KTDA itself does for tea producers. As farm size gets smaller with the splitting of farms as inheritance, these services may not be sustainable. On the other hand this presents a somewhat different model that may have lessons for other sectors.

The sugar sector faces a number of problems that are specific to it in addition to the general problems faced by the agricultural sector at large. In Figure 5.9 above, we compare the installed capacity of each factory as a proportion of the total national installed capacity versus the actual output as a proportion of total national output. Only West Kenya, South Nyanza, and Mumias—the two youngest and the largest plant—are able to produce a proportion that is close to or above their capacity as a proportion of national capacity.[10] The three oldest plants all produce below their capacity. This is due to a combination of poor yields due to the soil type (USDA 2006), out-dated machinery, and, as we will argue below, lack of economies of scale.

Figure 5.10 plots the installed capacity versus average yield. A positively sloped trend would suggest that larger factories can organize production in ways

Figure 5.10 Average Capacity and Production of Sugar Factories (indexed to 2005 levels)

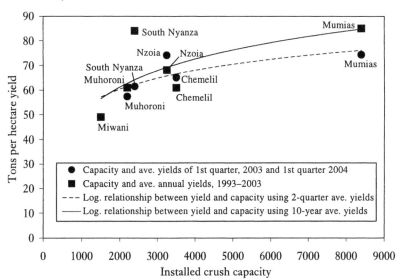

Sources: EPZ (2006), *Sugar Industry in Kenya 2006*, EPZ, Athi River, Kenya; USDA (2006), *Kenya Sugar Update 2006*, Gain Report No KE6004, USDA, Washington, DC.

that result in higher yields. This may come from cheaper bulk purchases of inputs, more efficient use of farm machinery, etc. There is a close fit between the trend lines and the points, demonstrating returns to scale at a decreasing rate. From this diagram it is clear that there are returns to scale that have not been exploited by most of the sugar factories. The one plant that has exploited the positive returns to scale is Mumias. This plant has enjoyed a 14.2 percent average return on assets over its 33-year history (Grosh 1991). This suggests that in South Nyanza a program of crop improvement and refurbishment of some of the factories may improve output and yields.

The decreasing size of farms that sugarcane is farmed on is an additional burden given the structure of the industry. Most subdivision of land occurs as fathers subdivide their land for their sons. Each new subdivision means that the factory loses some returns to scale in the provision of services to the growers and incurs some new costs to service the subdivisions. To give some context to this problem, take the case of Mumias, which presently operates with approximately 50,000 growers. This number could easily double in the next 20 years as sons start new families and fathers die off.

The industry as a whole also faces the problem of how to deal with imports. Sugar is produced in places such as the Sudan and Egypt at much lower costs than average costs in Kenya. With the exception of Mumias, it is unlikely that the other factories in their present state can compete with imports. At present Kenya produces only enough sugar to satisfy a little over two-thirds of its domestic demand. The gap is filled with imports, even though the importers face high duties. The high duty has served to encourage corruption as sugar brought into the country without duty can then be sold at tremendous profit. At present Kenya has been allowed by COMESA (Common Market for Eastern and Southern Africa) to impose the duty up to 2008 to give it time for its industry to become competitive.

Here again, despite significant challenges, the sugar industry also has significant opportunities. Sugar production elsewhere often produces two major by-products—alcohol both for human consumption and for fuel in the form of ethanol, as well as cogenerated electricity from the biomass waste. At present none of Kenya's factories exploit these opportunities. In the case of alcohol for human consumption, the present high tax regime does not make it worthwhile for the sugar factories to produce alcohol for human consumption. In the case of alcohol for energy, this would require a national policy to ensure demand sufficient for the factories to engage in the investment. This may become viable if oil prices remain at their 2006 peak levels. In the case of cogeneration of electricity, the Mumias factory has just started a project which will generate 25 megawatts (about 2 percent of national capacity) for the national grid using biomass produced in the refining process.

LIVESTOCK SECTOR

The livestock sector does not receive significant attention from policymakers, even though it is the largest single sector within agriculture in terms of output. Livestock accounts for over 40 percent of agricultural production but only receives about 1 percent of government expenditure (Government of Kenya 2004). While spending is low, certain aspects of livestock production, in particular large-scale dairy and ranching concerns, have received significant support. This government support comes through financing of the Kenya Cooperative Creameries, the Kenya Meat Commission, and the Agricultural Development Corporation.

Overall, the reasons for the low priority given to this sector are complicated, but can be reduced to two major factors. The first is that the livestock sector has never produced an export cash crop comparable to tea, coffee, and more recently, horticulture. The second is that much of the subsistence level livestock activities takes place in communities residing in the arid lands. These have been systematically ignored by all Kenyan governments. Fisheries, which also fall under the Ministry of Livestock, have suffered a similar fate.

The largest sub-sectors within the livestock sector are cattle, goats, and sheep. Chicken production is also significant, but because it is done mostly for household consumption, the numbers are not captured in the official statistics. In terms of households, more keep chicken than any other livestock (2006–07 KIHBS). As we would expect in a country where land is increasingly a limiting factor, there has been a shift from cattle to smaller stock—namely goats and sheep. In 1964, goats and sheep made up 54 percent of the national herd. In 2005 their proportion had gone up to 64 percent. This was at the expense of cattle which went from 44 percent to 35 percent. While the proportions have changed, the overall numbers for all three sub-sectors have grown. Between 1964 and 2005, the cattle, goat, and sheep herds increased by 62, 125, and 148 percent, respectively.

Despite the large increases in goats and sheep herding, cattle products have continued to dominate the sector both in growth and proportion. This is despite the collapse of the Kenya Meat Commission (KMC) and the Kenya Cooperative Creameries (KCC), the institutions created to support these sub-sectors. The production of cow's milk has increased by 300 percent since independence and cattle meat has increased by over 200 percent. This can be attributed to the improvement in stock that has occurred during the period. In the case of sheep and goat products, the increase has been more modest ranging from 140 percent in sheep's meat to 80 percent in goat's milk. The amount of sheep's milk produced is minimal. The result is that while cattle were only 44 and 35 percent of the national herd in 1964 and 2005, they made up 85 and 90 percent of the products respectively. This gap can be explained by the traditional bias in Kenyan livestock extension towards cattle. The present revitalization of KMC and KCC is an indication of the bias towards larger producers. This occurs despite the fact that the majority of livestock owners are smallholders. For example, over two-thirds of the cattle-owning households own four or fewer animals (2006–07 KIHBS).

While the sector has managed to do relatively well on little support it faces a number of problems. These include: the focus on cattle to the detriment of other stock; the bias in property arrangements toward those favoring private commercial ranching rather than the more sustainable nomadic transhumance (Githinji and Perrings 1993); the lack of safety nets and other institutional mechanisms to reduce risk in the drylands (Githinji and Perrings 1993); the lack of access to credit (Muriuki, Omore, Hooten, Waithaka, Ouma, Staal, and Odhiambo 2003); the diversion of dairy cess (tax) money to uses other than rural access roads; and the poor veterinary and breeding facilities (Muriuki et al. 2003).

LESSONS FROM SECTORAL ANALYSES

Learning from Successes

As we have seen, Kenya has experienced successes in agricultural in a number of important areas. In terms of sectors, tea, horticulture, and wheat stand out. The sugarcane producer Mumias is another important success story.

From these successes we can extract a number of valuable lessons that may be useful in thinking about agricultural policy. First, improvements have occurred when there is proper infrastructure and support for farmers or where farmers have sufficient capital to overcome structural impediments. Second, in some sectors it is possible for individual farmers or firms to exploit returns to scale to overcome impediments. This has been true, for example, in the flower sector among farmers who are sufficiently capitalized. Among smallholders, for this to occur, either a collective farmer organization such as KTDA or a firm such as Mumias has to harness the potential returns to scale. But nurturing organizations of this type will require some form of government intervention. These organizations have a large public good component to them, and therefore merit public support.

Adaptation rather than Replication of Past Successes

As we have seen, Kenya's agricultural sector was broadly successful from independence until about 1980. But this doesn't mean that simply recreating the institutional environment or policies of the early independence years will be adequate for recreating a positive agricultural growth path. This point is worth emphasizing because, at present, the government has embarked on a program of revitalizing some of the agricultural processing plants that collapsed in the 1980s and 1990s. Some of these plants did indeed collapse due to mismanagement. At the same time, many of the main supporting institutions, including the KMC and the KCC, were formed in the colonial era and structured to support big farmers. These institutions did not change substantially after independence. And while it is true that many of the reforms that were pursued in the 1980s and 1990s were poorly conceived, planned or implemented, some of them were guided by a positive agenda of addressing the previous bias toward large-scale producers. This includes, among other initiatives, the creation of the KGGCU. The aim of policy now should be to combine the management successes of the early independence years with a continued effort to promote the well-being of smallholders. The tea sector is the one major success story in the contemporary Kenyan economy that shows how capable management and the inclusion of smallholders can be successfully combined.

Understanding Resources and Capabilities of Smallholders

Most of Kenya's rural population has little in terms of resources or education. These are the farmers who need to become small commercial producers in order for poverty to drop significantly in the short- to medium-term. In order to service these farmers better, it is important for policymakers to recognize their capabilities and needs.

The first point is obvious—that most smallholders have had very limited formal schooling. This is despite the improvements in educational opportunities since the mid-1980s. As of 1998, only 10 percent of the heads of households had more than a primary school level of education among the poor and 40 percent had no formal education.

The lack of formal education puts smallholders at a distinct disadvantage in comparison to other participants in agricultural markets. Husbands et al. (1996) estimated that returns to primary education for rural agricultural households were between 8 and 12 percent per year. Assuring access to education for poor households would thus raise their agricultural productivity tremendously.

Female-headed households constitute about 38 percent of smallholders. Many of these may be defacto female-headed households created by migration of males to urban areas for work. Nevertheless, women participate actively in smallholding activities. At the same time, women have historically had less access to education. At present, both men and women need to receive greater access, and equal access, to education.

Designing Effective Extension Services for Smallholders

The need for increased educational opportunities becomes clear in terms of improving market access. There is certainly a need for improvements in market access, as many observers in government and among donor agencies emphasize. At the same time, it is equally important to recognize that to be capable of taking full advantage of the market opportunities that exist (for example, to export horticultural produce) requires a fair amount of human capital. In fact one of the reasons given for the failure of rural cooperatives is the low literacy of their members (Government of Kenya 2004).

This point becomes relevant also in terms of designing improvements in extension services. For example, a policy that aims to privatize extension is not likely to succeed with poor smallholders because they lack both the physical and human capital to make effective use of a private, demand-driven, extension service. Demand-driven extension works best for medium-scale and larger farmers who have specific problems to be solved (Schwartz 1994). Poor farmers tend to have larger problems that need more than a single visit and require systematic training.

Thus, for example, a large-scale farmer may already have the means and physical capital to pay for inputs, marketing, and transporting their crop and may only need extension to choose what variety of the crop they are interested in producing is the best for their area. These farmers will also have the wherewithal to obtain the complementary inputs that may be needed to grow the hybrid varieties frequently recommended by the extension services. On the other hand, a subsistence farmer who is planning on growing a commercial crop may need assistance with setting up a basic business plan, figuring out what crop is best, and how she or he can access marketing, transport, and credit networks. This kind of extension is not cost-effective for a private provider of these services, as they will tend to be more specialized, focus on specific crops and favor areas that are already well connected to the economy's basic infrastructure. What is needed is more generalized extension services that have both agricultural experts and business experts.

As an example of the current situation, Kenya presently runs a Training and Visit (T&V) extension service that is unable to reach the vast majority of smallholders. In 1988, for example, less than 28 percent of farmers met an extension worker once, either on their own or a neighbor's farm (Government of Kenya 1989). This is well below the program ideal, which is that 15 percent of all farmers should be meeting on a monthly basis with an extension officer. The extension officers have also had a bias towards larger and richer farmers, whom they hope will be role models for less well endowed farmers, and a bias against women farmers (Gautam 2000; Gautam and Anderson 1999). Alternatives to the T&V include the Farm Field Schools where farmers get together at one farm rather than receiving individual visits. This is more cost effective and there are examples presently practiced by non-governmental organizations (NGOs). A variation of this approach organized through a collective farmers organization may be a cost-effective way of providing additional extension.

There is a public aspect to extension that then provides a justification for increased government participation in extension. One factor is that extension is a form of education and thus is a public good. That is, a better-educated community is more productive because each individual's productivity affects overall productivity by bringing down the costs of goods that the individual produces and thus lowering costs for other producers in the community. In farming areas it has also been found that many farmers learn from each other, so improving the productivity of some farmers will tend to result in the spreading of the techniques to other farmers within the same socio-economic circles. Jayne, Yamano, and Nyoro (2004) show that farmers who have benefited from interlinked credit and fertilizer programs tend to have relatively high fertilizer use in crops not in the program, i.e. food crops. We would expect that extension for one crop would have similar spill-over effects to other crops.

Recently, the government has acknowledged the need for targeted public extension for the poor.[11] However, the fact that it hopes to fund this mostly through donor funding suggests that this is presently a low priority for the government. Otherwise, the government is moving towards privatizing extension services.

Returns to Scale and Agricultural Cooperatives

In our view, one of the key features to promoting successful agricultural production in Kenya is to take advantage of returns to scale. One way to promote more productive larger-scale operations is to provide improved employment opportunities in the non-farm economy. This will reduce the pressure for employment on the land, allowing for larger-sized farms. Of course, a central goal of our overall policy approach is to generate more non-farm employment, especially in the formal economy. But even assuming fairly steady employment needs within the agricultural sector, one can still obtain the benefits of larger-scale operations through improving the collective organization of smallholders.

The traditional collective organization for Kenyan farmers, both large and small, has been cooperatives. These have existed in the country since the early 1900s when settler farmers organized themselves into marketing cooperatives in order to get the best returns for their produce (Ouma 1989). While the early cooperatives catered mainly to larger farms in the 1950s and immediately after independence, the government encouraged smallholders to organize themselves into cooperatives for marketing and the purchase of inputs. By 2005 there were over 1.1 million members of 4,304 agricultural cooperatives (Government of Kenya 2005c). Assuming each member is the head of a household, and given an average household size of close to five, this works out to 5.5 million household members being connected to cooperatives. This amounts to roughly 25 percent of Kenya's rural population. This is a large share, particularly since cooperatives have traditionally been organized in Kenya only for cash crops, including coffee, cotton, pyrethrum, sugar, and dairy.

In particular, cooperatives in Kenya have been closely associated with coffee farmers, with close to 50 percent of all members of an agricultural cooperative belonging to a coffee society. Both the early successes and more recent failures of the coffee cooperatives have been taken to be representative of the experiences with cooperatives and their prospects for the future. This is particularly true with respect to the failures of the coffee cooperatives. In fact the mistrust toward cooperatives at present, linked to the experience in the coffee sector, appears so great that in the *Strategy for the Revitalization of Agriculture* (Government of Kenya 2004b), there was no discussion about how these cooperatives could be improved as a means of promoting higher productivity for smallholders. But, as we have discussed above, the failure of the coffee cooperatives was the product of specific circumstances. Moreover, elsewhere in the developing world, commercial agriculture has frequently been built on a foundation of farmers' cooperatives of various sorts. As such, we believe that in the right environment and with the correct support, cooperatives can play an important role in the improvement of agricultural output and productivity in Kenya.

Two crucial changes need to occur for cooperatives to play a successful role in agricultural development. The first is to create an effective regulatory body overseeing the operations of cooperatives and similar institutions. In 2004, for example, only 1 percent of all cooperatives were up to date in the audit of their accounts. Thirty-two percent were one year in arrears, while fully 60 percent were four years in arrears. These statistics suggest a weak capacity to audit and to enforce audits.

The second is increased public funding, probably through the Ministry of Cooperative Development and Marketing, to support the government's regulatory efforts, and to give positive guidance and support to these institutions. The 1997 Cooperative Act enabled farmers to obtain complete control over cooperatives, without any government regulatory oversight. It was the subsequent absence of any effective regulatory structure that encouraged mismanagement of the cooperatives, and the collapse of the coffee cooperatives.

The weak government support for cooperatives is the inevitable result of the severe cutbacks in the budget and staffing of the Ministry of Cooperatives (Government of Kenya 2004). From having 2,000 professional officers throughout the 1990s, the ministry now employs only 450 professionals. Some of the most severe cutbacks have occurred in the funding for extension services within the Ministry of Cooperative Development. In addition, the professional staffers that remain have only been minimally supported in terms of their professional development. For example, we were told at the Ministry of Cooperative Development that the Ministry's accounting system has become fully computerized, but the staff officers have not been adequately trained to use the computerized systems.[12]

Beyond the role played by the government in cooperative development and regulation, an increase in the role of the private sector in auditing cooperatives and credit rating would also be useful. Private-sector auditors could play an important role in providing information to potential lenders to the cooperatives. This improvement in the quality of information available will reduce the risk of lending to them. This should then increase access to credit.

Infrastructure Improvements

We will discuss below some proposals for improving Kenya's road and water infrastructure. Beyond these basic needs, there are also lessons to be learned from industries that have managed to absorb the increased costs imposed by poor infrastructure—particularly in terms of transportation and energy supplies—by taking advantage of returns to scale. This is particularly evident within the flower industry and KTDA. KTDA maintains a fleet of trucks that guarantee access to markets for its members, accepting that the costs are high (Wasike 2001). This is in addition to its efforts to maintain roads that are important for tea farmers, by assessing the farmers a fee of 1 percent of revenue. Similarly, individual wealthy Kenyans have responded to the poor state of Kenyan roads by purchasing four-wheel-drive vehicles that can traverse even the worst of the roads.

In the short term, one approach to dealing with the transportation problem and increasing market access for small farmers could be the organization of transport collectives. These cooperatives could be responsible for transporting smallholder crops to major urban areas and bringing back to the farmers the major inputs—seed, fertilizer, pesticides—which are generally more available and cheaper in the major urban areas. These collectives would not only provide cost savings for the farmers but would also create jobs. Each commercial vehicle in Kenya normally has a staff of a driver and at least one loader.

The main impediment to organizing such collectives would be the raising of capital to purchase the trucks. Through the SACCOs affordable credit could be made available from the main financial system. Given the high returns to market access and the ranking of transportation as the major impediment to improvements in agriculture, it would be worthwhile for the government not only to ensure that adequate credit is available for borrowing through the SACCOs for rural–urban transportation, but also to consider subsidizing these particular investments.

Cost of Capital and Access to Credit

The cost and access to capital has long been a problem for smallholders. It was assumed initially that lack of private title was the main cause of the inability for smallholders to get loans. However work in Kenya (Migot-Adholla, Hazell, Blarel, and Place 1991) and in Ethiopia (Gebeyehu 2000, Holden and Yohannes 2002, Shiferaw and Holden 2001) showed that the availability of titles did not increase the likelihood of credit access.

Apart from the high cost and difficulty of obtaining credit in the past there has been a bias against smallholders in terms of the amount and the duration of loans. For example, between 1980 and 1986, the most recent period for which data are available, large farmers received most of their loans with relatively long-term maturities of over seven years. By contrast, smallholders virtually never received long-term loans.

In the past, Kenyan farmers received credit by using their expected harvest as collateral. This was made possible because, until fairly recently, most commercial crops were purchased by a central marketing board or cooperative. This board could be relied on by financial institutions to remit the amount owed to financial institutions before sending payments to farmers. But this relationship has broken down with the deterioration of cooperatives as a central intermediary operating between farmers and banks (Nyoro 2002).

One approach out of this situation is to dramatically increase the provision of affordable credit through rural-based SACCOs and other microfinance enterprises, a topic that we consider at some length in later chapters.

NOTES

1. See Institute of Economic Affairs (2000) for a recent discussion of land reform in the Kenyan context.
2. Interview on March 13, 2006 with Mr. L. Tiampati, Managing Director of the KTDA, and Mr. D. Kimani, Finance Director, during a visit to KTDA headquarters.
3. Memorandum prepared by Mr. Bernard Sogomo, Managing Director of the Horticultural Crop Development Agency, 2006.
4. This average growth rate is somewhat deceptive, as crop yield is highly susceptible to rainfall. The growth ranged from 49.7 percent in 2001 to a low of -8.6 percent in 2000. However the three-year moving average trend line clearly shows the growth that occurred at least until 2003. The 2006 Economic Survey also reports a resurgence in growth in this sector (Government of Kenya 2006c).
5. After its turnaround in the late 1990s, Kenya Airways has become an efficient airline and is competitive internationally. In the last five years it has been one of the few airlines internationally making profit despite increased competition in the market to Nairobi, its main hub. For example in 2005 the net income for Kenya Airways, with a fleet of only 23 planes, was U.S. $69.7 million. Compare this to the most profitable airline in the U.S., Southwest, which had a net income in 2005 of U.S. $548 million and a fleet of 468 planes. Along with the success of Kenya Airways, the rehabilitation of Jomo Kenyatta International Airport and its increased use as a hub connecting other parts of Africa to Asia and Europe, increased flights by other carriers and the increase in tourism all have served to increase the availability of cargo space for the export of horticulture.
6. K. Bradsher, "Bouquet of Roses May Have Note: 'Made in China'." *New York Times*, September 25, 2006.
7. B. Kathuri, "Horticulture Earnings Drop Linked to the Strong Shilling." *East African Standard*, August 31, 2006 and C. Riungu, "Bad Times for Kenya Flower Sector." *The East African*, September 11, 2006.
8. Nalo, D., "Kenya Must Look beyond EU Markets." *The East African*, September 4-10, 2006.
9. Interview with Dr. Kiome, Permanent Secretary of Agriculture, on March 22, 2006, at Kilimo House.
10. For example, Mumias has an installed crush capacity of 8,400 tons. This works out to be equal to 41 percent of the total crush capacity installed in the country. Other things being constant we would expect that Mumias output would be roughly 41 percent of production. In fact, Mumias produces close to 55 percent of national production on average. That is, it produces a larger proportion of sugar than its installed capacity as a proportion of national installed capacity. This is partially due to the fact that larger plants are able to take advantage of their returns to scale and produce closer to their crushing limit than small operations. This then allows the larger firms to produce a larger proportion of national output.
11. K. Mugambi, "Governments Bold Plan to Aid Farmers." *Sunday Nation,* September 10, 2006.
12. Interview with Mr. J. Nyatich and Mr. M. Mbeka, Deputy and Senior Assistant Commissioners of Cooperatives, respectively, on March 16, 2006.

6. Investing in Roads and Water Infrastructure

According to the Medium-Term Budget Strategy Paper (MTBSP), a number of sectors have been prioritized within the Kenyan budget in order to meet development objectives and to make progress towards achieving the Millennium Development Goals (Government of Kenya 2006a). The targeted sectors include: health, education, agriculture, infrastructure, and food/water security.

Focusing on the area of infrastructure, the MTBSP states that, "The development and maintenance of physical infrastructure on a sustainable basis is a key prerequisite for rapid and sustainable economic growth and poverty reduction. The cost of doing business is to a large extent influenced by the state of infrastructure" (p. 38).

This is clearly the case. Infrastructure investments are central for raising productivity and thereby people's incomes. Improving the country's infrastructure is equally important in terms of promoting trade competitiveness. Finally, increased public spending in these areas can serve as a major source of job growth within the country's formal economy, as has traditionally been the case in Kenya as well as many other countries.

Most recent studies of the Kenyan economy point to the dilapidated road network as one of the major impediments to increasing agricultural and industrial productivity in Kenya. For example the World Bank points out that it is cheaper to transport a ton of maize from Iowa to Mombasa (U.S. $50) a distance of 13,600 km than it is to transport the maize from Mombasa to Kampala (U.S. $100) a distance of 1,100 km (IFPRI 2004).

Recognizing the centrality of investing in the country's infrastructure, the 2006 MTBSP commits to increasing the share of government resources going to physical expenditures from 19.2 percent in 2005–06 to 21.6 in 2008–09. In terms of the 2005-06 budget, this percentage increase would represent a budgetary expansion of about Ksh 10 billion, from a total of Ksh 80–90 billion. The MTBSP states its priority areas as being the expansion and improved maintenance of road networks and other public works. It has also prioritized increasing access to water resources, along with the provision of affordable energy.

This increased level of spending for the country's infrastructure is certainly needed. However, we believe that these expenditure commitments need to increase significantly beyond even these enhanced projected levels. To illustrate this point, we focus on the areas of transport and water infrastructure because these are the two most urgent areas of need.

ROADS

Transportation is central for raising productivity, containing costs and inflation, improving export competitiveness, securing access to markets, reducing spoilage and waste, and mitigating the risk associated with droughts and volatility in agricultural production.

Road transportation accounts for roughly 80% of all transport in Kenya. It is also the form of transportation with the most straightforward fiscal implications. By contrast, the issues surrounding ports and rail transport involve complicated questions of parastatal management and privatization/concessioning. Air transport has enjoyed a reasonable level of investment through Kenya Airways. In addition, the benefits of better air transport are restricted to a few sectors (e.g. tourism, horticulture, and high value-added exports) and a small, wealthy subset of the population. Furthermore, poor road quality negatively impacts these other transportation sectors (e.g. poor roads leading to the airport). Therefore, we focus here on road transport infrastructure as the single most important component of Kenya's transportation system.

The potential impact of improvements in the rural road infrastructure are large. Wasike (2001) quotes Obare (2000) as finding farm productivity went up when access to roads increased. In fact a decrease of 10 percent in transport costs resulted in savings of Ksh 14,000 per hectare in Nakuru district. In earlier studies in the 1980s completion of rural road programs was followed by a 29 percent increase in farm productivity and a 27 percent increase in income. Omamo (1998) points out that farmers are less likely to engage in commercial farming where roads are poor and thus access to markets is difficult.

According to the Physical Infrastructure Sector Medium-Term Expenditure Framework Report, 2006–07–2008–09 (Government of Kenya 2006b), expenditures on road development are scheduled to increase dramatically beginning in the 2006–07 fiscal year. We show these budgetary plans in Table 6.1. As we see there, most of this increase in expenditure will be used to construct new roads. In addition, the Kenya Roads Board repairs and improves the existing road network. Its budget is derived from the Road Maintenance Levy Fund and is not included in the budget projections of the Ministry of Roads and Public Works. Currently, annual expenditures of the Kenya Roads Board are approximately Ksh 8–9 billion per year.

Table 6.1 Planned Expenditures on Road Development, 2005–06 – 2008–09 (Ksh millions) (medium-term expenditure framework)

	2005–06	2006–07	2007–08	2008–09
Major roads	2,560	8,311	8,726	9,163
Other roads	2,389	7,050	7,403	7,773
Planning and design	100	167	175	184
Other expenditures	1,940	2,020	2,120	2,227
TOTAL	6,989	17,548	18,424	19,347

Source: Government of Kenya (2006b).

Kenya currently has 28,500 km of national and urban roads and an additional 150,000 of rural (mostly dirt or gravel) roads. According to the Kenya Roads Board, a 2002 survey found that approximately one-third of Kenya's national and urban roads are in poor repair.[1] The estimated cost of rehabilitating all these poor roads is Ksh 228 billion.[2] Suppose that we set a goal of rehabilitating all of these poor quality roads within 12 years. The real annual cost (not factoring in inflation or the cost of other repair activities) would be roughly Ksh 19 billion per year—i.e. approximately twice the current budget of the Kenya Road Board. This suggests that, despite the significant budget reprioritization to support road infrastructure, Kenya's roads will remain substandard in the foreseeable future unless additional resources are made available.

Lack of financial resources is only one of two basic problems that Kenya must overcome if it is going to significantly improve its transportation infrastructure. The other, equally serious concern, is the government's capacity to complete projects that already have received adequate funding allocations, with the funds at the Treasury waiting to be spent. We can see this in Table 6.2, which shows the budgetary allocations and actual expenditures for various aspects of road development and maintenance for the fiscal year 2004–05.

As the table shows, the single largest budgetary item here is for road maintenance. For 2004–05, Ksh 8.6 billion were allocated for maintenance, and virtually all of these funds were spent. The country's road maintenance program is evidently operating at a high level of efficiency. However, road construction programs, as well as the smaller planning and design programs, were unable to spend a high proportion of their allocations. The major road construction program, for example, was able to spend only 52 percent of its allocated budget of Ksh 4.5 billion. The two most cited reasons for low utilization rates in road development activities were slow and inefficient procurement processes and poor work progress (Government of Kenya 2006b).

Table 6.2 Budgetary Allocation and Actual Expenditure on Road Development and Maintenance, 2004–05 (Ksh million)

	Budgetary allocation	Actual expenditure	Actual expenditure as share of budgetary allocation
Maintenance of roads	8,627	8,328	97%
Construction of major roads	4,467	2,301	52%
Construction of other roads	2,586	1,604	62%
Roads 2000 programme	665	217	33%
Planning and design	108	43	40%

Source: Government of Kenya (2006b).

A few important points emerge from these figures. The first is that, because the maintenance program is operating so much more effectively than the other programs, it should therefore continue to receive the largest share of budgetary allocations. Second, in order to improve efficiency in the road building areas, the successes in the road maintenance program should be examined carefully for lessons that may be applicable to the construction projects. Finally, and related, the government needs to initiate measures to raise productivity linked to the completion of new road projects. Such measures could be regarded as one significant component of an overall program to "mainstream productivity" in all areas of the country's economic management.

Certainly one major factor—if not the whole explanation—for the success of Kenya's road maintenance program is the organizational structure of the KRB, the governmental agency that administers these activities. The Kenya Roads Board was established by an act of Parliament in 1999. The KRB is a statutory institute, capable of acting independently of other government structures, set up to maintain Kenya's roads and serve in an advisory capacity to the government. This includes overseeing the procurement process for road maintenance in Kenya. It also monitors the activities of other agencies associated with road development. When the KRB was established in 1999, considerable attention was already focused on ways of improving procurement and minimizing corruption in government operations. Thus, the KRB was deliberately maintained as a relatively small agency, with a significant amount of independence from any single ministry.[3] This administrative structure seems to be succeeding in achieving its initial purpose. As such, it would make sense for policymakers to consider ways of establishing similar structures in other areas of government procurement.

WATER

Kenya is a water-scarce country. Renewable freshwater endowments currently stand at 600–700 m³ per person per year. A country is categorized as "water scarce" if it has less than 1,000 m³ per capita in renewable freshwater resources.[4] In addition, water resources are unequally distributed across geographical regions in Kenya. The arid and semi-arid lands, which cover a large part of the land surface in northern Kenya, are particularly vulnerable due to a lack of water security.

Water insecurity was the single greatest problem associated with the recent famine in 2005–06. Lack of water and water storage threatened human life and caused enormous losses in terms of livestock in the northern part of Kenya. Scarcity of water was as important, if not more important, to the human and economic costs of the famine as was the scarcity of food.

Agriculture accounts for the largest share of demand for freshwater resources, approximately 76% of total consumption. At the same time, the agricultural sector's use of water is highly inefficient. The Ministry of Water and Irrigation estimates that half of all water used in agriculture is lost or wasted due to poor quality irrigation infrastructure.

Currently, Kenya has irrigation infrastructure in place to service about 105,000 hectares of agricultural land. This is less than one fifth of the estimated full irrigation potential of the country – about 540,000 hectares. The cost of expanding irrigation infrastructure to meet the country's full potential is high—involving physical infrastructure, compensation for the employees working on these projects, and purchase of land for the construction of irrigation facilities.

In addition to the deficiencies in the irrigation system, water storage facilities are also in poor condition in Kenya. Excluding hydroelectric facilities, the per capita water storage capacity in Kenya stood at just 4.3 m³ per person in 1999. In 1969, three decades earlier, the estimated water storage capacity was three times higher, at 11.4 m³. This 1969 level of storage capacity was itself low. But the fact that capacity has diminished in absolute terms since 1969 is a major matter of concern.

Estimates by the Ministry of Water and Irrigation suggest that raising water storage capacity to around 740 m³ per capita would cost approximately U.S. $16 billion per year over the next 30 years.[5] But to raise the country above the threshold for water security would not entail a budgetary allocation that large. Given that freshwater endowments are already at between 600-700 m³ per person, this means that around another 350 m³ in water storage capacity would be needed to deliver a total level of water access above the 1000 m³ water scarcity line. Financing an increase in water storage at this level would cost an additional Ksh 37.5 billion per year for 30 years, equal to about 2.5 percent of GDP.

Table 6.3 Planned Expenditures on Water and Irrigation Infrastructure

	Fiscal year			
	2005–06	2006–07	2007–08	2008–09
	Ksh billions			
Development budget for water	4.5	9.3	12.8	14.0
Recurrent budget for water	3.0	3.8	3.8	4.4
TOTAL budget for water	7.5	13.1	16.6	18.4
	Percent			
Water spending as a percent of total development budget	13.6%	16.7%	21.9%	22.2%
Water spending as a percent of total government spending	1.1%	2.0%	2.5%	2.6%

Source: Government of Kenya (2006a) and (2006b).

Medium-Term Budgets and Water Infrastructure

Table 6.3 presents budgetary data on water infrastructure projects through 2008–09. As the table shows, expenditures on water infrastructure currently account for about 14 percent of the government's total development budget and 1 percent of overall government spending. Over the next five years, the Treasury projects that substantially more resources will be directed towards the provision of water infrastructure. By 2008–09 spending on water is expected to rise to 22.2 percent of the government's development budget and 2.6 percent of overall government spending.

The relative increased level of funding for water infrastructure is an important step in the right direction. At the same time, even these enhanced expenditure commitments still fall well below the estimated budgetary commitments needed to move the people of Kenya above the level of water scarcity. That is, as the table shows, the combined development and recurrent budgets for water, as of 2008–09, is roughly Ksh 18.4 billion. Considering water storage alone, this amount is only about half as large as the Ksh 37.5 billion that would be needed on an annual basis for 30 years to bring the country above the water scarcity threshold. For the purposes of our costing exercises, let us assume that the water budget rises by Ksh 20 billion per year, bringing the total budget to Ksh 38.4 billion. This level of funding, if allocated efficiently, will bring Kenya's entire population above the water scarcity line within 30 years.

Of course, the issue of whether the funds will be utilized efficiently cannot be assumed away. As with the road construction projects, the successful completion of projects that have already received their funding allocation may be at least as much, if not more, of a problem than receiving the budgetary allocation itself. Actual spending falls short of budgeted spending in a number of areas. However, the efficiency of delivery varies from one category of water infrastructure to the next. For example, planned and actual expenditures are reasonably well matched for the construction and rehabilitation of dams, pans, and dykes and flood control projects (Government of Kenya 2006b). Slow disbursement of donor funds and delays in the procurement process are frequently cited reasons for inefficiencies in delivery.

It should also be noted that the development budget for water infrastructure is highly donor dependent. The Treasury is assuming that approximately half of the funds available for the development of water infrastructure are coming from loans or overseas grants. If these funds do not materialize, it is unclear how the development objectives set forth in the medium-term expenditure framework can be financed. We will consider in a later chapter the prospects for Kenya's development budget to become less donor dependent.

EMPLOYMENT EFFECTS OF EXPANDING ROADS AND WATER INFRASTRUCTURE SPENDING

For illustrative purposes, let us assume that all the road and water projects operate at a budgetary allocation as we have described in the foregoing discussions—i.e. at a funding level of roughly Ksh 40 billion greater than the current allocation levels projected through 2008–09 in the MTBSP. What would be the impact of this increased level of spending in terms of employment within the country?

This would first of all depend on the production techniques used in these road and water infrastructure projects. Infrastructure projects can be performed using a fairly wide range of production techniques, ranging from highly machine-intensive to highly labor-intensive. Countries like Kenya that are trying to maximize employment opportunities should of course attempt to utilize more labor-intensive methods, assuming these techniques are roughly equivalent to the more machine-intensive techniques in terms of overall productivity and costs. The distinguished South African civil engineer Robert McCutcheon has studied ways through which more labor-intensive methods of infrastructure construction and maintenance can be used efficiently while also producing large benefits in terms of creating job opportunities. Thus, in the case of road construction and maintenance, McCutcheon and colleagues have estimated that with a typical machine-intensive technique, the percentage spent on labor would range between 5–15 percent of total costs. But in using the most efficient labor-intensive methods, labor costs would rise to between 30–80 percent. Similarly

Table 6.4 Illustration of Direct Employment Effects of Increased Infrastructure Spending

	Level of increased annual spending (Ksh billions)	Low-wage labor as percent of total costs under labor-intensive methods	Direct jobs created at wage of Ksh 5000/month
Roads	20	60% (= Ksh 12 billion)	200,000
Water	20	40% (=Ksh 8 billion)	133,000
TOTALS	40	—	333,000

Source: Authors' calculations.

with water storage—McCutcheon and colleagues estimated that labor costs could rise from 5–15 percent of total project costs to a range of between 40–50 percent (Philips, et al. 1995).[6]

For purposes of illustration, let us assume that in Kenya, the road building and maintenance projects can be performed with wage labor costs at 60 percent of the total budget, and the water storage projects can be performed with wage labor at 40 percent of the total project budgets.

In Table 6.4, we can see the impact on employment of expanding road and water infrastructure spending by Ksh 40 billion per year above current allocation levels, combined with utilizing labor-intensive production techniques to perform the allocated work. As the table shows, we assume that the workers employed at these projects are paid Ksh 5,000 per month. This figure is just above the minimum wage of Ksh 4,638 for general laborers in Nairobi in 2005. Based on the assumptions in our exercise, we see that the Ksh 35 billion increase in infrastructure spending will directly produce 333,000 jobs, 200,000 in the roads sector and 133,000 in water storage. In addition, we roughly estimate that another 20,000 jobs in wage employment will be indirectly generated through multiplier effects—i.e. the increase in employment that comes from the 333,000 newly employed workers spending their wage income in Kenya's economy.[7]

NOTES

1. More precisely, 17% of roads are in good condition, 39% in fair condition, 27% in poor condition, and 16% cannot be rehabilitated and must be reconstructed (see www.krb.go.ke/roadconditions.php).
2. Based on an estimated cost of rehabilitation of roughly 24 million Ksh per kilometer. This figure is based on the estimated per kilometer cost of actual road rehabilitation projects as listed in the Physical Infrastructure Sector MTEF Report (Government of Kenya 2006b). We emphasize that this is a rough estimate, that does not take into account cost differences for different categories of roads.

3. The KRB is not governed within any single ministry of government. As was established in the 1999 Kenya Roads Board Act, the governing structure rather consists of the following: a chairperson, appointed by the President; an Executive Director (high-level management employee); the Permanent Secretary in the Ministry of Roads; the Permanent Secretary in the Ministry of Finance; the Permanent Secretary in the Ministry dealing with local authorities; the Permanent Secretary in the Ministry of Transportation; the Permanent Secretary in the Ministry dealing with regional coordination; eight representatives drawn from the following civil society organizations: Institution of Engineers of Kenya; The Automobile Association of Kenya; The National Chamber of Commerce and Industry; The Institute of Surveyors of Kenya; The Kenya National Farmers Union; The Kenya Association of Tour Operators; The Institute of Certified Public Accountants of Kenya; and The Kenya Transport Association. See also the website of the Kenya Roads Board for additional details on its operation (http://www.krb.go.ke/regsem11.php).

4. Countries with between 1,000 and 1,700 m³ of water per capita are considered "water stressed". Ministry of Water and Irrigation "Large-scale Water Infrastructure as a Platform for Economic Growth? The Kenyan Experience" (www.water.go.ke/article3.html), accessed October 2006.

5. Ministry of Water and Irrigation, "Large-scale Water Infrastructure as a Platform for Economic Growth? The Kenyan Experience" (www.water.go.ke/article3.html), accessed October 2006.

6. For an extensive list of the research of McCutcheon and his colleagues, see the useful ILO publication ASIST in Africa, which can be accessed at: http://www.ilo.org/public/english/employment/recon/eiip/asist/africa/papers/pap1996/pap966a.htm.

7. Our multiplier estimate is based on Lewis and Thorbecke (1992). They have estimated hired labor multipliers for Kutus Region production activities in a range of sectors. The fixed price multipliers show the Ksh increases in regional value added for a Ksh 1.00 increase in demand for each sector's output. For the transport sector, they find that a 100 percent increase in direct spending will yield a 6.5 percent fixed-price multiplier. If we assume that the increase in spending will yield a commensurate increase in employment, that suggests that a direct employment increase of 333,333 jobs will produce another 21,666 jobs indirectly.

7. Monetary Policy, Inflation Control and Interest Rates

In this chapter, we focus on three interrelated aspects of the broader policy approach—i.e., monetary policy, inflation control, and interest rates. In the next two chapters, we then consider two closely related subjects. Chapter 8 is concerned with the exchange rate, balance of payments and trade. In Chapter 9, we discuss restructuring the financial system to promote a more effective allocation of credit.

In this chapter, our purpose is to examine the current monetary policy regime and approach to inflation control, evaluating the extent to which it is able to promote sustainable economic development that significantly expands decent employment opportunities. In this broad context of promoting decent employment, government policymakers will, of course, also need to maintain a commitment to controlling inflation and the balance of payments. But establishing the appropriate mix of policies for expanding decent employment while also managing inflation and the balance of payments is a major challenge for policymakers in Kenya, as it is elsewhere in the world. In discussing how Kenyan policymakers can meet these challenges, we address in this chapter two areas in detail: (1) inflation dynamics in Kenya and the relationship between inflation and long-run growth; and (2) monetary policy targets and instruments, and their relationship to interest rate levels in Kenya. In the next chapter, we take up detailed issues around exchange rate dynamics, trade promotion and the country's external balance. In Chapter 9, we examine credit allocation policies in detail, considering further the issue of promoting private investment in Kenya through making affordable credit much more accessible to businesses of all sizes.

OVERALL CONTEXT REGARDING INFLATION CONTROL AND MONETARY POLICY

Kenya's current national development strategy, the *Economic Recovery Strategy for Wealth and Employment Creation* (ERS) (Government of Kenya 2003c), states the government's objectives in the area of monetary policy as follows:

The main focus of monetary policy is to ensure that growth in money supply is consistent with economic growth, employment creation, and a viable balance of payments position without putting undue pressure on inflation. In the last five years, monetary policy aimed at maintaining low stable inflation while providing adequate liquidity to enable the country to achieve its development needs. To a large extent the pursuit of low stable inflation was achieved. As a result, the shilling exchange rate, which since 1993 has been market determined, has been fairly stable, particularly in the last two years. Although interest rates remain a source of concern, considerable progress has been made in lowering them in line with reduced inflation (p. 4).

For the coming years, the ERS states that its focus will be on four goals:

1. contain inflation to below 5 percent;
2. maintain a competitive exchange rate consistent with an export-driven economic recovery;
3. maintain an interest rate structure that promotes financial savings and ensures efficient allocation of the same; and
4. ensure adequate growth in credit to the private sector.

There is no doubt that these are all important goals that are worthy in their own right. At the same time, this list raises a set of serious concerns that require careful attention.

1. Containing inflation below 5 percent could operate as a significant obstacle to promoting economic growth, employment expansion, and poverty reduction. As a case in point, the average inflation rate between 2004–06 in Kenya has been 11.3 percent. But as we discuss at some length below, this is due almost entirely to food and energy supply shocks. The issue of dampening inflation should be considered in terms of the primary factors causing inflation. The appropriate policies for controlling supply-shock and inertial inflation will almost always be distinct from those for controlling inflation resulting from excess demand. It is therefore imperative that policymakers pay attention to the particular sources of inflationary pressures, and devise policies to reflect these actual specific circumstances.
2. Maintaining a competitive exchange rate and promoting export growth is highly desirable. However, it is unclear how, under the current policy regime, the government can ensure that the exchange rate remains at a competitive level. Moreover, the economy of Kenya at present is heavily dependent on imports in the areas of energy products, chemicals, equipment, and machinery. Thus, the goal of promoting exports must be advanced within the framework of also reducing import-dependency in these areas.

3. Promoting an efficient allocation of financial savings and ensuring adequate growth in credit to the private sector are crucial to the country's growth prospects. But it is not likely that monetary policy by itself can reconcile these two goals, especially in the context of also attempting to maintain inflation below 5 percent. Other policy interventions will be needed to encourage an efficient allocation of credit to the private sector.

4. The need for an effective combination of monetary and credit allocation policies to support private sector investment become even more important in the context of the Kenyan economy's parallel need to promote public investment. We have argued in Chapter 6 for a substantial increase in public infrastructure investments for improving the country's road system and water supply. We identify these initiatives as key components of an overall program for employment expansion and poverty reduction. The level of expenditures that we propose is in the order of Ksh 40 billion per year beyond what the government has budgeted on an annual basis through 2008–09 (Government of Kenya 2006a and 2006b). In Chapter 10, we consider the necessary measures to finance these public investment expenditures. At the same time, for any such long-term public investment initiatives to be viable, it will be necessary for monetary and fiscal policy to operate in a coordinated, mutually supportive fashion.

As we will discuss at greater length, the primary monetary policy tool that the Central Bank of Kenya uses to achieve its goals is to target the growth rate of the aggregate money supply, or M3. The Central Bank allows the exchange rate to float and does not attempt to influence the value of the shilling by intervening in the foreign exchange market. The Central Bank will only intervene in the foreign exchange market in special circumstances—for example, if the level of foreign exchange is inadequate to meet external payment obligations. The reliance on a single policy target—the growth rate of the money supply—will likely be inadequate to achieve the multiple goals of monetary policy stated in the national development strategy.

BASIC TRENDS ON INFLATION AND INTEREST RATES

Inflation Trends

One of the current objectives of monetary policy is to maintain low rates of inflation. Figure 7.1 charts the movement in Kenya's consumer price inflation from 1965 to 2006. As we can see from the figure, the Kenyan economy has never been a high-inflation economy, in the sense that Kenya has never experienced a protracted hyper-inflation. In fact, the inflation rate has rarely risen

Figure 7.1 Consumer Price Index Inflation, 1965–2006

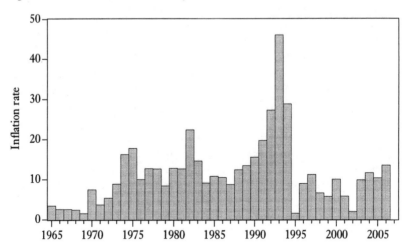

Source: National Bureau of Statistics.

above 20 percent. This is a strong overall performance relative to other developing countries throughout the world. The one exception to this positive experience in Kenya occurred in the early 1990s, when inflation rates soared to
approximately 45 percent. This bout of high inflation corresponded to a devaluation of the shilling associated with the implementation of a series of measures
to liberalize aspects of the economy, including the financial sector, exchange
rates, and trade.

We do also see that inflation has fallen below 5 percent only twice since
1973, in 1995 and 2002. Over the full decade 1997–2006, inflation averaged 8.7
percent, even after including the experience in 2002 when inflation fell to 2.0
percent. With respect to the goal of the ERS of maintaining inflation below 5
percent annually, the actual experience with inflation suggests some combination of the following conclusions: 1) Kenyan policymakers have not been effective in implementing the necessary measures to achieve the 5 percent inflation
target; 2) the structure of Kenya's economy makes it inherently difficult to achieve
this five percent inflation target; and 3) focusing on a 5 percent inflation target
may not be the most appropriate organizing principle for monetary and macroeconomic policy.

We believe that all three of these conclusions are accurate. As such, we will
focus our analysis on developing a new perspective and set of policies for controlling inflation at reasonable levels, such as those already achieved by Kenya
throughout almost all of its history since independence.

Figure 7.2 Nominal and Real Interest Rates on Loans, 1971–2006
(real interest rate = nominal rate—CPI inflation rate)

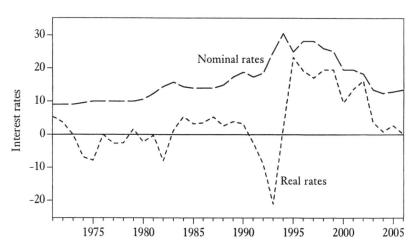

Source: International Monetary Fund (2007a), Central Bank of Kenya (2006).

Interest Rate Movements

Figure 7.2 shows the movement of nominal and real lending rates in Kenya between 1971 and 2006. The nominal rates are simply the rates on all loan documents that borrowers are committed to pay. The real rates are the nominal rates minus the rate of inflation. In measuring real lending rates, we therefore account for the depreciation in the value of the shilling that results from inflation, and the corresponding depreciation in the real value of the shillings that borrowers pay to lenders, relative to the shilling's value at the time a loan was made.

As we see, for the most part, real lending rates in Kenya had remained below 5 percent until 1993, and sometimes fell into negative figures. One consequence of the financial liberalization policies that were introduced in the first half of the 1990s was an unprecedented increase in real interest rates that persisted from 1994–2002. The real lending rate was 24 percent in 1994 and remained as high as 16.4 percent in 2002. But as inflation rose after 2002, the real lending rates correspondingly fell, to 1.5 percent in 2004, 3.2 percent in 2005, and 0.1 percent in 2006.

Higher real lending rates raise the cost of credit to businesses, reducing investment and curtailing access to working capital. In addition, many smaller enterprises, particularly in the agricultural sector and among own-account workers, face credit constraints that limit the potential for productivity-enhancing investments. The lack of productivity improvements keeps earnings low and limits the quality of available employment opportunities.

To our knowledge, there is not solid evidence demonstrating how much high real lending rates inhibit the growth of private investment and consumption. From the range of interviews we conducted with private business representatives, bankers, and government officials, the consensus view is that high interest rates are indeed a significant constraint on growth. In any case, we do know which way the direction of effect operates—that is, lowering interest rates will lower the costs of investment for business and will make the purchase of expensive consumer goods more possible for consumers.

INFLATION CONTROL AND ECONOMIC GROWTH

The government of Kenya has stated strongly its commitment to attacking the country's severe problems of poverty, unemployment, and underemployment. At the same time, as the Economic Recovery Strategy emphasizes, the government is also committed to maintaining a low-inflation environment. Clearly, the government holds to the idea that maintaining a low-inflation environment is a necessary foundation for attacking poverty, unemployment, and underemployment in a sustainable way.

High inflation is not a desirable end in itself. Given the choice between high inflation and strong economic growth or low inflation and equally robust growth, policymakers should opt for low inflation. However, it is important to examine the premise that low inflation rates are, by themselves, conducive to economic growth. More specifically, we want to consider here what the effect is likely to be of allowing the Kenyan economy to operate at a target inflation rate above its current 5 percent target. Of course, the only reason for relaxing this target inflation rate is that faster economic growth may occur in correspondence with a somewhat higher inflation rate. This would be because tight monetary policies generally will lead to high interest rates. High interest rates, in turn, dampen economic growth, and thereby, the expansion of decent employment opportunities in the formal sector.

Indeed, the past few years in Kenya have offered some useful evidence on these points. The government has not achieved its 5 percent inflation target since 2002. At the same time, real lending rates have fallen, to close to zero in 2006, when both inflation and nominal interest rates were at around 13.5 percent. The high level of inflation was due to energy and food supply shocks. The decline in the real lending rate to nearly zero, relative to the 13.5 percent nominal rate, could therefore not have been entirely anticipated by the country's financial markets participants—either the borrowers or lenders. Nevertheless, economic growth did improve in the previous two years, reaching 5.7 percent in

2005 and 6.1 percent in 2006. This recent experience strongly suggests that the government should reassess its stated commitment of maintaining a 5 percent inflation target and refocus its policy aims to build upon the relatively successful growth experiences of the past two years.

To provide some analytic background in support of such a reassessment, we will first review some relevant literature on the relationship between inflation and growth throughout the world. We will then consider the evidence in Kenya that relates the effects of supply shocks—in particular large spikes in the prices of energy, food, and transportation—on overall inflation in the country.

What Is the Relationship between Inflation and Growth?

Answers to this question vary widely in the professional literature. Some of the most influential recent studies were those produced by the late Michael Bruno, along with his colleague William Easterly. Bruno had been Chief Economist at the World Bank at the time he conducted his studies.

In his 1995 research, Bruno studied the relationship between inflation and economic growth for 127 countries between 1960 and 1992. Bruno found that the average growth rates fell only slightly as inflation rates moved up to 20–25 percent. Of particular importance, Bruno found that during 1960–72, economic growth on average increased as inflation rose, from negative or low rates to the 15–20 percent range. This is because, as Bruno explained, "in the 1950s and 1960s, low-to-moderate inflation went hand in hand with very rapid growth because of investment demand pressures in an expanding economy" (Bruno 1995, p. 35). Thus, according to Bruno's findings, inflation that results directly from expansionary economic policies will not create any significant barriers to further growth.

Bruno's 1995 findings were challenged by other researchers, who did indeed find that inflation leads to lower economic growth. However, in responding to these critics, Bruno and Easterly (1998) found that the clear negative relationship between inflation and growth only operates at very high inflation rates—what they define as in the range of 40 percent or above. Once these experiences of very high inflation are considered separately from those of moderate inflation, Bruno and Easterly again found that, for the moderate inflation cases, no clear relationship existed between inflation and economic growth.

Still again, other researchers have produced findings contradictory to Bruno and Easterly, even after separating out the experiences of high (i.e., 40 percent or more) inflation from moderate inflation. For example, IMF economists Ghosh and Phillips (1998), drawing from a data sample of IMF member countries over 1960–96, found evidence of a negative inflation/growth threshold at 2.5 percent. But they also acknowledge that thresholds of 5–10 percent generate statistical results very similar to their 2.5 percent threshold.

Their particular conclusions aside, the work of Ghosh and Phillips is within a widely accepted current stream of research that distinguishes the relationship to growth of different levels of inflation—observing how the effects of inflation on growth will vary at, say, 5, 10, 20, and 30 percent inflation rates. These researchers rely on nonlinear econometric estimating techniques to distinguish the growth/inflation effects at these alternative threshold levels. What is also especially relevant for the case of Kenya is that this most recent stream of researchers now also consistently finds that the growth/inflation relationship is different for industrialized countries and developing countries.

For example, a 2001 study by another team of IMF economists, Moshin Khan and Abdelhak Senhadji, identified the threshold point for industrial countries at which inflation reduces economic growth at a very low 1–3 percent. But their threshold point for developing countries was between 11–12 percent. This distinction in threshold points was also found in a 2004 study by Burdekin, Denzau, Keil, Sitthiyot, and Willett. They also utilized non-linear estimating techniques. However, they reached conclusions nearly opposite to Khan and Senhadji: that the negative inflation/growth threshold was higher for industrial countries, at 8 percent, than the threshold for developing countries, which was 3 percent.

Robert Pollin and Andong Zhu (2006) recently developed another model that estimates the effects of inflation on economic growth. This model includes inflation as one potential factor influencing economic growth, after controlling for a range of other potential influences.[1] The growth/inflation estimates are based on data from 80 countries from 1961 to 2000. As with the more recent literature generally, the Pollin/Zhu model includes a non-linear component to capture the differential effects of relatively low versus relatively high levels of inflation. In addition, the models follow Bruno and Easterly (1998) in excluding inflation episodes in excess of 40 percent. Finally, this model examines the inflation/growth relationship for the full set of countries in different ways. It provides separate sets of results for OECD countries, middle-income countries, and low income countries. It also considers the full sample of countries within four separate decades from 1961 to 2000. This study then utilizes four different estimating techniques with each of the various country- and time-period groupings, to test for the robustness of findings using any given technique.

The main results of these exercises can be summarized quickly. Considering the full data set, they consistently find that higher inflation is associated with moderate gains in GDP growth up to a roughly 15–18 percent inflation threshold. But the results do diverge when they divide the full data set according to income levels. With the OECD countries, no clear pattern emerges in terms of identifying a negative inflation/growth threshold. With the middle-income countries, including South Africa as the one sub-Saharan African country in this grouping, the results again become consistently positive between inflation and growth up to a 14–16 percent threshold, though these results are not statistically significant. The positive inflation/growth relationship holds more strongly and consistently with low-income countries, including Kenya as one of 18 sub-Saharan African low-income countries in this grouping. With the groupings by decades, the results indicate that inflation and growth will be more positively correlated to the degree that macroeconomic policy is focused on stimulating demand; that is, a finding consistent with Bruno's (1995) observation that growth and inflation were more positively correlated over 1960–72, when active demand management policies were being widely practiced in support of maintaining high employment.

In short, the results from Pollin and Zhu's model are broadly consistent with Bruno's earlier World Bank studies, despite substantial differences between methodological approaches. That is, there is no statistically robust evidence in the Pollin/Zhu model suggesting that moderate inflation, in the range of less than 20 percent, will have a negative influence on economic growth. There was rather some evidence to support the view that such moderate inflation is associated positively with growth.

Considering the findings from all the studies, nothing close to a consensus has been reached on this question, even while increasingly sophisticated estimating techniques have been deployed to control for various non-linearities in the inflation/economic growth relationship. At the same time, a few basic conclusions from these various studies that are relevant for the Kenyan case do seem warranted. A first basic conclusion is that regardless of whether researchers observe a negative growth/inflation relationship emerging in the low or high double-digit range for developing countries, only one study found a clear negative relationship between growth and single-digit inflation specifically for the developing countries. This suggests that for Kenya, setting an inflation target below five percent is not likely to offer benefits in terms of the economy's growth performance. If Kenya chooses to follow the low-end finding within the professional literature on the inflation/growth trade-off, that would still suggest an inflation target in the range of 8 to 9 percent.

A second basic conclusion is that, despite the wide range of techniques now being used to estimate the growth/inflation trade-off, no researcher has challenged one important point emphasized by Bruno in his initial 1995 work—namely, that the relationship between inflation and growth will be different depending on what is causing the economy's inflationary pressures. As Bruno found, demand–pull inflation, resulting from a process of economic expansion, will be positively associated with growth as long as the inflation rate remains moderate. Thus, if Kenya pursues an aggressive jobs program, one would expect that the inflationary pressures that may then emerge would not be harmful to growth, as long as, again, the inflation remains moderate.

By contrast, following the logic of Bruno's findings, inflation that results from excessive price mark-ups over costs by businesses, supply shocks, or exchange rate volatility will be associated with negative growth effects. But these negative growth effects will not be due to the inflation per se, but rather to the monopolistic pricing power of businesses or from the economy's attempt at adjusting to the effects of supply shocks or volatile movements of the shilling.

Supply Shocks and Kenyan Inflation Control

We have already shown that the Kenyan economy has never been a high-inflation economy. In fact, according to the research we have just reviewed, the inflation rate in Kenya has been in the range consistent with strong, stable economic performance during most of the post-independence period.

Despite Kenya's generally positive performance with inflation control, it is still the case that supply-side shocks have a major impact on inflationary dynamics in Kenya. As one important example, food price inflation, due to droughts or other breakdowns in the country's food production, raises the country's overall inflation rate and lowers living standards, particularly of poorer households. Rapid increases in global oil prices have similar effects on the Kenyan economy. Tightening monetary policy in response to such events in order to maintain low inflation rates runs the risks of worsening the economic impact of these shocks.[2] Therefore, it is important to understand the impact of exogenous price shocks on inflation dynamics in Kenya and to design policies that may mitigate the impact of these shocks without resorting to macroeconomic tightening.

One way of exploring the impact of exogenous price shocks on inflationary dynamics is to analyze the relationships that exist between the different components of the consumer price index (CPI). Table 7.1 lists the various components of the Kenyan CPI and describes the goods and services included under the different categories.[3] The table also shows the relative weights assigned to each broad category of the CPI, with the categories listed in order of their relative rankings. As we see, food prices are by far the most significant component of the overall CPI, with a weight of 50.5 percent of the overall CPI basket. Housing and clothing are the next most significant components of the overall CPI, with weights of 11.7 and 9 percent respectively. Thus, in combination, food, housing, and clothing comprise over 70 percent of Kenya's overall CPI.

Policymakers in Kenya, as elsewhere, sometimes make a distinction between "headline inflation," the rate of increase of the overall CPI, and "core inflation," the rate of increase of the CPI excluding food and energy components. This distinction is not generally illuminating in the Kenya setting. This is first of all because, as we have just seen, food prices alone account for more than half of the overall CPI. The figure is even higher, at 56 percent, for lower-income households in Nairobi.

Table 7.1 Components of Kenya's New Broad Category Consumer Price Index

Components	Relative weight in overall CPI (percentages)	Examples of goods and services included
(1) Food	50.5	Grains, fruits, vegetables, meat, non-alcoholic drinks, meals away from home
(2) Housing	11.7	Rented houses, rented flats, land rates
(3) Clothing and footwear	9.0	Men's, women's and children's clothes, school uniforms, nappies, material costs for home production, shoes, shoe repair
(4) Education & recreation	6.0	School fees, college fees, textbooks, radios, televisions, cinema, newspapers
(5) Household goods & services	5.8	Furniture, appliances, utensils, cleaning supplies, candles, bedding
(6) Transportation & communication	5.7	Petrol, diesel, car service, insurance, taxi fare, bus fares, matatu fares, postage, phone calls
(7) Energy (fuel and power)	4.2	Electricity, water, paraffin, cooking gas, charcoal
(8) Alcohol & tobacco	3.0	Cigarettes, beer, traditional liqueur, miraa
(9) Personal goods & services	2.4	Soap, haircut, toothpaste, watch, umbrella
(10) Medical goods & services	1.6	Pain killers, anti-malaria tablets, bandages, dental services, consultation fees

Source: Government of Kenya (2002).

With respect to energy prices, the primary source of supply-shock inflation in Kenya, as elsewhere, are spikes in the global price of oil. These spikes in global oil prices are reflected in two components of Kenya's CPI that we see in Table 7.1:

1. *transportation and communication* (5.7 percent of overall CPI), including petrol, diesel, car service, insurance, taxi fare, bus fares, matatu fares,[4] postage, and phone calls; and
2. *energy (fuel and power)* (4.2 percent of overall CPI), including electricity, water, paraffin, cooking gas, and charcoal.

In addition, the prices of both "Transportation & communication" and "Energy" feed into other costs of doing business, and thereby affect the other components of the CPI indirectly. It is therefore unclear whether any measure of "core inflation" actually removes the effects of spikes in the prices of food and foreign oil.

To understand more clearly how food and oil price shocks affect the overall CPI in Kenya, we estimated a vector autoregression (VAR) model that includes the ten components of the Kenyan CPI as variables. The data consist of monthly estimates of the revised CPI series from January 1991 to December 2005. We present a technical summary of the model in Appendix 2. Here we offer a brief non-technical summary of the principal findings of the exercise, focusing on the effects throughout the economy of shocks in the prices of three components of the Kenyan CPI: Food, Transportation & communication, and Energy. We focus on both the Transportation & communication and Energy components of the Kenyan CPI, since, as we have discussed above, they are the two categories within the CPI through which foreign oil price shocks get transmitted throughout the Kenyan economy.

Food price shocks

The results of our VAR model show that food price shocks appear to have few systematic effects on inflation rates in the rest of the economy. Even within the food sector itself, the cumulative impact of the shock on food price inflation dwindles significantly after two years. The only other sector that shows any significant response to an exogenous increase in food prices is the transportation sector. In other words, food price shocks appear to be fairly transitory with little systemic impact on inflationary dynamics in Kenya. This finding is especially relevant given the recent drought, which led to a 44 percent increase in food prices between October 2005 and March 2006. According to our model, we would not expect that this spike in food prices will have any longer-term impact on inflation in Kenya.

Transportation and Communication Price Shocks

Shocks to transportation costs have systemic effects on other prices in the Kenyan economy, even though they constitute only 5.7 percent of the overall CPI. Recall here from Table 7.1 that the index of transportation and prices includes fares for car services, taxis, buses, and matatus, as well as petrol and diesel prices. As such, this component of the CPI does not simply reflect changes in global oil prices. It will clearly be strongly influenced by oil prices, but it will also include, for example, the labor and material costs associated with each of the various modes of transportation.

From our VAR model, we found that a transportation price shock unleashes inflationary pressures throughout Kenya's economy. Moreover, the effects of the shock also appears to lead to accelerating inflation, even after two years, in certain other components of overall CPI, including the prices of clothing and a range of services. This finding has significant implications for the issue of overall inflation control. It suggests that lowering transportation costs will contribute to sustainable lower inflation rates overall.

Energy price shocks

According to our model, a one-time energy price shock—including here, again, electricity, water, paraffin, cooking gas, and charcoal prices—does raise the inflation rates of the other CPI components and these higher inflation rates are often sustained over time. This is true even though the energy component constitutes only 4.2 percent of the overall CPI basket. This result confirms the high degree to which energy prices affect business costs, which in turn get passed onto consumers by raising the overall CPI over a sustained period of time.

Conclusions

The findings from our VAR model suggest the following policy implications:

1. Food price shocks do have a major direct impact on overall "headline" inflation in the short-run. And because food prices constitute over 50 percent of the overall CPI basket, these effects can impose serious hardships, especially for lower-income households. At the same time, these effects are transitory. These two results imply the need for immediate policy interventions to counteract the short-term impact of food price shocks, but that such interventions need not be sustained over longer time periods.

    The most effective approach would be for the government to utilize its existing underutilized grain storage facilities throughout the country to provide an effective buffer stock of food that is readily accessible. This buffer stock should of course be accumulated during periods when food prices are relatively low. This buffer stock of food could then be distributed throughout Kenya in response to any period of rapid increases in food prices, regardless of the source of the price increases. It is also the case that, by purchasing food for the buffer stocks when prices are low, this will serve to set a floor on food prices. Overall, then, the buffer stock system will contribute to food price stability by counteracting both upward and downward price fluctuations.

    Note here that, precisely because the effects of the food price shocks are transitory on the overall economy, the period of time over which the food reserves would need to be drawn down would be relatively short.

2. Transportation and communication price shocks, are, of course, heavily affected by global oil prices. The most direct channel is through the petrol and diesel price components. But car service, taxi fares, bus fares, and matatu fares will also be affected by an oil shock, though less fully than petrol and diesel prices, since these services also include significant labor and material costs other than oil. It would not be feasible for the Kenyan government to

create oil buffer stocks comparable to the food buffer stocks we are proposing as a means of mitigating the effects of food price shocks. This is because Kenya imports all of its oil, and because building an oil buffer stock will likely be far more expensive than what could be developed for a food supply.

At the same time, the Kenyan government could pursue initiatives to directly reduce the price of transportation, both in the short run, after a global oil price spike has occurred, and in the longer term. In the short term, the most effective means of counteracting the effect of global oil price shocks would be for the government to quickly increase its subsidy for public transportation, including bus and matatu fares. Over the longer term, investments in the country's transportation infrastructure, especially its roads system, will lower the overall share of transportation costs in the CPI, and thereby mitigate the effects on the overall CPI of a short-term oil price shock.

3. Energy price shocks—including here again, electricity, water, paraffin, cooking gas, and charcoal prices—also have a sustained, systemic impact on inflation in Kenya. As with the Transportation and Communications component of the CPI, the only way that the government can counteract the effects of a global oil price spike would be to subsidize the prices of these components of the CPI in the short run. This would short-circuit the long-lasting effects of these price increases on the overall CPI.

Overall, the challenge for policymakers in Kenya in this area is therefore to identify how best to provide short-term subsidies in both the "Transportation & communication" and "Energy" components of the CPI, such that the longer-term effects on overall inflation can be minimized.

ADDITIONAL INFLATION CONTROL TOOLS

As we have seen, the weight of the professional literature suggests that, as Kenya continues to advance an aggressive program of employment expansion, it should not weaken the program as long as inflation remains moderate, i.e. basically within a single-digit range. But what happens if inflation accumulates inertial momentum, such that a rise to a 10 percent inflation rate leads to still greater inflationary pressures? This happens most commonly when wage and price increases spiral upward together, as labor and business both try to protect their real incomes from the very inflationary forces to which they themselves are contributing. Should Kenya then revert to stringent growth in the money supply as a means of raising interest rates? In fact, other policy tools are available for their use, through which Kenya could contain inflation within a moderate range, without having to rely on high interest rates as its primary control mechanism.

One useful policy tool to consider is "incomes policies." Incomes policies have been developed in various specific ways, as we discuss briefly below, but the basic idea is straightforward: that wage and price increases are negotiated over on an economy-wide basis between labor and business in the formal economy. Through such negotiations, labor and business agree to restrain wage and price increases. This then serves to break the inertial wage-price spiral. To the extent that such agreements are effective, this will then reduce inertial inflationary pressures in the economy. This will be true as a matter of course, since "inflationary pressures" are, by definition, simply efforts by business to raise prices on the products they sell to consumers.

The experience with various types of incomes policies as applied in developing country settings is usefully described in a 1991 paper, "Moderate Inflation," by Rudiger Dornbusch and Stanley Fischer.[5] One case Dornbusch and Fischer consider is the successful effort by South Korea in the early 1980s to move from an environment where inflation had consistently remained in double-digits between 1963–81, to an environment of single-digit inflation thereafter. The primary measure for achieving this, according to Dornbusch and Fischer, was incomes policies. They write:

> Wage increases in the government sector were reduced in 1981 and 1982; by convention and with the assistance of jawboning, the private sector followed. In addition, a mass education campaign, undertaken at the end of 1980, "stressed the need for restraining the demand for excessive wage increases and for a higher government purchase price of rice" (p. 51; the internal quote is from a paper by Nam 1984).

In this Korean case, the government was clearly focused on restraining the wages of workers, as opposed to combining wage restraint with price constraints on business. Indeed, as Dornbusch and Fischer note, the Korean government in this same period also agreed to *increase* the price that they would pay for rice while imposing wage restraints on workers. As such, in this case, incomes policies were clearly also a means of redistributing national income away from workers and toward business.

However, it is not necessarily the case that incomes policies need to also encourage a regressive redistribution of national income. Thus, Dornbusch and Fischer also describe the disinflationary program pursued in Indonesia in the mid-1970s. In this case, the government imposed fiscal restraints with redistributive fiscal measures favoring the poor. They write that "Sales taxes on luxuries were raised while those on essentials were reduced; imports of rice and fertilizer were heavily subsidized, and it was decided to aim for a budget surplus" (p. 54). Demand for luxury goods would thereby fall, lowering the prices for luxury goods. Meanwhile the demand for imported necessities, such as rice and fertilizer, was allowed to rise, without producing higher prices, since the government was subsidizing these prices.

Overall, incomes policies represent what Dornbusch and Fischer call a "non-market" tool for restraining inflationary pressures generated by inertia—i.e. by a wage-price spiral. Breaking such inertial inflationary forces entails some combination of restraints on both wages and prices, or some reconfiguration of the government's budget, as in Indonesia, to effectively achieve a comparable effect on inertial inflationary pressures. With such policies, there will always be an issue of which social classes are restrained to a greater or lesser extent in their efforts to keep up with the wage-price spiral. This is ultimately not a technical matter of economic policy, but rather a question of which groups have more or less political power. At the same time, the ability of an incomes policy to be sustained over time as an effective inflation control tool will depend on representatives of labor and capital achieving at least a minimally workable consensus as to the equitable distribution of wage and price constraints.

In the case of Kenya, there is some precedent for the types of negotiations similar to those needed for operating an effective incomes policy. This is the extensive set of negotiations that take place every year to establish the range of minimum wage rates for different occupations and different regions of the country. However, to date, these negotiations have not seriously taken up the issue of how wage-setting decisions may also be linked to issues of inflation control. But there is no reason why these negotiations might not be expanded to consider incomes policies.[6]

In addition, the establishment of the Productivity Centre of Kenya—which is being done precisely through negotiations between representatives of business, labor, and the government—could offer a forum through which the issue of linking wage growth, productivity growth, and inflation control might be fruitfully explored. That is, the Productivity Centre could undertake productive discussions around an egalitarian set of incomes policies, with restraints shared equitably by both workers and businesses.

One potential barrier to establishing effective incomes policies in Kenya is the fact that the negotiations we are describing above would primarily occur among only those social groups operating in the formal economy. As we have seen, formal sector employment represents only about 15 percent of total employment in Kenya. But clearly the formal economy is the key for maintaining control over energy and transportation prices, and also has a strong influence over food prices. Thus, establishing some institutional basis for price control within the formal economy should help weaken inertial inflationary forces from spreading throughout the informal sectors and agricultural self-employment.

RETARGETING MONETARY POLICY

We have seen in the previous section how interventions apart from monetary policy can be used to control inflation within a single-digit range. However, the current monetary regime in Kenya relies on monetary instruments to meet its 5 percent inflation target, despite the fact that it has not achieved this target since 2002. It clearly seems an appropriate time to re-evaluate the goals and techniques of monetary policy in Kenya.[7]

Although the Central Bank formulates monetary policy based on its ultimate objective of maintaining low inflation, the specific intermediate target used in its daily operations is to control the growth rate of the money supply. Specifically, monetary policy targets the growth rate of broad money, defined as M3 (previously called M3X). In Kenya, M3 is composed of currency in circulation outside of the banking sector, demand deposits, savings deposits, certificates of deposit (CDs), the deposits of non-bank financial institutions, and the foreign currency deposits of Kenyan residents.[8]

The economic theory behind this operating procedure is the quantity theory of money, with its well-known formula:

$$\text{(money supply growth)} \times \text{(velocity of circulation of money)} =$$

$$\text{(inflation rate)} \times \text{(real GDP growth)}$$

The quantity theory of money holds that the velocity of circulation of money is constant, and that real GDP growth can be taken as given for the purpose of this formula. This therefore means that the growth rate of the money supply should be closely linked to the country's inflation rate. The Central Bank operates with the assumption that its target money supply growth rate should be approximately equal to the country's inflation target plus the expected growth rate of real GDP. As such, in recent years, the target growth rate for broad money has generally ranged between 6 and 11 percent (Central Bank of Kenya, *Annual Reports* 2000–06).

In fact, the Central Bank of Kenya does not directly control the growth rate of its money target, M3. This is true not only for the Kenyan central bank, but for all central banks. The central bank can influence the growth of a more narrow band of financial assets which are called "high-powered money" or "reserve money." Reserve money consists of currency in circulation plus reserves in the banking system. It therefore excludes the other components of M3 as policy targets—i.e. demand deposits, savings deposits, CDs, the deposits of non-bank financial institutions, and the foreign currency deposits of Kenyan residents.

In other words, in practice, the Central Bank establishes a growth rate for reserve money that it decides is consistent with low inflation, with the idea that this reserve money target will in turn lead to a growth rate of M3 that is consistent with low inflation and adequate liquidity to the private sector.

This current operating procedure for the Central Bank of focusing on reserve money targeting differs significantly from that which prevailed prior to financial and monetary liberalization in the late 1980s and early 1990s. Instead of targeting the growth rate of reserve money, with the aim of controlling M3 growth in turn, monetary policy before liberalization involved direct regulatory interventions in credit markets and was closely tied to fiscal policy. The Central Bank extended credit to the public sector to finance budget deficits. In addition, the government maintained credit controls and administratively determined interest rates. Relatively comprehensive monetary and financial reforms began to be implemented in 1989 and were comprised of numerous components: reduction in direct financing of budget deficits, gradual liberalization of interest rates, harmonizing and strengthening the regulation of financial institutions, and removal of direct credit controls (Ngugi 2000). These changes had a significant impact on the banking sector, interest rates, and the conduct of monetary policy.

Trends in Monetary Aggregates

Figure 7.3 shows trends in the money supply as a percent of GDP from 1980 to 2005.[9] Measures of broad money (e.g. M2 or M3) increased as a share of GDP on average until the late 1990s at which time broad money, relative to GDP, began to decline modestly.[10] The narrowest definition of the money supply, M1, exhibits a different pattern. M1 as a share of GDP remains relatively constant through much of the period illustrated in Figure 7.3. However, beginning in the late 1990s, M1 rises as a percent of GDP while M2 and M3 decline.

One possible explanation for the pattern observed since the mid-1990s is that individuals and businesses in Kenya are increasingly moving their financial assets out of the banking system and purchasing non-bank assets – including domestic and foreign stocks, bonds, and derivatives, as well as real estate. Such asset purchases require additional cash. This would mean that the demand for narrow money would rise while the demand for M2 and M3—such as savings deposits and CDs—would fall. However, if this type of pattern is prevailing, it means that wealth-holders are moving their assets into and out of the banking sector on a regular basis.[11] Under such circumstances, the Central Bank's control over M3 will diminish. In addition, large amounts of money and financial assets currently circulate in the Kenyan economy outside of the banking sector. The Central Bank has virtually no influence over these resources.

Furthermore, the monetary aggregates in Kenya, like M3, respond to the demand for credit generated by the economy. If the broad money supply responds to changes in credit demand, the Central Bank will not be able to independently determine the growth rate of monetary aggregates by altering the

Figure 7.3 Alternative Measures of Money Supply as Percentage of GDP,
1980–2005

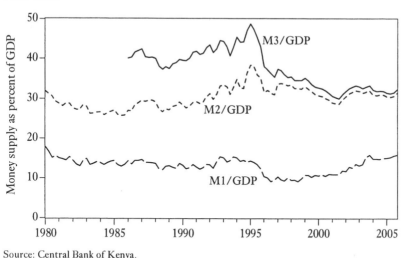

Source: Central Bank of Kenya.

supply of high-powered reserve money. Figure 7.4 charts the growth rate of M1 and M3 in the Kenyan economy from 1997 to 2005. Although the two monetary aggregates move together in terms of general long-run tendencies, broad money (M3) often does not respond directly to changes in the monetary base. This suggests that the Central Bank cannot target monetary aggregates with precision, even if monetary policy may be able to influence to some extent the general rate at which the money supply expands.

Intensifying Rather than Dampening Cyclical Instability

The current inflation target and the tools used to achieve this goal, if utilized inflexibly, have the potential to make cyclical instability in the Kenyan economy worse. In other words, under the current policy regime, the Central Bank has a tendency to pursue an expansionary policy when the economy is growing rapidly and, correspondingly, to pursue a tight monetary policy when the economy is contracting or growing slowly.

We see an example of such a bias in monetary policy in the 2002 *Annual Report* of the Central Bank of Kenya. Real GDP growth was initially expected to be 2.6 percent for the financial year 2001–02. However, economic performance was worse than expected and the GDP growth estimate was revised downward to 1.4 percent (p. 12). The Annual Report describes the response of monetary policy as follows:

Figure 7.4 Quarterly Growth Rates for M1 and M3, 1997.1–2005.4

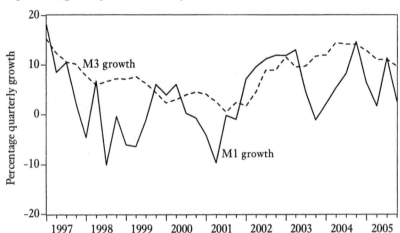

Note: Quarterly growth figures are reported as annualized.
Source: Central Bank of Kenya (2005) and (2006).

In line with these developments, a revised monetary framework, *which adopted a tighter monetary policy framework*, was designed and implemented ... (p. 12, emphasis added).

The logic behind this kind of intervention follows from the Central Banks operating according to the quantity theory of money. According to this approach, the Central Bank cannot control the real growth rate of the economy. If real GDP growth is slowing down for other reasons, then the Central Bank needs to also reduce the growth of the money supply. If money supply growth were to exceed the growth of GDP in this situation, the reasoning goes, an acceleration of inflation would ensue.

But there is a serious problem with this approach. This is that reducing the availability of credit and raising interest rates may discourage economic growth exactly when it would be beneficial for the central bank to promote growth through lower interest rates and greater overall access to credit. That is, a tight monetary policy such as that described in the statement above may slow down GDP growth by reducing consumption and investment through increases in the real interest rate. The reduction in liquidity during an economic downturn may worsen growth performance instead of reigning in inflationary pressures.

A similar bias in monetary policy may be introduced by the 5 percent inflation target itself. As we have seen, the inflationary pressures which the Kenyan economy faces often are triggered by adverse supply-side shocks, such as poor agricultural performance, or high fuel and petrol prices. Such supply-side shocks raise inflation, but they also slow economic growth. Tightening monetary policy in response to these shocks introduces a similar anti-growth bias into the conduct of macroeconomic policy.

The Monetary Policy Statement of the Central Bank of Kenya, December 2005, demonstrates the risk of this anti-growth bias. The document states:

> It was clear that the threat of rising oil prices and strong expansion in credit to the private sector challenged the Bank in its pursuit of the five percent inflation objective. Consequently, the Bank considered it prudent to continue with a tight monetary policy (Central Bank of Kenya, *Annual Report* 2005, p. 2).

The Monetary Policy Statement does go on to acknowledge that the tight monetary stance was later deemed inappropriate and a revised policy was implemented, due to faster than expected economic growth. Moreover, the basic evidence on economic growth and inflation over the previous two years—with inflation ranging between 10–13 percent and real GDP growth between 5.7–6.2 percent—shows that the Central Bank clearly did not follow its own stated policy aim of maintaining inflation at 5 percent. Nevertheless, the Statement still shows the basic stipulated approach at the Central Bank, operating on the basis of the quantity theory of money. It is this basic stipulated approach, rather than the Bank's actual, on-the-ground practice, that merits rethinking.

Interest Rate Spreads between Deposit Rates and Lending Rates

The spread between the rates that banks pay to their depositors relative to the rates the banks charge to borrowers increased significantly in Kenya following the liberalization of the banking sector and credit markets in the mid-1990s. Figure 7.5 charts the trend in the lending/deposit rate spread. The spread increased dramatically at the time of liberalization, spiking in 1996 at 14 percent. However, the spread then diminished to lower levels. Nevertheless, as of 2006, the spread remained in the range of 8 percent. This remains an extremely large spread, despite the clear downward trend since the early 1990s. These spreads suggest that bankers, in their capacity as lenders, are making very large profits on loans as long as the borrowers continue to service these loans. At the same time, these figures suggest that depositors are receiving very little interest on their deposits. In fact, for the most part, depositors are seeing the value of their bank deposits depreciate in real value.

This becomes especially clear when we consider that even in 2006, when the real lending rate was close to zero, the spread between deposit rates and lending rates remained above 8 percent. This means that, if the real return banks were receiving in 2006 was zero, the return to depositors was negative eight percent. The depositors may not have immediately experienced their 8 percent

Figure 7.5 Interest Rate Spread Between Bank Lending and Deposit Rates,
1971–2006

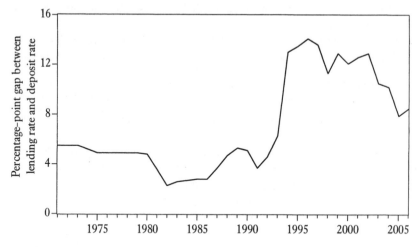

Source: International Monetary Fund (2007a). Central Bank of Kenya: statistical download from
website: http://www.centralbank.go.ke/downloads/statistics/interestRates/timeseries2.xls

loss. In nominal terms, depositors were receiving a positive 5.5 percent interest payment from their bank. But with inflation at 13.5 percent, this brought their real return to negative 8 percent.[12]

There are three factors at work in generating these large spreads, and the fact that depositors—not lenders—are bearing the brunt of the costs of such spreads, through receiving negative real returns on their bank deposits. They are: 1) lack of competition among commercial banks in Kenya; 2) financial liberalization, which has enabled the banks to impose higher risk premiums on their loans; and 3) high transactions costs associated with inflation, shortages of information, and related inefficiencies in the financial sector. We return to this issue in Chapter 9.

For now, we should note that, in general, the increase in real lending rates and the widening of the spread between lending and deposit rates following financial liberalization is not unique to Kenya. Many other countries in sub-Saharan Africa have experienced similar interest rate developments following similar reform processes (Reinhart and Tokatlidis 2003). This suggests that financial liberalization, by itself, is not capable of resolving the broader structural and institutional problems of the financial sectors in many, if not all, African countries (see, for example, Aryeetey 2001, Nissanke and Aryeetey 1998). In the case of Kenya, without deeper institutional reforms to strengthen the developmental role of banks and other financial institutions, liberalized financial markets will not be able to deliver the predicted benefits of reform. We also explore this policy question in more depth in Chapter 9.

There is another important implication to this evidence on spreads between deposit and lending rates. It is to reinforce the fact that the Central Bank can exercise only limited control over the setting of interest rates throughout the Kenyan economy. The Central Bank does have the ability to control overnight lending rates. But there are large and variable spreads between overnight rates, that carry little default and inflation risk, and other, higher-risk, market rates. This limits the effectiveness of the Central Bank's policies of manipulating the overnight rates, since, ultimately, the point of the Central Bank's efforts is not simply to manage the overnight rate but the range of market rates as well. The market rates, of course, are the rates that are faced by businesses and consumers as they make calculations about the affordability of increasing their borrowing to help finance investment and consumption.

It is also important to recognize that the effectiveness of monetary policy and the reform of the financial sector are closely interconnected. The financial sector is the primary conduit through which monetary policy affects real economic outcomes, and monetary policy determines, to some extent, the amount and distribution of resources available to financial institutions. Therefore, monetary policy must be coordinated with financial sector interventions that are directly aimed at promoting more rapid economic growth, employment expansion and poverty reduction.

CONCLUSIONS AND POLICY RECOMMENDATIONS

Our analysis suggests that the current tools used to address the challenges Kenya faces with regard to its monetary policy, inflation-control and interest-rate objectives are inadequate. The ultimate goal of monetary policy should be to promote a macroeconomic environment that is both stable and also supportive of economic growth, the expansion of decent employment, and the reduction in poverty. The current policy regime does not support this combination of objectives to the extent that is possible today through undertaking some changes in policy direction. Based on the foregoing discussion, we propose four basic changes in the conduct of monetary and inflation-control policies in Kenya. The recommendations are:

1. *Use a core short-term real interest rate as an intermediate monetary target.* The Central Bank of Kenya should move away from targeting the growth rates of monetary aggregates. The Bank has little direct control over monetary aggregates and the links between monetary growth and macroeconomic performance, as defined by the quantity theory of money, are too weak to form

the basis of a development-oriented monetary policy. Targeting real interest rates will have a more direct influence in promoting private investment, economic growth and employment.

2. *Remove the anti-growth bias in monetary policy.* This involves a shift in the ways in which the goals and procedures of monetary policy have been framed. Specifically, monetary policy should be prepared to (1) provide economic stimulus during a contraction; and (2) treat inflationary experiences differently depending on whether inflation is resulting from excess aggregate demand or a combination of supply shocks and inertia. In particular, it appears that policymakers in Kenya recognize these distinctions and have acted appropriately in light of the recent food and energy supply shocks. But it is still important that the overall policy framework be re-examined, rather than continuing to deviate from the stated policy targets on an ad hoc basis.

3. *Diversify the toolkit for addressing inflation in Kenya.* Using monetary policy alone for controlling inflation will almost always entail high costs in terms of restraining output and employment growth, in Kenya and elsewhere. In Kenya, this is especially likely to be true when inflation emerges as the result of supply-side shocks. Responding to such shocks by reducing the growth rates of monetary aggregates or pushing up short-term real interest rates is unlikely to be effective. Multiple tools are needed to simultaneously control inflation and support a poverty-reducing development agenda. Specific categories of goods and services contribute disproportionately to overall inflation—for example, energy and transportation. Policies aimed at smoothing price fluctuations in strategic sectors can be combined with incomes policies to help manage inflation at levels consistent with long-run growth.

4. *Institute reforms to the financial sector to channel credit to socially productive uses.* The Kenyan banking sector has resources at its disposal that could be more effectively mobilized to facilitate the attainment of development objectives, such as employment creation, increasing productivity-enhancing investments, and supporting poverty reduction. However, at present, the financial structure fails to channel credit to many socially productive uses. A variety of interventions could be implemented to mobilize these resources more effectively: strengthen development banking, build linkages between commercial banks and less formal credit institutions (such as the SACCOs), and implement a credit guarantee scheme to lower risk premiums and channel resources towards priority activities. These are topics we consider in Chapter 9.

NOTES

1. These other potential influences include 1) the initial level of GDP; 2) the share of investment spending in GDP; 3) the share of government spending in GDP; 4) the fiscal deficit; 5) the level of overall health, as measured by life expectancy; 6) the international economic environment; 7) the effects of natural disasters; and 8) the effects of wars.
2. From our discussions with policymakers at the Central Bank of Kenya, it seems clear that they are aware of these tensions. They do not appear to believe that it is necessary to tighten monetary policy in response to food or oil price shocks. It is apparent that in 2006, they did not attempt to tighten excessively in 2006 when food and energy supply shocks raised CPI "headline" inflation to 13.5 percent.
3. The discussion of the CPI in the 2002 report (Government of Kenya 2002) is based on the 1997 revision of the Kenyan Consumer Price Index. Note that we are referring here to the "New Kenya CPI," and are reporting here on the "Broad Category Weights for All Kenya." The New CPI breaks down the "All Kenya" consumer basket by areas of the country and income groupings—specifically into lower-income and middle- or upper-income groups for Nairobi, which then is aggregated into an all-Nairobi category; and a "rest of Kenya" grouping.
4. A matatu is a type of informal, low-cost public transportation, usually a minibus in urban areas or a pick-up truck in outlying areas.
5. Fischer is the former Director of Research at the IMF and currently Governor of the Bank of Israel.
6. The fact that the Productivity Centre has recently proposed to abolish minimum wage statutes has no direct relationship to our proposal that they be involved in considering how to develop a workable set of incomes policies as an inflation-control tool. Nevertheless, as we have emphasized, the key to a successful set of incomes policies is that they be implemented within an egalitarian policy framework. The Productivity Centre's proposal to abolish minimum wage statutes is not likely to promote such an egalitarian policy framework in Kenya.
7. The general approach that we propose is similar to that in Ouma et al., 2006.
8. Previously, this definition of M3 applied to M3X. Under the older definitions, M3 excluded foreign currency deposits and M2 excluded deposits in non-bank financial institutions. Under the new definitions, the new M3 corresponds to the old M3X and the new M2 corresponds to the old M3.
9. Because of issues of data availability, the older definitions of the money supply are used. That is, M1 includes currency outside of the banking sector and demand deposits. M2 includes M1 plus savings deposits and CDs. M3 includes M2 plus deposits of non-bank financial institutions.
10. Note that the gap between M2 and M3 narrows significantly over this period. The gap represents deposits of non-bank financial institutions. Due to regulatory reforms, many non-bank financial institutions (which were previously able to avoid some of the regulations of the banking sector) were transformed into banks. This purely regulatory change would have caused M2 to increase faster than M3, closing the gap between the two series.
11. See Pollin and Schaberg (1998) for a discussion of this pattern as it affected the U.S. economy.
12. That is, if the deposit rate is +5 percent, but the inflation rate is +13.5 percent, the real deposit rate is 5 percent - 13 percent = -8 percent.

8. Exchange Rate Policy and Foreign Trade

Any discussion of Kenya's situation with respect to its exchange rate policy and foreign trade accounts must begin with the fact of the country's structural trade deficit. We reviewed the trend for the trade deficit in Chapter 1. We obtain a fuller sense of the situation through Figure 8.1, which shows the movements of Kenya's imports and exports along with the trade balance figures—the trade balance data being, of course, the net effect of the difference between the country's imports and exports.

As Figure 8.1 shows, Kenya has experienced periods of sharply rising exports as a share of the country's GDP, most notably from the late 1980s to the early 1990s. Exports/GDP have also been rising moderately since 2000. The problem is that imports/GDP have been rising more sharply over that same period. It is clear from these patterns that, in order to close its structural trade deficit, Kenya would need to address both the import and export side of its foreign trade accounts.

Considering how to accomplish this most effectively is the focus of this chapter. We first provide some historical background on Kenya's exchange rate and trade policies since independence. We then consider the role of exchange rate policy, and in particular the problems presented as Kenya maintains an overvalued shilling. Indeed, as we will see, as of 2005, the extent of shilling overvaluation has risen to its highest level since 1994. We then consider Kenya's relationships with its trading partners, and explore possibilities for export expansion, especially among neighboring countries in sub-Saharan Africa.

HISTORICAL PERSPECTIVES ON EXCHANGE RATE AND TRADE POLICIES

Kenya has pursued a variety of exchange rate regimes since gaining independence (Ndung'u 2000, Ndung'u and Ngugi 1999). From independence until the early 1980s, the shilling was fixed relative to the U.S. dollar or Special Drawing Rights, the quasi-currency created by the International Monetary Fund as a tool for promoting its global policy management initiatives.[1] Beginning in 1982,

Figure 8.1 Kenya's Imports, Exports and Trade Balance as Percentage of GDP, 1980–2005

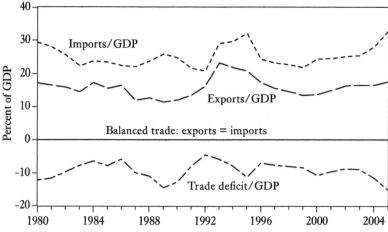

Source: International Monetary Fund (2007a).

the exchange rate regime was shifted to a crawling peg. The crawling peg was in place until 1990, when a dual exchange rate system was implemented. In October 1993, the official exchange rate was merged with the market rate and a floating exchange rate, primarily determined by market forces, was put into place.

In many respects, the overall approach to trade policy mimicked trends with regard to Kenya's exchange rate regimes – that is, moving, from purposeful intervention towards market-based liberalization. In the 1960s and 1970s, Kenya followed what can be characterized as an import-substitution development strategy (Jenkins 2005, Wagacha 2003, Bigsten 2002). In the early post-independence years, the Kenyan government aimed to expand domestic productive activities and to "indigenize" production—i.e. increase the role of Africans in the ownership of enterprises and management of productive activities (Wagacha 2003, Bigsten 2002). In the early 1970s, Kenya ran into balance of payments problems. The government intensified efforts at import substitution in order to deal with the shortage of foreign exchange. However, these efforts turned out to be unsustainable.

The import-substitution regime was biased against agriculture and production for export (Wagacha 2003). Meanwhile, Kenya remained highly dependent on imported intermediate inputs and capital goods (Bigsten 2002), a constraint that could not readily be corrected through import-substitution efforts alone, certainly not in the short- to medium-term. The bias against agriculture—which accounted for the majority of employment and economic activity—limited the growth of the domestic market and placed significant con-straints on the expansion of productive activity. The bias against exports and the continued dependence on imported inputs meant that the demand for scarce foreign exchange expanded faster than the supply. These twin constraints—the limited domestic market and scarce foreign exchange—eventually crippled the import-substitution strategy in Kenya.

In the 1980s, Kenya adopted structural adjustment programs as a condi-tionality of the country's borrowing from the International Monetary Fund. During this time, there was a move away from the import-substitution model towards a model of export-oriented growth. However, many forms of trade pro-tection remained in place. In addition, the allocation of foreign exchange was largely controlled by the state and its distribution favored particular sectors (Bigsten 2002). The allocation of foreign exchange was not always supportive of broader developmental objectives such as the diversification of exports or the generation of employment.

In the early 1990s, a policy of broad-based liberalization was adopted, in-cluding the liberalization of trade, the financial sector, and foreign exchange mar-kets. In addition, specific export-promoting policies were implemented (e.g., tariff rebates for exporters, export subsidies, and the establishment of export process-ing zones, or EPZs). The result of the combined policy of liberalization and ex-port-promotion was a notable, once-off, increase in the volume of trade, as we have seen in Figure 8.1. Although trade volumes expanded after liberalization, the structure of trade was not transformed. In particular, the structural trade deficit was not reduced, indicating that imports expanded along with exports.

Research has suggested that the overall effect of the liberalization of trade and exchange rates on employment has been negative (Jenkins 2005, Manda and Sen 2004). That is, despite the significant growth in exports following liber-alization, the increase in import penetration has offset these gains. Apart from a few significant sectors, horticulture in particular, exports from Kenya are not more labor-intensive on average than import substitutes (Jenkins 2005). In ad-dition, the quality of employment opportunities may have diminished with lib-eralization, with the rise of part-time and casual labor jobs as opposed to full-time modern sector opportunities (Jenkins 2005). The persistence of structural im-balances in the Kenyan economy suggests that liberalization has failed to ad-dress significant constraints on economic performance. Specifically, it raises the possibility that market-determined exchange rates could be misaligned and do not automatically adjust to eliminate external imbalances.

Is the Shilling Overvalued?

Exchange rate movements affect economic growth, employment, living stan-dards, and the distribution of resources between sectors that trade on global markets (tradables) and those that produce only for domestic consumption (non-tradables). Therefore, appropriate exchange rate policies are critical in designing an economic program that can succeed in promoting economic growth, employment expansion, and poverty reduction.

Recent literature suggests that overvalued real exchange rates—that is allowing a country's currency to rise too high in value relative to those of its trading partners—has negatively impacted long-run growth and compromised development in a number of developing economies, including countries in sub-Saharan Africa (Gala and Lucinda 2006, Frenkel and Taylor 2005, Ghura and Grennes 1993, Dollar 1992, Cottani, Cavallo, and Khan 1990).[2] Maintaining an overvalued exchange rate means that the price of a country's exports is relatively high in global markets, making it more difficult to succeed in selling exports. At the same time, an overvalued exchange rate also means that imports become relatively inexpensive. This creates difficulties for domestic producers to compete against importers within their own domestic markets. As such, maintaining a competitive real exchange rate in Kenya may be an important policy tool for raising Kenya's growth performance and employment opportunities.

But what does it mean for any given currency, and for the shilling in particular, to be "overvalued?" This is the question we now consider. We have developed a technical econometric analysis of this problem, which we present in Appendix 3. In this main text, we present a brief overview of the principle findings of our technical analysis. The details of the methodology used are explained more fully in Appendix 3.

Figure 8.2 shows trends in the nominal value of the Kenyan shilling—that is, before adjusting for domestic and international price levels—relative to the currencies of Kenya's largest trading partners.[3] Figure 8.2 also plots on the same graph movements in Kenya's price level, as measured by the CPI.[4]

As the graph shows, the nominal value of the shilling falls steadily when the domestic price level rises. This is of course what we would expect theoretically. Inflation means that the purchasing power of a currency is diminishing. Therefore, holding everything else equal, the value of the currency will fall relative to other currencies as a result of inflation.

This inverse relationship—the value of the shilling falling as the price level rises—is particularly close in the years prior to 1993. The shilling was fully liberalized in October 1993, that is, it was permitted to float according to market forces (Ndung'u 2000, Ndung'u and Ngugi 1999). But before the Central Bank of Kenya floated the shilling, they undertook an initial devaluation. The sharp fall in the value of the shilling, and the corresponding rise in inflation, are both evident in Figure 8.2. However, after this one-time devaluation, we see that the inverse relationship between the value of the shilling and inflation weakens somewhat. Specifically, the Kenyan CPI begins to rise faster than the value of the

Figure 8.2 Nominal Exchange Rate and Price Level (CPI), 1980–2005

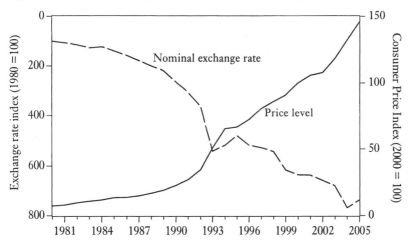

Source: International Monetary Fund (2007a).

shilling falls. Thus, the value of the shilling and inflation in Kenya begin to diverge in the period since the exchange rate was liberalized.[5]

Figure 8.3 presents an index that shows the *real value* of the Kenyan shilling over the same time period. The difference between this data series and the series in Figure 8.2 showing the *nominal* value of the shilling is that, with this *real* value series, we control for relative changes in inflation rates between Kenya and its major trading partners.[6] The real value of the shilling begins to fall in the mid-1980s, indicating a real depreciation of the shilling. The sharp devaluation of the shilling that the Kenyan central bank undertook just prior to liberalization is also evident in Figure 8.3. However, as the graph also shows, the effects of this devaluation were short-lived. After the exchange rate liberalization, the fact (as we saw in Figure 8.2) that the nominal exchange rate no longer responded as strongly to domestic price increases meant that the real value of the shilling remained high relative to the values of the pound, U.S. dollar, and mark.

This is the background for considering whether the shilling is in fact overvalued at present, even though its value is mainly determined by market forces. This is a difficult question to answer. There are many ways to assess the degree of exchange rate misalignment. For this study, we have built models based on two alternative techniques that are frequently used in the professional literature, a "price parity" approach and a single-equation econometric technique. We present both of our models in Appendix 3. For the discussion here, we simply summarize the main findings of these models.

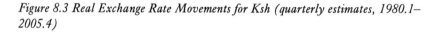

Figure 8.3 Real Exchange Rate Movements for Ksh (quarterly estimates, 1980.1–2005.4)

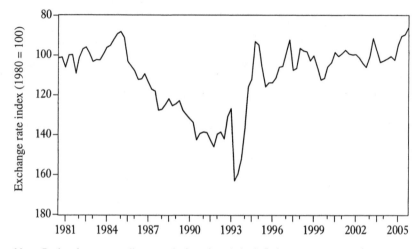

Note: Real exchange rate adjusts nominal rate by relative inflation rate movements between Kenya and its main trading partners.
Source: Appendix 3.

Our overall conclusion from both models is that the shilling is indeed overvalued. In Figure 8.4, we present our estimate of the extent of this overvaluation, as generated by the single-equation econometric technique. As we can see in Figure 8.4 according to our estimate, a sharp level of overvaluation occurred soon after the financial markets adjusted to the liberalization and one-time devaluation of the shilling in 1994. The overvaluation spikes in 1995 at 20.9 percent. After 1995, the extent of overvaluation fluctuates sharply through 2005, including a brief period in 2003.4 when, according to our estimate, the shilling is marginally undervalued. However, the real value of the shilling has appreciated rapidly since then. By the end of 2005, we estimate that the shilling was about 25 percent overvalued.

Real Exchange Rate Appreciation and Liberalization: Contributing Factors

What factors have contributed to the overvaluation of the shilling since 1995? Why might the nominal exchange rate have failed to depreciate when domestic prices rose after liberalization, leading to an appreciation of the real exchange rate? There are a number of possibilities.

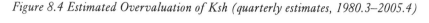

Figure 8.4 Estimated Overvaluation of Ksh (quarterly estimates, 1980.3–2005.4)

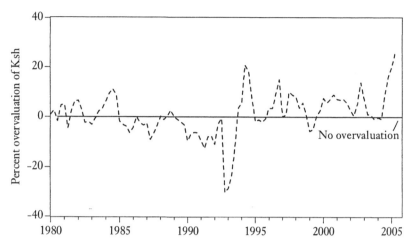

Source: Appendix 3.

1. *Liberalization of cross-border financial flows combined with low inflation targets.* This may produce overvalued exchange rates if high real interest rates are the primary means of controlling inflation. This is because the high real interest rates will attract financial investors to purchase bonds denominated in shillings, given the prospects of high returns on these bonds. But to buy these bonds, investors first have to purchase shillings. This would drive up the value of the shilling, all else equal.

2. *Inflation resulting from supply-side shocks.* As we have already discussed, inflationary pressures in Kenya often result from supply-side shocks that rapidly drive up the prices of, in particular, energy, food, and transportation. Such supply-side shocks increase the pressures for the shilling to remain overvalued. This is because the supply-side shocks lead to a rapid increase in inflation. However, the inflation is not likely to produce an equivalent depreciation in the shilling. This is because, for the most part, high interest rates maintain support for the value of the shilling despite the rise in inflation. Correspondingly, any short-run fall in the real interest rate that might occur due to a rapid spike in supply-shock inflation does not necessarily lead to a significant reduction in the real exchange rate. This is because purchasers of shilling-denominated bonds may calculate that the spike in inflation will not be sustained at that high level and therefore would not have a permanent impact on the value of their investment.

3. *Factors leading to increased financial inflows.* There is evidence that factors beyond the high nominal interest rates are contributing to maintaining the overvalued shilling. These factors include the possibility that remittance flows into the country have grown substantially. This drives up the value of the shilling, all else equal, since Kenyans living abroad that send money back home have to sell the euros, pounds, U.S. dollars, or other currencies that they earn abroad, and buy shillings in exchange. This increases the demand for shillings, pushing up its relative price. Unfortunately, remittances are not documented within the balance of payments account, making it difficult to confirm whether or not this effect is large in magnitude. But in combination with any impact from remittances, Kenya has also emerged as a financial center within East Africa, providing a stable institutional environment lacking in some of the region's countries that have experienced higher levels of conflict (e.g. Sudan, Somalia, Burundi, and Rwanda). Here again, this will increase the demand for shillings, independent of the interest rates available on shilling-denominated bonds.

   Figure 8.5 shows net capital inflows plus current transfers as a percent of Kenya's GDP for the period 1980 to 2005.[7] As we see, Kenya experienced a dramatic decline in inflows at the time of the devaluation and subsequent liberalization. However, after the floating exchange rate was introduced, net inflows increased. This suggests that capital inflows and foreign transfers could be playing a role in the strengthening of the real exchange rate post-liberalization. But of course we cannot conclude anything definitively from this figure itself.

4. *Global commodity price boom.* Since Kenya is a major exporter of primary tea and coffee, and other commodities to a lesser extent, higher commodity prices could raise export revenues and strengthen the nominal exchange rate relative to domestic prices. Our formal econometric model, discussed below, offers some evidence that higher global commodity prices contribute to a rise in export revenues that could support an appreciated exchange rate.

We have already discussed policy interventions that can serve to counteract the pressures for real exchange rate appreciation. In particular:

1. the lower interest-rate environment and more relaxed inflation targets that we propose will reduce the attractiveness for financial market traders to favor the shilling; and
2. improved control over supply-shock inflation will reduce the possibility for imbalances in the relative movements of Kenya's inflation rate and the value of the shilling.

Figure 8.5 Net Capital Flows and Foreign Transfers into Kenya as Percentage of GDP, 1980–2005

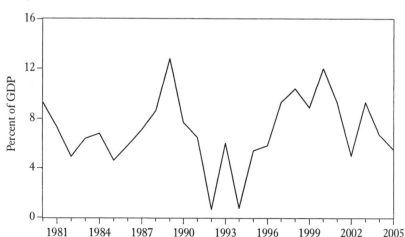

Source: International Monetary Fund (2007a).

EXCHANGE RATES AND REGIONAL TRADE

Kenya has a structural trade deficit with the rest of the world. However, Kenya is a net exporter to the rest of the African continent. In addition, the share of Kenyan exports going to African countries has grown, particularly following liberalization in the early 1990s, while the share of exports going to industrial countries has fallen. We show the trends in the shares of Kenyan exports in Figure 8.6.[8] Imports from African countries have not increased proportionately.[9] This suggests that expanding regional trade may be an important component of an overall strategy, both for export expansion, and more broadly, for economic growth and employment expansion.

The real exchange rate index that we have been analyzing thus far is based on exchange rate and price trends with Kenya's three largest trading partners from 1980 to 2003, the U.K., the U.S, and Germany. It has been useful in considering the overall exchange rate position of Kenya in global trade. But it tells us little about whether Kenya is positioned competitively specifically with respect to its major African trading partners.

To address this question of Kenya's regional exchange rate position, we have constructed a specific real exchange rate index for Kenya's three largest trading partners in Africa, which are Uganda, Tanzania, and South Africa. Figure 8.7 presents the Africa-specific and the overall real exchange rate indices for Kenya over the period 1985 to 2003. As we see in Figure 8.7, the African real

Figure 8.6 Share of Kenya's Exports by Major Country Groups, 1982–2005 (figures are three-year moving averages)

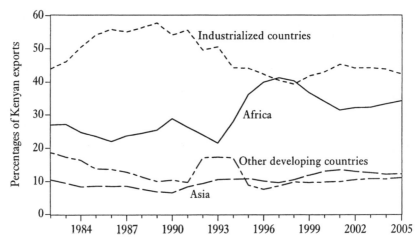

Source: International Monetary Fund (2007b).

exchange rate index is significantly more volatile than the overall real exchange rate index. Moreover, as we see, the Kenyan shilling has appreciated somewhat more over the past several years relative to the country's African trading partners than the appreciation relative to the pound, U.S. dollar, and mark. Specifically, in the post-liberalization period, both real exchange rate series behave similarly, but the African real exchange rate exhibits a somewhat stronger appreciation during the most recent years analyzed here. This suggests that Kenya's exchange rate regime may be a barrier to greater success in exporting within Africa, despite the strong potential for Kenya to succeed as an African exporter.

The Structure of Kenyan Trade

For years, Kenyan exports have been dominated by the primary commodities of tea and coffee. Kenya has also established a practice of refining imported petroleum and then exporting the higher value-added products, including to the East African market. The fastest growing exports in Kenya in recent years have been horticultural products. The value of horticultural exports has exceeded that of coffee and may overtake tea as Kenya's most important export. Diversification into manufactured exports, as happened in the fast-growing countries of East Asia, remains relatively insignificant in Kenya. Figure 8.8 shows Kenya's major exports, by commodity group, from 2001–05.

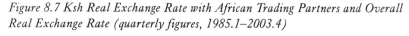

Figure 8.7 Ksh Real Exchange Rate with African Trading Partners and Overall Real Exchange Rate (quarterly figures, 1985.1–2003.4)

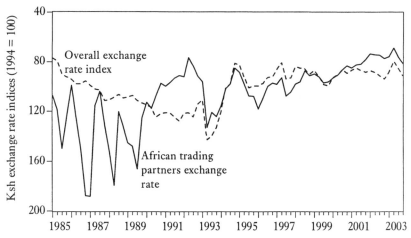

Source: Appendix 3.

The horticultural sector provides an interesting example of how export performance may be linked to employment creation and poverty reduction. The prime products of the horticultural sector are fresh fruits, vegetables, and cut flowers. Almost all of this horticultural production is sold on the European market, with the U.K. currently being the most important market for fresh fruits and vegetables (Jenkins 2005). The growth of the horticultural sector in Kenya has been propelled by the expansion in European demand for fresh, high-quality produce that is available year–round. In addition, trade preferences improve Kenya's access to the European market. A less favorable preferential treatment could create serious difficulties for Kenya's export performance (Jenkins 2005).

The employment effects of the rapid expansion of horticultural production include the growth in production of smallholder farms and increases in the number of workers on large commercial operations. In terms of wage employment, the majority of the workers are women (between 60 and 70 percent) and most of the workforce is young. Fully half are 20 years old or younger. Employment in the horticultural sector does appear to reduce poverty and raise living standards among households, when compared to those households that do not participate in the sector. The effect is particularly strong in the rural areas. Despite these positive employment and poverty outcomes, it is important to also emphasize that a significant proportion of the jobs generated through horticultural exports are casual and seasonal, and employment income is volatile (Jenkins 2005). This

Figure 8.8 Share of Total Exports by Major Commodity Grouping, Kenya, Average 2001–05

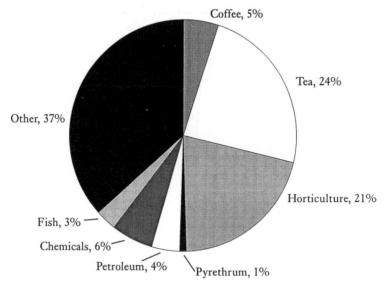

Source: Central Bank of Kenya (2005).

---

fact reinforces one of the overarching arguments of this study, which is to focus not simply on the expansion of employment, whatever the quality of the jobs created; but to create *decent* employment opportunities, in the horticultural export sector, as elsewhere.

Overall, the horticultural sector in Kenya shows how poverty-reducing employment may be a result of greater global integration. At the same time, the number of jobs generated by the sector in the near future is likely to be relatively small compared to the employment challenge Kenya currently faces. For example, continued growth of the fresh vegetable sector and on-going development of local processing and packaging operations may generate between 10,000 and 20,000 jobs over the next five years (Humphrey, McCulloch, and Ota 2004). Therefore, the policy objective should extend beyond supporting the continued growth of horticulture in Kenya, to provide similar support to other labor-intensive sectors that could replicate horticulture's success. Some possibilities here include garments and leather.

Turning from exports to imports, Kenya remains dependent on imported inputs, particularly in terms of energy products, chemicals, equipment, and machinery. In addition, Kenya imports more general manufactured goods than

Figure 8.9 Share of Total Imports by Major Commodity Grouping, Kenya Average 2001–05

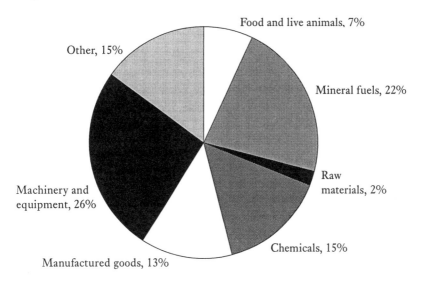

Food and live animals, 7%

Other, 15%

Mineral fuels, 22%

Raw materials, 2%

Machinery and equipment, 26%

Chemicals, 15%

Manufactured goods, 13%

Source: Central Bank of Kenya (2005).

it exports. Kenya's policy of import-substitution industrialization, adopted in the 1960s and 1970s, focused primarily on producing consumer goods and did not develop local capacity for supplying capital goods and intermediate inputs (Bigsten 2002). Not only did this limit the development of a strong network of upstream and downstream linkages within the Kenyan economy, it also increased the demand for foreign exchange when production expanded. This dependency on imported inputs remains entrenched today. Figure 8.9 shows Kenya's major imports, by commodity group, from 2001–05.

The Determinants of Kenyan Exports and Imports

The real exchange rate represents the relative price of tradables to non-tradables. Therefore, a depreciation of the Kenyan shilling would generally benefit the country's tradable sectors—export-producing sectors and sectors competing with foreign imports. This is because a depreciation would make Kenya's exports cheaper in foreign markets and its imports more expensive within the domestic Kenyan economy. However, other variables also affect import and export performance, including income growth in foreign markets, fluctuations in the relative terms of trade between Kenya and its trading partners, domestic income growth, and trade, industrial, and agricultural policies. Therefore, it is important to assess the responsiveness of imports and exports to movements in the real exchange rate along with these other possible influences to determine the potential impact of an overvalued shilling.

To address these concerns, we have constructed another formal econometric model to estimate the effects on imports and exports of changes in Kenya's real exchange rate. As with the exchange rate overvaluation model above, we present our full formal model in Appendix 3. We provide a brief summary of the main findings here.

Beginning with the analysis of exports, our model finds that real depreciation of the shilling is associated with higher export earnings. Increases in the world prices of major commodities (in this case, coffee and tea) also raise export earnings, suggesting that demand for these commodities is fairly price inelastic—that is, to some significant extent, foreign customers will generally keep purchasing Kenyan tea and coffee even when the prices of these commodities rise. We find that increases in the real incomes of Kenya's primary trading partners positively impacts export earnings. Specifically, this means that Kenya's trading partners, such as Britain and the U.S., will buy more Kenyan products when their national incomes rise. This effect is to be expected. But we also find that its impact is very weak (i.e. statistically insignificant). As such, Kenyan exports appear to respond strongly to price changes (i.e. the real exchange rate and global commodity prices), but more weakly to income growth in their primary markets.

The story with imports appears to be different. As expected, imports do go down when the shilling depreciates, since this means that it becomes more expensive for Kenyans to purchase imports relative to domestic substitutes. In addition, sharp increases in petroleum prices raise the overall value of imports. This means that when the price of imported oil goes up, Kenyans continue to buy virtually the same quantities of oil at the higher prices. This is because, at present, there are few substitutes in Kenya for oil as an energy source. However, these price effects have only a weak (i.e. statistically insignificant) effect on imports. On the other hand, we do find a strong positive effect on demand for imports when the incomes of Kenyans go up. Our findings indicate specifically that economic growth will be accompanied by an even larger growth rate for imports, all other factors remaining equal.

This apparent high level of import demand in Kenya raises concerns about the sustainability of faster economic growth in the country. Given the estimates presented here, a depreciated real exchange rate provides only a partial counterweight to import dependency. That is, exports do appear to respond favorably to a depreciated shilling. Import demand may also fall modestly when the shilling depreciates. However, this falling import demand linked to a shilling depreciation will most likely be small relative to income effects associated with faster growth—that is, faster income growth means even greater demand for imports in Kenya. The end result of this dynamic could very well be that faster income growth can mean that imports are growing faster than exports. This in turn will bring a growing trade deficit and eventual balance of payments problems.

Reducing Kenya's dependency on imported inputs would help address the country's structural trade problems. Consider the case of inorganic fertilizer. Kenya depends on imported inorganic fertilizer as an input into agricultural production. Depletion of soil nutrients is commonplace in Kenya, which in turn negatively affects the country's overall agricultural productivity (Omamo and Mose 2001). Therefore, the availability of inorganic fertilizers is important for addressing the larger challenge of increasing agricultural productivity. Building the capacity to manufacture inorganic fertilizers within Kenya could be an important component of an overall strategy to boost productivity and earnings in the labor-intensive agricultural sector in a way that is sustainable and does not feed into persistent balance of payments problems.[10]

Building the capacity to produce certain strategic intermediate inputs and capital goods requires a broad set of policy tools. As discussed in the previous section, price-based interventions, such as maintaining a competitive exchange rate, may facilitate this type of industrial diversification. But exchange rate interventions by themselves are not sufficient. Moreover, expecting liberalized markets to coordinate the realization of these fundamental structural changes is also unrealistic. What is needed is a coordinated development strategy that uses the tools that we have focused on above—primarily infrastructure development and providing cheap and accessible credit for business—to promote the growth of a healthy balance between exports and imports.

SUMMARY AND CONCLUSIONS

Over the past several decades, Kenya has moved towards increasingly market-determined trade and exchange rate regimes. The import-substitution strategy of the 1960s and 1970s, with its protectionist measures to encourage domestic production, has been gradually replaced by a stronger export-orientation, with reductions in tariffs and quantitative restrictions. At the same time, Kenya's fixed exchange rate regime was replaced by a crawling peg which, in turn, was eventually replaced by a floating regime. Despite an expansion of trade in the early 1990s, these reforms have not been successful in addressing Kenya's structural problems, including sustained trade and current account deficits. Moreover, trade liberalization appears to have had a net negative impact on employment opportunities, with important implications for poverty reduction.

With regard to exchange rate policies, the evidence suggests that, after the shift to a market-determined rate, the shilling has become overvalued, although the real exchange rate shows a great deal of volatility. This runs contrary to the predictions of the proponents of non-intervention in the foreign exchange market. Although overvaluation may make imported inputs cheaper and could reduce inflation, it has had an adverse effect on exports. While the precise degree of overvaluation is difficult to assess, the analysis presented here suggests that the misalignment has not yet been overly severe. However, the degree of overvaluation may be stronger with respect to Kenya's major trading partners in Africa. This could be a barrier preventing Kenya from capturing the benefits of greater regional trade integration.

There are reasons to think that overvaluation may continue to be a concern in the future. Inflows of capital and remittances into Kenya appear to have increased on average in recent years. In addition, the world boom in commodity prices may produce so-called "Dutch disease" effects, in which the shilling becomes increasingly overvalued with negative consequences for the domestic economy. The data presented here suggests that the shilling was relatively more competitive when Kenya was targeting its exchange rate using a crawling peg.

Analysis of the determinants of export performance and import penetration indicate that exports tend to respond more strongly to changes in prices as opposed to changes in incomes within the economies of Kenya's main trading partners. The reverse holds true for imports. Kenya's imports rise and fall sharply along with increases and declines in Kenya's own national income. However, price increases in imported products such as oil do little to reduce the demand for oil imports. Therefore, managing the real exchange rate through active policy interventions may be important for promoting new and more diverse types of exports. However, exchange rates appear to have less of an impact on imports. This raises the question of how Kenya's excessive dependence on imported inputs and capital goods could be reduced. Targeted policies such as the credit allocation schemes discussed above that actively underwrite the country's industrial expansion could be instrumental in addressing these structural problems.

In summary, three broad directions for policy emerge from the analysis presented here:

1. A targeted exchange rate policy—such as the crawling peg that existed prior to 1993—is an important macroeconomic instrument for ensuring the competitiveness of Kenya's exports. It could also provide an appropriate economic environment for diversifying Kenya's export base. The Central Bank does have the capacity to implement a targeted peg policy, since the exchange rate can be manipulated through adjusting overnight interest rates as well as active interventions in currency markets.
2. Kenya should focus on developing regional trade within the African continent. Kenya remains a net exporter to the continent and should remain

competitive in this region as long as the shilling does not become overvalued. Moreover, regional growth can have important positive feedback effects in the Kenyan economy.

3. Targeted interventions aimed at promoting industrial expansion are needed in order to generate employment that reduces poverty in a way that is sustainable in the long-run. Here we move into the role of subsidized credit policies to promote activities that can be competitive in export markets.

NOTES

1. The shilling was fixed relative to the dollar until 1974. Balance of payments crises in the early 1970s led to devaluations of the shilling, after which the shilling was fixed relative to Special Drawing Rights.
2. Easterly (2001) questions whether overvalued real exchange rates help to explain the poor growth performance of many developing countries during the so-called "lost decades" of the 1980s and 1990s.
3. Kenya's most important trading partners were determined by looking at each country's share of the sum of Kenya's exports and imports. The countries with the largest shares on average over the period in question were determined to be Kenya's most significant trading partners. In the analysis presented here, those countries were Britain, the U.S., and Germany.
4. Exchange rates with the U.K., the U.S., and Germany over the period 1980–2003 were used to construct the index. Shares of total trade volume (the value of exports plus imports) were used to measure the relative importance of trading partners. Data were taken from the IMF's International Financial Statistics and Direction of Trade Statistics. See Appendix 3 for a more detailed discussion of the context for this analysis.
5. The correlation coefficient between the nominal exchange rate index and the CPI is -0.99 from the first quarter of 1980 to the third quarter of 1993—prior to the introduction of a floating exchange rate. From the fourth quarter of 1993 to the fourth quarter of 2005, the correlation between the two series drops to -0.89. This is clearly still a strong association, but it also indicates a growing tendency for the nominal exchange rate and the average price level to diverge after liberalization.
6. GDP deflators for the U.K., the U.S., and Germany were used to estimate changes in the foreign price level. The domestic CPI was used to measure changes in the Kenyan average price level. Data were taken from the IMF's International Financial Statistics and Direction of Trade Statistics.
7. Errors and omissions in the balance of payments accounts are included in the estimation of total net capital inflows and current transfers.
8. The establishment of Common Market for Eastern and Southern Arfica in 1994 may have had an impact on the growth of Kenyan exports to other African countries (see Musila 2004).
9. Imports from African countries did increase beginning in 1994, but much of this growth is explained by imports from South Africa following the end of the apartheid regime.
10. Reforms to the domestic marketing and distribution systems for inorganic fertilizers are also needed if accessibility is to be enhanced (Omamo and Mose 2001).

9. Restructuring Kenya's Financial System

The financial system in Kenya today presents a mixed picture in terms of its overall performance and contributions to a broadly-shared development path for the country. At the same time, its potential for contributing in the future to broadly-shared development in Kenya is substantial. The aim of any new policy proposals for the financial system is therefore straightforward: to nurture the substantial potential that already exists. To be more specific, it is already within the reach of Kenya's existing financial institutions to give far more support to small and medium-sized enterprises (SMEs), which would also entail bringing a higher proportion of such enterprises into the realm of the formal economy; to also extend far more credit on reasonable terms to rural smallholders; and, more generally, underwrite a development path for the country that promotes faster economic growth, an expansion of decent employment opportunities, and a reduction in poverty. All of these ends can be accomplished in a way that will also be profitable for the country's leading banks and other financial firms.

But tapping into this potential will entail some important new policy initiatives. We will consider such initiatives in this section, in particular, a measure to develop an extensive system of government-financed loan guarantees for commercial banks when these banks, in partnership with the country's extensive set of microfinance institutions (MFIs), devote resources to providing credit for small and medium-sized enterprises and rural smallholders. We will show how this system can be made to operate with relatively modest overall costs, while also giving large incentives to the banking system to combine with microfinance entities to promote broadly-based development initiatives.

In the first part of this section, we describe the major features of the Kenyan financial system today, as we understand it. In the second section, we develop our proposal for the government to provide loan guarantees to private banks in exchange for the banks becoming more connected to the country's development needs.

OVERALL PERSPECTIVE ON KENYA'S FINANCIAL SYSTEM

As noted above, Kenya's financial system already has some important positive features. These include:

1. Kenya's commercial banking system is generally well-developed, and by some standard performance measures, is more focused on lending to the private sector than is the case in other sub-Saharan African countries.
2. Kenya is developing as a regional financial center, with emerging securities markets.
3. Kenya has a widespread system of microfinance institutions already in place and operating. SACCOs are the most important of these institutions. But there are others, both formal and informal, client- and member-based. These include institutions such as the KREP (Kenya Rural Enterprise Program bank; formal and client-based) and ROSCAs (Rotating Savings and Credit Associations; informal and member based).

Despite these positive features, the contributions of the financial system to promoting economic growth, employment expansion and poverty reduction are inadequate. In our view, the main reasons for this inadequate performance are as follows:

1. As we saw in Chapter 7, interest rate levels are high in *nominal* terms—that is, before making any adjustments for inflation (Figure 7.2). Rates are not necessarily high in *real* terms—i.e. after subtracting the inflation rate from the nominal interest rate. But knowing whether *real* interest rates are high or low depends on movements in the rate of inflation. This creates considerable uncertainty in the financial system.
2. More significant than problems with interest rate levels are the spreads between deposit and lending rates, which are extremely wide, as we also reviewed in Chapter 7 (Figure 7.5). Again, depending on how one calculates a real interest rate, most deposit rates are actually negative. There is therefore no incentive to save in formal financial markets. These wide interest rate spreads indicate lack of competition in the commercial banking system.
3. The commercial banking system lends more than one-third of its deposit base to the government. This of course reduces the availability of funds for businesses, especially small and medium-sized enterprises (SMEs) and small farmers.
4. More generally, the farming, SME, and informal sectors are starved for credit. This is due to the fact that a) commercial banks do not generally lend to these sectors; and b) the SACCOs and other MFIs do not have

sufficient resources to provide large-scale funds. Moreover, the largest share of the lending done by the MFIs is for personal household purposes or family emergencies.

Given this combination of positive and negative features of the Kenyan financial system, the solution to the problem, at a fundamental level, seems straightforward: to somehow bring into much closer alliance the formal commercial banking system and the MFIs. In fact, proposals along these lines have been suggested by, among others, the World Bank in a 1994 study on Kenya specifically, and the International Monetary Fund in a more general 2005 study on sub-Saharan African finance. This idea has also been raised in some previous research papers by Kenyan scholars (e.g. Atieno 2001). What remains is to flesh out a large-scale program that could be realistically implemented on a short-term basis, but that is also capable of enabling a longer-term transformation of the Kenyan financial system. The proposal that we present here will create a pool of subsidized credit at a level equal to roughly 20 percent of the current level of private investment in Kenya; with a cost to the government of about 5 percent of the fiscal budget.

Though our focus in terms of policy will be on this particular measure, other complementary initiatives worth considering include:

1. reviving cooperative-type institutions to build collateral for SMEs and smallholders. We discuss this in more detail in Chapter 5;
2. revitalizing the public investment banks, such as the Industrial and Commercial Development Corporation (ICDC) and the Agricultural Development Bank, perhaps as private/public partnerships;
3. utilizing the Postbank as a lender to SMEs, an idea that has already passed the Parliament; and
4. indexing loans so as to shift at least in part inflation risk from lenders to borrowers.

We briefly discuss some of these additional proposals at the conclusion of this section.

STRENGTHS OF KENYA'S CURRENT FINANCIAL SYSTEM

Commercial Bank Portfolios

1. *Bank Credit to Private Sector.* As we see in Table 9.1, commercial bank lending to the private sector in Kenya stood at 20.3 percent of GDP in 2003.

Table 9.1 Bank Credit to Private Sector and Non-Financial Public Enterprises as Share of GDP, 2003

Kenya	20.3%
South Africa	82.7%
Tanzania	7.6%
Uganda	7.6%
Ghana	14.7%
Ivory Coast	14.8%
Brazil	28.1%
Morocco	56.0%
Mexico	16.8%
Chile	61.7%
Peru	20.8%

Source: Sacerdoti (2005).

As the table shows, this is a fairly high ratio, relative to other sub-Saharan African countries. For example, in Tanzania and Uganda, the comparable ratios are 7.6 percent. In Ghana and the Ivory Coast, the ratios are 14.7 and 14.8 respectively. South Africa is much higher at 82.7 percent, but that is the exception. Kenya is in line with Latin American countries such as Brazil, Mexico, and Peru.

2.   *Bank Liquidity Ratios.* As we see in Table 9.2, as of 2003, Kenyan commercial banks were holding a significantly smaller share of their assets in liquid reserve accounts than other sub-Saharan African countries.[1] They are holding 16.7 percent of their assets in liquid reserves, as opposed to Tanzania's 49.7 percent, Uganda's 33.5 percent, Ghana's 24.8 percent, and even South Africa, at 23.0 percent. All else equal, this indicates a level of confidence by Kenyan commercial banks in the lending opportunities available. At the same time, even this level of liquid reserve holdings is high, and represents lost opportunities to provide loans for productive activities.

Development of Securities Markets

The stock and bond markets are emerging steadily in Kenya, and the country is being transformed into a regional financial center. There are clear benefits to this development. Most generally, they affirm the fact that Kenyans are operating a sophisticated financial system, fully capable of undertaking a wide range of financing activities. More specifically, the rising level of activity in Kenya's securities markets has enabled large Kenyan firms to successfully raise funds to finance their investment projects. For example, in April 2006, KenGen, the

Table 9.2 Bank Liquidity Ratio, 2003

Kenya	16.7%
South Africa	23.0%
Tanzania	49.7%
Uganda	33.5%
Ghana	24.8%
Ivory Coast	27.6%
Brazil	55.8%
Morocco	15.5%
Mexico	61.9%
Chile	29.4%
Peru	38.5%

Source: Sacerdoti (2005).

country's biggest power supplier, put out an Initial Public Offering (IPO), hoping to raise Ksh 7.6 billion. They ended up raising Ksh 26 billion, over three times what they were seeking. The success of KenGen's IPO had been preceded by a series of oversubscribed IPOs in Kenya over the past eight years, though not to the same extent at the KenGen case.[2]

These successes with IPOs have enabled the government to begin planning to utilize the bond market to raise funds to promote infrastructure investments in the country. As reported in *The East African* on June 26, 2006, Finance Minister Amos Kimunya said the government "would resort to the bond market to mobilize resources for infrastructure on a long term basis and secure a sovereign rating from the Standard and Poors agency."[3] This could represent a major positive development for Kenya, if such bond offerings are handled carefully, given the country's major needs in the area of infrastructure. We discuss this issue in more depth below in our discussion of fiscal policy.

At the same time, the development of active securities markets also poses serious challenges for the Kenyan economy, in particular, with Kenya becoming an attractive target for speculative financial investors. Thus, *The East African* reported in May 2006 that:

> Hot money is flowing into Kenya in a big way as the country emerges as the latest target in Africa for international fund managers looking for high returns on equities and bonds in emerging markets. Since January this year, hundreds of billions of shillings from emerging market funds have been pumped into the local bond market, precipitating a mini-boom (May 17, 2006).

The development of Kenya as a target for speculative finance creates three serious concerns:

1. A demand from bond holders to maintain high interest rates. This of course raises their rate of return, but it discourages borrowing and lending within the country, especially to small business owners and rural smallholders.
2. All else equal, it raises the value of the shilling in international currency markets, as we have discussed in Chapter 8. This is detrimental to promoting Kenya's exports.
3. "Hot money" by its nature can flow out of a country's financial markets just as quickly as it flows in. This can lead to volatility in the operations of the markets, which then can contribute to instability in the non-financial spheres of the economy.

In short, the development of securities markets in Kenya has the potential both to promote and undermine the country's development, in terms of supporting employment expansion and poverty reduction. To promote the benefits of these developments, what is needed are policies that explicitly link the security markets to the country's developmental needs. This clearly is the logic behind Finance Minister Kimunya's proposal for financing infrastructure projects.

Microfinance Institutions

Perhaps the single most promising feature of the Kenyan financial system is its extensive system of microfinance enterprises. The largest of these are the SACCOs, which are the largest grouping of credit unions in sub-Saharan Africa. But the SACCOs themselves are part of a broader system of microfinance institutions (MFIs).

The different types of MFIs in Kenya are described well in Hospes, Musinga, and Ong'ayo (2002):

> Depending on the purpose, two approaches are generally used to categorize the different providers of micro finance services in Kenya. The first and most commonly used one is on the basis of formality where providers are categorized as formal or informal depending on the extent to which the provider is registered and regulated under formal law and transactions are governed under the various statutes of the law of contract or rather by self-regulation or group-based rules. The second categorization is based on the customer/provider relationship in the management and ownership of the financial service-providing entity. Under this categorization, micro finance providers could be dichotomized into client-based micro finance agencies and member-based micro finance agencies (MMFAs) (p. 23).

This same study defines SACCOs themselves as follows:

> The SACCO system is a mutual membership organization. It involves pooling of voluntary savings from members in form of shares. The savings/shares form the

Table 9.3 Typology of Microfinance Enterprises in Kenya

	Formal	Informal
Client-based	K-REP Bank, KWFT, Faulu Kenya, etc.	Traders, shopkeepers, money-lenders, family and friends
Member-based	SACCOs, FSAs	ROSCAs, ASCRAs

Note: From Hospes et al.: "Rotating Savings and Credit Associations (ROSCAs) and Accumulating Savings and Credit Associations (ASCRAs) are also locally known in Kenya as merry-go-rounds ... Some of them are registered at the Ministry of Social Affairs, others are not. As self-regulation or group-based rules provide the most decisive regulatory framework for ROSCAs and ASCRAs, they are all labeled as informal here—whether registered or not," p. 23.
Source: Hospes et al. (2002).

basis for extending credit to members. Credit is usually based on three times the level of savings/shares. SACCOs are regulated by the Cooperatives-Societies Act. SACCOs respond to people's need for food and food production, housing, education, small enterprise, transport, medical care, clothing and expenses in marriage, birth, and death (p. 24).

Table 9.3 provides a typology developed by Hospes et al. (2002) of the various types of microfinance enterprises in Kenya.

How extensive is the system of MFIs? It is difficult to establish a firm figure for this, in part, of course, because many of the institutions are informal. However, various researchers do all agree that the SACCOs are the largest and most prominent set of MFIs. According to the official figures based on District Annual Reports, there were 3,187 SACCOs operating in 2005, and 1,491 dormant SACCOs. According to this document, total membership in 2005 was 1.6 million. This is significantly lower than the reported peak of 2.1 million in 2001.

In contrast with these official figures, a recent press account states that there are 8.5 million members of SACCOs in Kenya.[4] Three separate research papers offer estimates ranging between 1.3 and 2.9 million members (Evans and Radu 2002, Hospes et al. 2002, and Argwings-Kodhek 2004). However, even if we accept the low estimate, this is still a very extensive network. As Evans and Radu (2002) note, "Given a national population of 30.8 million with half of the population under the age of 18, Kenyan SACCO membership of over 1.5 million covers a significant portion of Kenya's economically active population."[5] That is, at the very least, about 10 percent of Kenya's working-aged population are members of SACCOs.

Based on this evidence alone, there does appear to be at least the rudiments in place of a financial infrastructure capable of meeting the needs of small businesses, rural smallholders, and the informal sector.

WEAKNESSES OF KENYA'S CURRENT FINANCIAL SYSTEM

Interest Rate Levels

Lending rate

Interest rate levels in Kenya are difficult to interpret. This becomes clear in considering the situation with the lending rates of commercial banks, i.e. their "loans and advances" interest rate. The average lending rate for 2006, as we have seen, was 13.6 percent. One would normally regard this as being quite high. However, as always, a major issue in interpreting interest rate levels is the impact that inflation plays in establishing real returns to creditors for making loans, since inflation diminishes the purchasing power of loan repayments that are paid in fixed nominal terms. The official overall CPI inflation rate in the country for 2006 was 13.5 percent. That means that, calculating the simplest possible real interest rate (equal to the current loan rate minus the current overall inflation rate) the real lending rate for 2006 was 0.1 percent—essentially a zero real interest rate for Kenya's borrowers.

However, as we can see from Figure 9.1, since the end of the inflation spike in 1995, the nominal lending rate was substantially above the inflation rate through 2002. The gap between the rates begins to close in 2003 before falling to near zero in 2006. Still, even with a zero-rate for 2006, for the full period 1995–2006, the average real lending rate—as measured, again, simply as the nominal rate minus the contemporaneous inflation rate—was 8.4 percent, while the range was between 23.5 percent and -12.8 percent.

It is obvious that real interest rates have been unstable. But the ways in which they are unstable depends on how people experience inflation. As we discussed in Chapter 7, the biggest single source of recent inflationary pressures has been food and energy price shocks. For wealthy households—i.e. those most likely to be involved as creditors or debtors in the formal financial market—the impact of energy and food price shocks will be smaller than the impact experienced by the poor majority.[6] Hence, relying on a simple calculation of a real interest rate based on the aggregate CPI—inclusive of food and energy prices—may not be the most appropriate measure.

The volatility of inflation is also a relevant concern in establishing what constitutes a real interest rate. As we have discussed earlier, Kenya has not been a particularly high inflation country. Except for the spike between 1992 and 1994, inflation has remained within single digits or very low double digits. One could say that inflation has ranged widely within, or only somewhat above, the single digit range since 1995—with a mean inflation rate of 7.8 percent and a standard deviation of 3.7 percent. Even a standard deviation in that range would tend to make it difficult to build in an inflation premium

Figure 9.1 Nominal Deposit and Lending Rates and Inflation Rate in Kenya, 1992–2006

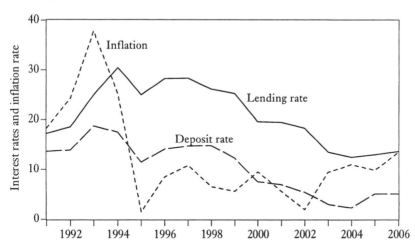

Source: Central Bank of Kenya (2005).

into interest rates that generates something like a stable real interest return to lenders.

One way to address this problem is to build indexation into credit contracts. This is something we will discuss in the policy section below. For now, the main point to establish is that Kenya operates at high nominal interest rates, with real rates fluctuating strongly based on inflation.

Lending–deposit rate spread

However we may interpret the lending rate level, what is clear is that the interest rate spreads are very high. We have reviewed the basic data on this from 1971–2006 in Chapter 7 (Figure 7.5). But it will be useful here to examine this set of data again, focusing now on the period since the liberalization of financial markets, i.e. from the early 1990s to the present. Figure 9.2 shows the movement in the difference between the commercial banks' 0–3-month demand deposit rate and their loan and advance rate. The spread was less than four percentage points before liberalization, in 1991, then rose sharply, to a peak of 14.1 percentage points in 1996. The spread has come down substantially since 1996. But at 8.5 percentage points in 2006, it is still very high.

What are the causes of this large spread? At a strictly accounting level, we need to again raise the issue of inflationary effects and real versus nominal rates. This is especially relevant in considering the deposit rate figures. The nominal

Figure 9.2 Spread Between Lending and Deposit Rates, 1991–2006

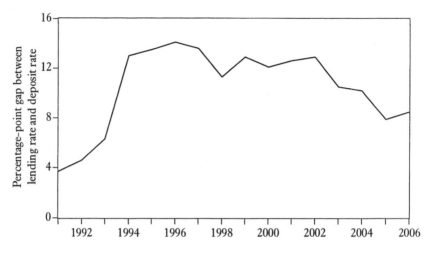

Note: Deposit rate is 0–3 month demand deposits; lending rate is commercial bank loans and advances.
Source: Central Bank of Kenya (2005).

deposit rate for 2006 averaged 5.1 percent. This means that the real deposit rate for 2006—again, establishing the real rate based on the contemporaneous CPI inflation rate—was -8.4 percent, with the overall inflation rate at 13.5 percent. In this sense, it is not surprising that the spread should be so large, to the extent that the inflation rate is indeed capturing something significant about price behavior in Kenya. In this context, the primary question then is, why are deposit rates so low, i.e. roughly five percentage points below inflation?

Ngugi (2001) addresses the overall question of large spreads, not the low deposit rates per se, in her paper, "An Empirical Analysis of Interest Rate Spread in Kenya." She explains the increasing spread in the post-1991 liberalization era as follows:

> Variations in the interest spread are attributable to bank efforts to maintain threatened profit margins. For example, banks that faced increasing credit risk as the proportion of non-performing loans went up responded by charging a high risk premium on the lending rate. High non-performing loans reflect the poor business environment and distress borrowing, which is attributed to the lack of alternative sourcing for credit when banks increased the lending rate, and the weak legal system in enforcement of financial contracts. Fiscal policy actions saw an increase in treasury bill rates and high inflationary pressure that called for tightening of monetary policy. As a result, banks increased their lending rates but

Table 9.4 Differential Deposit Rates in December 2006

Commercial banks 0–3 mos	Commercial banks savings rate	Hire purchase companies and merchant banks	Mortgage finance companies (various deposits)	Post office savings bank
5.13%	1.36%	5.13% – 7.10%	1.34 %– 2.10%	2.50%

Source: Central Bank of Kenya (2006).

were reluctant to reduce the lending rate when the treasury bill rate came down because of the declining income from loans. They responded by reducing the deposit rate, thus maintaining a wider margin as they left the lending rate at a higher level. Thus, there was an asymmetric response of lending rates to treasury bill rates (p. 33).

In short, Ngugi identifies three major factors producing the large spreads: 1) lack of competition in the banking sector; 2) high default risk, and certainly the perception that risk is high; and 3) tight monetary policy, producing high lending rates.

These factors can certainly explain large spreads in general. But it still does not seem clear as to why, to a significant extent, the large spreads would be manifested in the specific form of strongly negative deposit rates. Why would people deposit their money in banks, only to see these funds lose value? Part of this is likely tied to the point we raised above—i.e. the lack of clarity as to the effects of inflation on the economy.[7]

Large differentials between deposit rates

Table 9.4 shows the figures for December 2006 in terms of different deposit rates in the Kenyan banking system. As we see, there are extremely large disparities in these various deposit rates. These disparities no doubt reflect strong differences in institutional structures and instruments being offered to bank clients. For example, there is more than a four percentage-point gap between even the commercial banks' own "savings rate" and their 0–3-month deposit rate. We also see the wide ranges of rates with the hire purchase companies and the mortgage finance companies, reflecting the same disparities that are present with the commercial bank deposit rates. Finally, the situation with the Post Office Savings Bank is a matter of serious concern, with the savings rate at the Post Office Banks at 2.5 percent. This is 13 percentage points below the aggregate inflation rate. The Post Office Bank is where a high proportion of Kenyans make any connection with the formal financial system, and perhaps the formal economy more generally. But by accepting a deposit rate at this low level, savers at the

Post Office Bank are clearly committing themselves to a major financial loss, after accounting for inflation.

This figure for the Post Office Savings Bank is particularly important in light of the news reported in July 2006 that the Postbank "may soon give loans in the villages" (Murithi). In principle, this is a welcome development. However, in practice, if the Postbank is to extend its operations into lending, there needs to be care taken that this not be done through depositors massively subsidizing either the borrowers or the government via strongly negative deposit rates.

Lending to Government vs. Lending to Private Sector

According to the IMF study by Sacerdoti (2005), Kenya ranks high relative to other developing countries in terms of the proportion of loans that commercial banks make to the government, as opposed to private borrowers. We can see this from Table 9.5.

It is true that Uganda and Ghana are even higher than Kenya here. But note that South Africa is much lower, at 10.8 percent, and Tanzania is also lower at 17.5 percent. We can see this same relationship in further analysis by Sacerdoti. He shows Kenya as holding relatively low liquidity ratios, but being only reasonably well placed in terms of lending to the private sector. This appears to be a case of what we may term "direct crowding out"—where a high level of loans to the government is a straightforward substitute for lending to private businesses.

As noted by Argwings-Kodhek (2004):

> Most banks continue to hold large amounts of government paper at extremely low interest rates while agriculture and the rural sector are starved of credit and other financial services. Put another way: the commercial banks have 100 billion of deposits they wish they did not have lying in low performing instruments. Some are reportedly considering charging for holding deposits and taking active measures to discourage further customer deposits. Deposit interest rates below one percent do not seem to have done the trick (p. 3).

Lack of Access to Credit for Small Businesses and Farmers

It would appear to be something of a paradox that despite an extensive system of micro credit—both formal institutions such as SACCOs and informal ones such as ROSCAs—all evidence suggests that small businesses are starved for credit. For example, in 1999, only 5.8 percent of MSE (micro and small enterprise) owners interviewed in a survey in 1999 even applied for a loan, despite the fact that:

> About 90 percent of MSEs perceive borrowing as necessary for business. Only a small percent do not like credit. Furthermore, most of them would borrow to save their businesses from collapsing if and when that became necessary. Only a small

Table 9.5 Bank Credit to Government as Share of Bank Deposits, 2002–04

Kenya	36.7%
South Africa	10.8%
Tanzania	17.5%
Uganda	47.3%
Ghana	45.8%
Ivory Coast	24.2%
Brazil	90.8%
Morocco	24.8%
Mexico	8.4%
Chile	42.1%
Peru	14.7%

Source: Sacerdoti (2005).

proportion would rather allow their businesses to collapse than borrow (Kimuyu and Omita 2000, p. 13).

These problems appear particularly acute among rural smallholders. An estimated 77 percent of rural Kenyan households have no access to financial services.

Why is there inadequate credit going to SMEs?

The short answer is that commercial banks are simply reluctant to move into this line of banking. They obviously do not now see this as a profitable endeavor, or they would pursue it. The question therefore is why this is not regarded as profitable for them. Here is a sampling of views from the literature:

> The formal segment of Kenya's financial sector is dominated by a few commercial banks. Some of the banks have roots in the colonial period and were historically oriented towards meeting the financial needs of external trade and large-scale commerce. These banks therefore do not have a track record of lending to small enterprises and smallholder agriculture (Kimuyu and Omiti 2000).

> On the credit side, one only has to note the minimum Ksh 40,000 monthly income for unsecured (salary deduction facility) loans at Standard Chartered to conclude that the credit union is the more accessible institution for poor, low-income and lower-middle income people in Kenya (Evans and Radu 2002, p. 21).

> Commercial banks operate purely on a commercial basis and they are reluctant to lend to the MSE sector because MSE borrowers seldom have a credit history or marketable assets to use as collateral. Despite innovative methodologies for lending to the sectors that have emerged in the recent past, existing banking regulations do not allow for a loan portfolio with borrowers whose characteristics are substantially different from those of typical institutions specialized in the provision of micro

finance. Consequently, only a few commercial banking institutions have endeavored to provide financial services to MSEs. However these few have not been very successful in reaching the wide spectrum of MSEs requiring credit, particularly in rural areas (Hospes et al. 2002, p. 31).

Commercial banks and other formal institutions fail to cater to the credit needs of smallholders, however, mainly due to their lending terms and conditions. It is generally the rules and regulations of the formal financial institutions that have created the myth that the poor are not bankable and since they can't afford the required collateral, they are considered uncredit-worthy (Atieno 2001, p. 1).

Problems with micro lenders

There are five basic problems with the MFIs as a significant source of credit in advancing an agenda for decent employment and poverty reduction. They are:

1. a small asset base;
2. a focus on making personal loans as opposed to business loans;
3. much stronger presence in urban areas, especially with SACCOs;
4. the rural SACCOs and other MFIs are primarily available in communities with traditional cash-crops;
5. MFIs tend to exclude the poor;[8] and
6. poor regulatory oversight.

The overall effect of these factors is well summarized by Hospes et al. (2002):

> In spite of the heavy investments in technology development, micro-finance as an industry has hardly found appropriate answers to substantially increase outreach and to address poverty on a large scale in Kenya. Also, fully fledged financial intermediation in the micro-finance market has hardly evolved in Kenya. Some players in this market concentrate either on savings mobilization or disbursement of small loans. Finally, micro-finance in Kenya, in particular the category of client-based micro-finance agencies, is biased towards urban and/or densely populated areas hosting large numbers of micro-entrepreneurs in a relatively small area (pp. 118–119).

POLICY PROPOSAL: A SYSTEM OF LOAN GUARANTEES FROM COMMERCIAL BANKS TO MFIS

We are proposing a large-scale policy intervention to link the formal commercial banking system with the SACCOs and other micro finance entities. The MFIs are much more capable of making loans to small businesses, farmers, and the informal sector—and can utilize more flexible systems of collateral for such loans.[9] As we noted above, something along these lines has been proposed in at least some documents of both the IMF and World Bank. Here is Sacerdoti of the IMF (2005), writing about sub-Saharan African finance in general:

In some countries, more mature MFIs appear well adapted to lend to SMEs, and may have a competitive advantage, as they can use risk assessment techniques and information acquired through dealing with clients that began as micro-entrepreneurs. However, to put these advantages to good use would require that MFIs obtain adequate resources through credit lines from banks, and be able to provide credit at rates below those that apply to micro-credits.

The provision of credit to small farmers faces major obstacles, due to the limited availability of collateral. Efforts must be made for farmers to regroup in strong cooperatives, which can provide adequate guarantees to banks, as indicated above (p. 21).

The earlier World Bank study focused on the Kenyan financial system is equally specific in endorsing some version of a credit guarantee program for Kenya (Fafchamps, Biggs, Conning, and Srivastava 1994, p. 88). This point is also the main policy conclusion of the excellent 2001 paper by Atieno. She writes:

Given the relatively abundant financial resources of the formal institutions compared with informal credit sources, there is a need for policy measures to increase access to SMEs to formal credit. This can be achieved through the establishment of credit insurance schemes protecting the financial institutions against default risks, which result in credit rationing. The formal financial institutions should also be encouraged to diversity their loan portfolios so as to be able to cater for the different financial needs of SMEs (p. 38).

Atieno also intriguingly reports that loan guarantee programs are already being implemented in Kenya, though she does not supply sufficient details. For example, she describes a program at Barclays Bank that offers loans for women entrepreneurs both as individuals and as groups.

Key Elements of Proposal

We propose a loan guarantee fund similar to the one that Atieno reports Barclays Bank had been operating on a small scale. That is, we propose a loan guarantee system, in which the government offers commercial banks something on the order of a 75 percent guarantee on loans that they make to SACCOs and other micro finance entities. The commercial banks would have to demonstrate that the SACCOs are capable of making business loans, rather than simply emergency loans and personal loans. SACCOs would also need to have the flexibility to lend to non-members, relying on new forms of collateral such as that which we describe below.

For the program of this sort to be successful at promoting decent employment and reducing poverty, it needs to operate at a large scale. Of course, any such program will need to be phased-in gradually. But as a matter of principle, it is important to show that it could operate on a large scale without placing excessive strains either on the government budget or the capacities of the financial system.

Scale of operation

Consider a program of roughly the following scale when fully operational. Private investment in Kenya in 2004 (the most recent year with non-provisional GDP data) was roughly 15 percent of GDP:

2004 GDP in Market Prices = Ksh 1.3 trillion
2004 Gross Private Domestic Investment = Ksh 200 billion

Let us assume that the loan guarantee program is roughly equal to 20 percent of 2004 gross private domestic investment of Ksh 200 billion. Thus,

Total loans being guaranteed = Ksh 40 billion (in 2004 prices)

Following the model from Barclay's Bank (as reported by Atieno 2001), let us assume that loans are guaranteed at a 75 percent rate. That means that the government is guaranteeing Ksh 30 billion in loans.

Let us also assume a default rate on these loans of 30 percent. This is a very high rate, roughly equal, in fact to the actual "alarming" rate reported for 2004 in what had been a confidential memo prepared by former Central Bank Governor Andrew Mullei to former Finance Minister David Mwiraria.[10] According to the official District Annual Reports, the default rates on SACCOs between 2001 – 2005 ranged between 2.8 and 7.5 percent. For the purposes of our exercise, we deliberately assume a very high default rate. This establishes a plausible outer limit of the costs of the loan guarantee program.

Working with an assumption of a high default rate also underscores a key point of this proposal: that for commercial banks to make loans to micro finance entities will entail real risks. Indeed, the initiative will not be useful unless the commercial banks are willing to accept greater risks and the fact that defaults will occur. At the same time, precisely because the banks will have a large share of their own funds committed to the guaranteed loans, they will operate with care in entering arrangements with microfinance enterprises, even though 75 percent of their loans would be guaranteed by the government.

The cost to the government of a 75 percent guarantee with a 30 percent default rate on Ksh 40 billion in guaranteed loans can be calculated as follows:

Ksh 40 billion x 0.75 x 0.3 = Ksh 9 billion

Thus, the direct annual expense of the guarantee program of this magnitude, and building in the assumptions that we have would amount to Ksh 9 billion per year. The total government budget for 2004 was Ksh 188.9 billion in 2004 prices. Thus, at the 2004 level of economic activity and government spending, the loan guarantee program, at full operations, would be equal to somewhat less than 5 percent of the Kenyan general government budget. If we allow for a lower default rate, at, say 15 percent, then the costs of the loan guarantee program correspondingly fall, to Ksh 4.5 billion.

We will consider in Chapter 10 the ways through which this roughly 5 percent increase in government spending could be covered.

Extent of credit subsidy

The terms of the subsidy must meet four criteria:

1. Subsidies must be large enough such that the program will succeed in building the necessary links between the commercial banks and the SACCOs and other MFIs.
2. The program must still be seen as providing potential profit opportunities for both commercial banks and the microlenders.
3. The loan terms must be broadly consistent with the structure of interest rates, rewards, and risks within the Kenyan financial market as it currently operates.
4. The terms must be understood simply by participants in the financial system.

A logical starting point for establishing an appropriate interest rate on subsidized loans is the government bond rate. With respect to default risk, government bonds are the least risky asset within the Kenyan financial system. At the same time, the Kenyan government bond rate reflects everything about the general level of risk in Kenya, including both inflation risk and country risk.

A subsidized loan from a commercial bank to a microcredit lender would also incorporate general levels of country risk and inflation risk. The default risk on a subsidized loan would then depend on the credit profile of the individual borrower and the extent of the loan guarantee. Based on this, the rate on concessionary loans should be set as an increment above the government bond rate. How large an increment above the government bond rate should then depend on the borrowers' profile and the extent of the government guarantee on loans. To make this clearer, we can stipulate that a government bond issue in shillings faces virtually zero default risk. Thus, the interest rate on a private loan with a 100 percent guarantee should be set at exactly the government bond rate. By contrast, the appropriate rate on a loan with no guarantee is, by definition, the market interest rate on that loan. As such, the government bond rate and the market interest rate define the range within which concessionary rates should be set.

The appropriate concessionary rate can therefore be derived simply as follows:

$$I^{lg} = i^m - LC, \text{ where}$$

$$LC = C(i^m - i^b),$$

and I^{lg} is the rate on loan guarantees, i^m is the market interest rate for a loan of a given risk class and maturity, i^b is the government bond rate for a given maturity, and C is the percentage of a loan that the government is guaranteeing.

To illustrate this calculation with an example, consider a case, which closely approximates actual Kenyan financial market conditions in July 2007, in which the government 3-year bond rate is 8 percent, and the commercial bank rate is 13 percent. In such a case, and assuming a 75 percent loan guarantee program, the concessionary loan rate I^{lg} would be 9.25 percent. Of course, the concessionary loan rate would rise if the government guarantee were less. Thus, if we assume that the loan guarantee is 50 percent rather than 75 percent, the concessionary loan rate rises to 10.5 percent.

For the program to operate successfully, the subsidized lending rate that commercial banks make to SACCOs and other MFIs would then also have to be incorporated into the rate at which the SACCOs themselves make retail loans to small businesses and farmers. Establishing the details of this retail lending rate would have to take account of the specific operations of the micro credit units, including the means through which they establish collateral. Given the large number of microcredit units operating in Kenya, it may be possible that establishing appropriate spreads for subsidized retail lending rates could result through market competition alone. This is a matter to consider in detail later. For now, it is sufficient to recognize the basic principles presented here on which subsidized lending—at both the wholesale and retail levels—should be established.

Creating Disincentives to Defraud the System

The obvious way to defraud the system of loan guarantees is for borrowers and lenders to collude in obtaining guaranteed loans from the government, then deliberately defaulting on these loans to collect the government guarantee. As colluders in such an enterprise, the borrower and lender would then share the government guarantee payment.

As a simple example, consider a case in which a commercial bank makes a Ksh 1,000 loan to a SACCO, which then will purportedly lend the money to small business owners. But in fact, the commercial bank and SACCO are colluding to collect funds from the SACCO defaulting on the loan. Once the default is accepted as legitimate by the government, the government is then obligated to pay the commercial bank Ksh 750, assuming a 75 percent guarantee on the loan. The borrower and lender can then split these funds. Of course, the commercial bank and SACCO would have also earlier worked out an arrangement for sharing the Ksh 1,000 in fraudulent "loan funds."

A loan guarantee system can be designed to minimize such opportunities for fraud. The first type of disincentive would entail creating an escrow account on the loan, to be held by the government. Having established such an escrow fund, this fund can be used to minimize the incentives for fraud. Thus, if the loan does not go into default, then the escrow funds are released to the borrower when the loan matures. But if the loan does go into default, the government only releases the escrow account funds back to the commercial bank after the conditions of the loan default have been investigated. In addition, this set of incentives can be combined with strict penalties for fraud as well as rewards for people who discover and report on such schemes. We now illustrate these considerations through the following example. We present this example in Table 9.6.

As the table shows, the main parameters of this case are as follows:

1. amount of loan: Ksh 1,000
2. terms of loan: five years at 5 percent annual simple interest
3. government guarantee: 75 percent of principle on loan
4. escrow account: SACCO contributes Ksh 100; commercial bank contributes Ksh 200
5. amount of funds for SACCO expenditure: Ksh 800.

No Default Case
With this loan, if there is no default, the SACCO pays Ksh 50 per year in interest plus the repayment of the principal. At the end of five years, the SACCO also receives the Ksh 300, plus accrued interest, on the escrow account.

Default Case
The SACCO is out Ksh 100 of its own money, plus loses the opportunity to receive the Ksh 200 in the escrow funds. The commercial bank is out Ksh 250, receiving Ksh 750 from the government guarantee.

Incentive to Defraud the System
Assume that the SACCO and the commercial bank are in a conspiracy to defraud the government of the Ksh 750 of the loan guarantee. Their arrangement is that each will receive half of the money coming from the government guarantee, i.e. each receives 375 Ksh from loan guarantee.

The net outcomes are as follows:

SACCO: Nets Ksh 275 (= Ksh 375 from the guarantee—the Ksh 100 contribution to the escrow fund).

Commercial bank: Nets Ksh 175 (= Ksh 375 from the guarantee—the Ksh 200 contribution to the escrow fund).

This incentive to defraud the system could be large enough to encourage this type of fraudulent operation. If so, aside from the punishments to be faced

Table 9.6 Numerical Example on Collateral and Escrow Fund

Loan Terms: R1000, 5 years at 5 percent
Government Guarantee: Varies, 75 percent versus 50 percent
Escrow Contributions: Constant at 10 percent borrower; 20 percent lender

| | (figures are in Ksh) | |
	Case 1	Case 2
Guarantee	750	500
Escrow		
Total escrow	300	300
Borrower contribution	100	100
Lender contribution	200	200
If default, government pays	750	500
Net gains from fraud		
Borrower gain	275 (=375–100)	150 (=250–100)
Lender gain	175 (=375–200)	50 (=250–200)

if the fraud were discovered (more on this below) the way to weaken such incentives would, straightforwardly, entail some combination of either reducing the level of the guarantee or increasing the escrow fund obligations for both the borrower and lender.

If we assume that the guarantee is only 50 percent of the loan, but the escrow commitment remains the same, the incentives reduce to the following:

Borrower: Nets Ksh 150 (= Ksh 250 from the guarantee—Ksh 100 contribution to the escrow fund).

Lender: Nets Ksh 50 (= Ksh 250 from the guarantee —Ksh 200 contribution to the escrow fund).

We go through these two examples in Table 9.6.

From these examples, we can see that by reducing the size of the guarantees or increasing the amount of the escrow commitments, incentives for fraud are diminished. But by pursuing such measures, one also obviously weakens the benefits to be accrued from the loan guarantee program, and thereby the prospect that the program could be used as a major financing tool contributing to economic growth and employment expansion.

Incentive-based monitoring

The way to sustain a more expansionary loan guarantee program—i.e. including a higher guarantee ratio and lower escrow contribution ratios—is to also create severe penalties for fraud along with strong incentive for "whistleblowers" to report abuses of the system. This means mobilizing incentives to monitor the system rather than relying primarily on government investigators to prevent fraud. This approach to monitoring financial market regulations was developed by Dean Baker (2003) with respect to the so-called Tobin Tax—a tax on speculative transactions in global currency markets. A variation on Baker's idea could be applicable here. For example:

In the case of a Ksh 1,000 loan with a 75 percent guarantee:

1. minimum penalty to commercial bank for gaming the system: "treble damages"—i.e. Ksh 2,250
2. reward for whistleblowing: Full amount of guarantee—i.e. Ksh 750

In addition, both the commercial bank and the SACCO would lose their licenses to operate.

Through combining the escrow system with the incentive-based monitoring approach, it should be possible to establish a workable set of incentives in place to operate the loan guarantee program.[11]

Additional Financial Market Reform Initiatives

We believe that a loan guarantee program of this sort is both feasible and highly desirable, and indeed can serve as the foundation for linking Kenya's well-developed commercial banking system with its similarly well-developed micro-lending institutions. But operating on its own, this measure will not be sufficient to move Kenya's financial system onto a sustainable developmental path. As we noted at the outset, other initiatives will also provide important support. These include the following:

1. *Reliable credit-rating operations.* Initiatives along these lines are being pursued by private firms in Kenya.[12] Once these initiatives reach a critical mass, they will serve as the conduit through which information on credit risks will get transmitted among lenders. Having such information available will thereby reduce informational gaps in financial markets. This in turn will help close existing gaps between deposit and lending rates, to the extent that these gaps reflect excessive risk premiums due to informational deficiencies.

2. *Index bond rates to inflation.* As we have discussed, uncertainty as to the effects of inflation on the real returns to lenders is contributing to the high risk premium in the Kenyan financial system, and thus again to the large gap between deposit and lending rates. Indexing bonds to inflation is a well-developed measure of protecting the value of bonds against changes in inflation. At the same time, building indexation into loan contracts also raises concerns that need to be addressed. These include the following:

    a. At the simplest level, a system of bond indexation assumes that the government is providing an accurate measure of inflation on which to base the indexed adjustments. We have discussed above the difficulties of measuring inflation accurately, especially given the problems presented by supply-shock inflations from food and energy price volatility;

    b. Even if we could assume an accurate Consumer Price Index, the indexation of loans builds complexity into credit relationships. This would discourage SMEs and rural smallholders from borrowing. Thus, if Kenya were to introduce inflation-adjusted interest rates, perhaps it should be done only in relationships between commercial banks and MFIs; and

    c. Full indexation shifts the burden of inflation risk from lenders entirely onto borrowers. As such, even if Kenya were to introduce inflation-adjusted rates, the equitable way to do it would be through an arrangement that shares inflation risk between borrowers and lenders.

3. *Utilizing the Postbank as a small-scale lender.* The issue of narrowing the deposit-lending rate gaps is highly relevant with respect to converting the Postbank into a lending institution. For this new initiative to succeed over time, the Postbank cannot be in the position of financing its small-scale loan program through providing negative real returns to its equally small-scale depositors. The returns to depositors need to be positive, and this, in turn, means both reducing the informational gaps in Kenya's financial market, and establishing better means of controlling the impact of inflation on the value of financial assets.

4. *Revitalizing public investment banks.* Public investment banks in Kenya, such as the ICDC and the Agricultural Development Bank, had played central roles in Kenya's development in the early years after independence. Their importance in Kenya was similar to the experience of other developing countries. This becomes clear in the illuminating discussion of development banking by Alice Amsden in *The Rise of "the Rest": Challenges to the West from Late-Industrializing Economies.* Amsden begins her discussion of this topic with the general observation that:

The state's agent for financing investment was the development bank. From the viewpoint of long-term capital supply for public *and private* investment, development banks throughout "the rest" were of overwhelming importance (p. 127).

Of course, a major problem with the Kenyan development banks in the 1980s and 1990s was their lack of objective criteria for providing loans. This suggests that perhaps converting the banks into public–private partnership arrangements would accomplish two things. First, it would create profit-driven criteria for lending decisions, with private investors having put up funds that are at risk to revitalize these institutions. Second, it would still allow for a strong public goods component to lending decisions, given that the banks would remain partially controlled by the government. As such, the lending activities of these banks would parallel the loan guarantee programs operating through the commercial banks and MFIs. Both would be underwritten by government support, but both would also require private initiative and risk-taking.

NOTES

1. The bank liquidity ratio is defined as liquid reserves, including required reserves, plus foreign assets of banking institutions, over demand and time deposits of such institutions.
2. Tom Mogusu, "KenGen IPO Nets Over Sh26 billion," *The Standard*, April 29, 2006.
3. Peter Munaita, "Kimunya Sees Kenya's Future in the Bond Market," *The East African*, June 26, 2006.
4. "Plight of SACCOs Put in the Spotlight," *Tomorrow's Nation*, October 4, 2006.
5. Here are the relevant passages: Evans and Radu (2002): "As of December 2001, there were 1.3 million credit union members belonging to Kenyan Union of Savings and Credit Cooperatives Limited. In addition, there are 350,000 or more direct members of the rural SACCO association, Kenya Rural Savings and Credit Societies Union (KERUSSU)." Hospes et al. (2002) write: "available information shows that there were about 4,000 SACCOs by the end of 1999 with a total of 2.9 million active members" (p. 35). Argwings-Kodhek (2004) writes: "Currently there are 3,200 SACCOs in Kenya serving 1.3 million savers and 1 million borrowers." Argwings-Kodhek goes on to say, quite significantly that "There has been a flurry of activity in setting up micro-finance institutions in Kenya to meet the financial needs of the majority of citizens. However, after 25 years their total client base is in the range of only 200,000 of Kenya's 5 million households" (2004, p. 7).
6. Thus, with the New Kenya CPI Broad Category weightings, food prices account for 56 percent of total inflation for lower-income households in Nairobi, but only 32 percent for middle- and upper-income households (Government of Kenya 2002, p. 12).
7. If this is so, Kenya would hardly be the first economy to experience difficulties in interpreting the impact of inflation on financial assets. See, for example, Modigliani and Cohn (1979) and Campbell and Vuolteenaho (2004) on the problems faced by U.S. financial markets in interpreting financial asset values in a high-inflation environment.
8. For references, see Sacerdoti 2005, Argwings-Kodhek 2004, and Evans and Radu 2002.
9. However, a study released in August 2007 by KERUSSU finds that SACCOs are not succeeding in competing with commercial banks and other MFIs in terms of providing services to consumers. The report found that "the SACCO movement has limited sources of finances thereby inhibiting it from raising sufficient funds to strengthen its capital base and service needs of its members." See Geoffrey Irungu, "Banks Outsmart SACCOs in Loans Market," *Business Daily*, August 22, 2007.

10. "Three out of 10 Debts Gone Bad as 'Serial Defaulters' Run Amok in Kenya's Banks," August 3, 2006.
11. These views are consistent with the concern expressed by the World Bank that credit guarantee systems also maintain workable methods of contract enforcement. The authors of the World Bank study write, for example, that "The difficulty, however, is that any credit program, directed or not, is bound to run out of funds if sufficient care is not given to contract enforcement issues.... Directed credit must therefore rely on innovative contract enforcement mechanisms, whether group lending, credit guarantee schemes, hire-purchase, computerizations of credit history, and chattel mortgages. The approach currently adopted by the Kenya Industrial Estates, as we understand it, espouses many of these innovations. It should be encouraged and imitated," (Fafchamps et al. 1994, p. 92).
12. See for example, Vitalis Omondi, "Credit Reporting Takes Root in Kenya," *Daily Standard*, January 28, 2006. The story focuses on the initiative of Sam Omukoko, the founder and managing director of Metrropol East Africa, a credit reporting firm that he began in 1999.

10. Fiscal Policy: How to Pay for New Pro-employment Initiatives

We have proposed a series of additions to the government's expenditure commitments, in the areas of infrastructure, subsidized credit, marketing, grain storage, and cooperatives. The major issue we consider now is how these additional programs are to be financed, especially alongside the government's other priorities, both in terms of spending and fiscal management.

To begin with, it will be useful to analyze current priorities in terms of fiscal policy in a broader historical context. Figure 10.1 shows public expenditures, government revenues, grants, and budget deficits in Kenya from 1970 to 2005, all expressed as percentages of GDP. Government spending increased as a share of the economy on average throughout the 1970s, reaching a peak of nearly 35 percent of GDP in the mid-1990s. Spending generally averaged between 25 and 30 percent of GDP from 1980 until the late 1990s, at which time expenditures fell to an average of 22 percent of GDP from 2000 to 2005. The budget deficit was correspondingly reduced over these years.

The most recent May 2006 Medium-Term Budget Strategy Paper (MTBSP) from the Ministry of Finance presents actual and targeted values for public expenditures, revenues, and the budget deficit for the fiscal years 2004–05 through 2008–09. These figures are presented in Table 10.1. The MTBSP calls for an expansion of spending to approximately 25–26 percent of GDP over this period, with revenues remaining in the range of 20–21 percent of GDP. The goal is to keep the budget deficit to 2–3 percent of GDP. Revenues and domestic borrowing will not be sufficient to finance the additional expenditures outlined in the Budget Strategy. Increases in grants are expected to rise in order to fund the shortfall without driving up domestic borrowing. In addition, external borrowing will rise slightly to reduce the pressures on domestic borrowing.

Considering the sectoral distribution of these funds, the MTBSP has prioritized a number of sectors in order to meet its development objectives and to make progress towards achieving the Millennium Development Goals (MDGs). The targeted sectors include health, education, agriculture, infrastructure, and food/water security.

All of these sectors are, of course, crucial for social and economic development, poverty reduction, and risk reduction for vulnerable populations. In ad-

Figure 10.1 Public Expenditures, Total Revenues, Grants, and Budget Deficits as Percentage of Kenyan GDP, 1970–2005

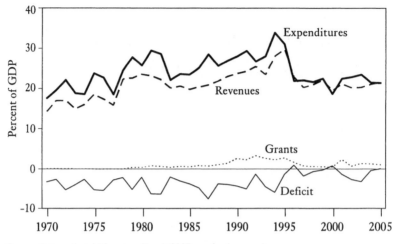

Source: International Monetary Fund (2007a, and prior years).

dition to what the government has already budgeted, we have proposed three areas that in our view warrant further significant budgetary increases. These are, again:

1. road and water infrastructure: Ksh 40 billion per year;
2. accruals on credit subsidies: Ksh nine billion per year;
3. marketing, cooperatives, extension services, and grain storage. Here we have not been able as yet to provide a well-grounded budget estimate. As a first approximation, we are working with a figure of Ksh three billion per year for all of these interrelated areas.

We have shown elsewhere how we derived these cost estimates. If the government were to pursue all three of the initiatives that we propose, this would entail an increase in government expenditures to around 28 percent of GDP for 2008–09. This figure is of course greater than what the government has projected to date. However, as we have seen, spending 28 percent of GDP on public sector activities is still well within the range of Kenya's historical experience.

The MTBSP puts forward several cost-saving measures in addition to proposals for budget reprioritization. Two of the most important cost saving measures are (1) reduction of the public sector wage bill; and (2) reduction of direct transfers and subsidies to parastatals. In terms of transfers and subsidies to

Table 10.1 Actual and Projected Budget Indicators for Fiscal Years 2004–05 Through 2008–09, Kenya (central government only)

Variables (percent of GDP)	2004–05 Provisional	2005–06 Estimated	2006–07 Projected	2007–08 Projected	2008–09 Projected
Total expenditures	22.2	26.4	25.9	25.5	25.2
Total revenues	21.2	20.7	20.7	20.9	21.0
Overall budget balance (excluding grants)	-1.0	-5.7	-5.2	-4.6	-4.3
Overall budget balance (including grants)	0.1	-3.5	-3.1	-2.5	-2.2
Net domestic borrowing	-0.5	2.0	1.6	1.3	0.8
Net external borrowing	0.0	0.4	0.9	1.3	1.2

Source: Government of Kenya (2006a).

parastatals, the proposal is to freeze these expenditures in nominal terms, maintaining them at their 2005–06 level. It is expected that such subsidies will amount to just 1.1 percent of GDP by 2008–09, down from the current level of 1.5 percent.

The public sector wage bill currently stands at 7.8 percent of GDP. The goal is to reduce this to 6.6 percent by the fiscal year 2008–09. Reductions in the public sector wage bill would be realized by the Voluntary Early Retirement scheme and by enforcing stricter wage guidelines.

Of course, the measures we are proposing would entail an increase in the number of public sector employees and the overall public sector wage bill. However, most of the expansion in employment that we are proposing would be for workers on public infrastructure projects. We have proposed that these workers be paid an average of Ksh 5,000 per month. This figure is a bit above the statutory minimum wage for general laborers in Nairobi, which was Ksh 4,638 in 2005. These projects would also entail a modest increase in supervisory workers. These costs are built into the budget projections for these projects.

To achieve the objective of more efficiently utilizing public resources, the government has produced a pay policy document that outlines recommendations for adhering to target wage levels.[1] We support the government's initiative to establish stricter wage guidelines for public sector employment. Specifically, we would support the idea of maintaining public sector real wage increases to a rate roughly commensurate with improvements in private sector productivity. Of course, the aim of our proposal, as with much of the government's own program, is to improve formal private sector productivity. To the extent that these government initiatives are successful, this will create opportunities for public sector wages to rise.

ADDITIONAL REVENUE SOURCES

As we have seen, we are proposing three major new areas of public policy initiative, which would entail additional expenditures of around Ksh 50 billion per year in 2005 prices, which is equal to about 3 percent of GDP.

For the fiscal year 2007–08, the Treasury has estimated total expenditures at 25.5 percent of GDP and revenues of 20.9 percent of GDP. This implies a deficit of 4.6 percent of GDP, with the projection that this deficit will fall to 4.2 percent of GDP in 2008–09. How would we propose to finance these existing expenditures? We need to consider this question in the context of two other important considerations: 1) the Treasury is committed to reducing its level of outstanding debt, which stood at an estimated 41.4 percent of GDP as of 2005–06—of this total, 18.2 percent was domestic debt while 23.1 percent was external debt; and 2) The current budget projections assume donor support, in the form of grants and loans, amounting to about 4.3 percent of GDP as of 2007–08 and 2008–09. It is probably not prudent to assume that this figure could or should rise much higher.

There are five ways in which additional public revenues could be made available to finance the policies that we are suggesting. They are:

1. increased collection of taxes from domestic sources;
2. increased domestic borrowing;
3. increased external borrowing;
4. debt relief or complete forgiveness by foreign creditors; and
5. overseas development assistance providing direct budget support.

As we will discuss below, the two most viable sources for generating increased tax revenues in both the short- and longer-term are the two domestic sources, i.e. higher domestic tax revenues and maintaining, rather than cutting, existing levels of domestic borrowing. For various reasons that we will discuss briefly at the end of this chapter, the three external sources are all less promising. Still, they each may be useful in generating small supplemental streams of increased government revenue.

Increased Tax Collection from Domestic Sources

In recent years, Kenya has made efforts to improve the efficiency with which it collects revenues from domestic sources. According to the 2006 MTBSP, total tax revenues are expected to amount to over 19 percent of GDP in the fiscal years 2007–08 and 2008–09. This figure is high relative to many other countries in sub-Saharan Africa. Moreover, as we show in Figure 10.2, the share of income tax collected as a percent of GDP has increased in recent years, from

Figure 10.2 Income Tax Revenues as Percentage of Kenyan GDP, Fiscal Years 1998–2009

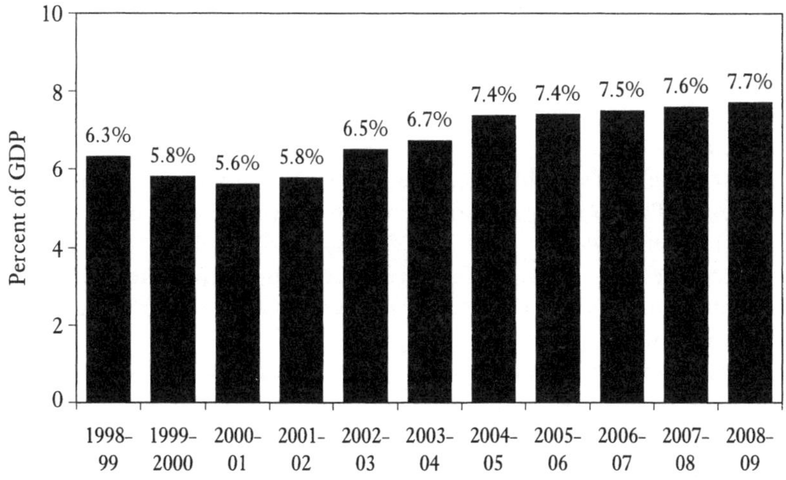

Source: International Monetary Fund (2007a), Government of Kenya (2006a)

approximately 5.5 percent in 2000–01 to 7.5 percent in 2006–07, with still further modest gains expected through at least 2008–09. This relative success at mobilizing domestic resources should certainly continue. Ultimately, it is this sustainable revenue base that provides the foundation for sound fiscal policies. Many countries in sub-Saharan Africa have improved revenue collection through a diverse array of approaches.[2] These include preventing the erosion of traditional sources of revenue (e.g. taxes from international trade), improving the efficiency of tax collection, maintaining a diverse set of tax instruments, and exploring ways of raising domestic non-tax revenues (e.g. licensing fees for access to natural resources).

The informal sector represents probably the largest single new source of additional tax revenues for Kenya. This is true even if we assume that the informal sector becomes formalized only to a modest extent. Of course, one of the defining features of working in the informal, as opposed to the formal, economy is that those in the informal economy do not pay taxes. At the same time, Kenyans working in the informal economy would be less resistant to paying taxes if they felt they were receiving tangible benefits from government programs. The informal sector workers might then be induced to accept the burden of tax obligations as an acceptable trade-off for the benefits they would be receiving from government policies.

The employment expansion policy initiatives we are proposing aim to increase the share of the formal sector of Kenya's economy in the following ways:

1. Providing loan guarantees that will connect the country's vibrant but under-capitalized microcredit sector with its already established commercial banking system should serve to increase the number of small business investments, both to establish new enterprises and expand existing ones. For firms to be eligible for subsidized loans, they will need to be registered and pay taxes. The opportunities to receive subsidized loans will create incentives for them to do so.
2. Promoting exports through improved marketing support, exchange rate policies and infrastructure investments should also lead to an increase in the formal economy.
3. Directly increasing the number of formal jobs by roughly 350,000 through transportation and water infrastructure investments will correspondingly expand the number of people that pay income and value-added taxes.

How extensive would such revenue increases need to be to support our proposed expenditure increases? In fact, the relative expansion of the formal sector would need to only be modest to fully cover the costs of the programs we have proposed. We can see this through the following simple exercise.

As of the 2005–06 KIHBS, roughly 86 percent of the total workforce in Kenya was employed in either the informal sector or agricultural self-employment, with only 14 percent in the formal economy. For the purposes of this exercise, we round these proportions to 85 percent informal and agricultural self-employed vs. 15 percent formal. We then make the following assumptions:

1. All tax revenues come from the formal sector, none come from either the informal sector or agricultural self-employment. Moreover, each unit of output in the formal sector generates a comparable increase in tax revenues. At present, total tax revenue is roughly 20 percent of GDP, coming from a formal sector that employs only 15 percent of workers. Thus, as a rough illustration of the situation, we can say that Ksh 100 of formal sector output produces Ksh 20 in revenue.
2. Let us now allow that the proportion of formal sector workers rises from 15 to 20 percent, while the share of informal/rural workers falls to 80 percent. This then increases the base of tax revenues. The increase in tax revenues will be in proportion to the increase in the share of formal employment. Thus, a rise from 15 to 20 percent formal workers represents a 33 percent increase in the number of formal workers in the economy. The rise in the tax revenue should be comparable. If 15 formal sector workers produced

Ksh 20 in revenue, then 20 workers would produce Ksh 27 in tax revenues, a 33 percent increase.

3. The 2005–06 level of government revenue is Ksh 325 billion. If it is true that raising the relative size of the formal sector by 33 percent would also generate 33 percent more revenue, that means that the increase in the formal sector from 15 to 20 percent of total employment would also generate about Ksh 108 billion in new revenue. Even if we were to cut this revenue increase estimate in half, we still are left with a new flow of revenue of Ksh 54 billion.

As we have seen, the programs we are proposing would entail an annual budgetary increase on the order of Ksh 50 billion. In short, a relative shift of Kenya's economy in favor of the formal sector from 15 to 20 percent of the economy would itself, in all likelihood, fully pay for the increased expenditures we are proposing, if the assumptions that we have made are even broadly reflective of the actual conditions in the Kenyan economy.

Overall then, it is reasonable to expect that Kenya could fully cover the costs of the programs we have proposed through continuing its modest but steady gains in revenue collections within the existing formal sector, while also expanding the relative size of the formal sector from, say, 15 to 20 percent of total employment.

MAINTAINING CURRENT LEVELS OF DOMESTIC BORROWING

Total domestic borrowing by the Kenya Treasury in 2005–06 amounted to about Ksh 32 billion, equal to about 2 percent of GDP. The outstanding stock of net domestic debt carried by the Kenya Treasury as of 2005–06 amounted to approximately 18.2 percent of GDP during fiscal year 2005–06. The Treasury is proposing that domestic borrowing fall to 0.8 percent of GDP as of 2008–09. With the economy operating at its 2005–06 level, the cut from a 2 percent level of domestic borrowing to 0.8 percent would mean a decline in funds available for development projects of roughly Ksh 20 billion per year.

We believe the Kenyan Treasury can prudently maintain a level of borrowing at approximately 2 percent of GDP. This way, the benefits of increasing tax collection revenues would not serve largely as an offset to the decline in funds generated by a reduction in domestic borrowing.

It is crucial to emphasize in this regard that Kenya's level of domestic debt is not high by international standards. We can see this in Table 10.2, which shows domestic debt as a share of GDP for Kenya and a series of comparison countries. As we can see from the table, about half the countries we have included for comparison are in sub-Saharan Africa, including Swaziland, Rwanda, Burundi, Sierra Leone, Cameroon, and Mauritius. We have also included other countries

Table 10.2 Domestic Debt as a Percentage of GDP and Average Per Capita Growth Rates, Selected Countries, 1994–2004

	Country years	Domestic debt as a percent of GDP	Average annual growth rate of per capita GDP
Kenya	**1997–2004**	21.8%	0.0%
Burundi	1997–2004	15.3%	-0.1%
Cameroon	1994–2001	27.3%	1.4%
Mauritius	1997–2004	28.8%	3.8%
Nigeria	1997–2004	7.3%	1.5%
Rwanda	1996–2003	12.1%	2.0%
Sierra Leone	1997–2004	15.5%	-2.5%
Swaziland	1996–2003	1.4%	0.3%
Costa Rica	1995–2002	26.8%	1.7%
El Salvador	1994–2001	8.8%	1.6%
Honduras	1997–2004	5.7%	0.6%
India	1994–2001	48.1%	4.3%
Indonesia	1994–2001	0.5%	1.7%
Malaysia	1994–2001	32.7%	3.0%
Sri Lanka	1997–2004	58.3%	3.6%

Note: For each country, figures are reported for the most recent seven-year period for which data are available.
Source: International Monetary Fund (2007a, and prior years). World Bank World Development Indicators (2006).

that are now or have recently been at roughly comparable levels of development, including Honduras, Costa Rica, Malaysia, India, and Sri Lanka. Of course, many within this latter group of countries have experienced successful growth trends in recent years.

As we can see, Kenya is basically in the middle of the sample of countries. It is well above Indonesia or Swaziland with their ratios of 0.5 and 1.4 percent of GDP. But Kenya is also substantially below Costa Rica, Malaysia, and India, among others. Based on these figures, there is no reason for Kenya to assume its debt levels are too high.

What about the relationship between domestic debt levels and economic growth among these countries? In fact, there is no evidence among this sample of countries that low domestic debt levels correspond with faster economic growth. We can see this both in Table 10.2, which reports the per capita growth figures for each of the countries, and more clearly still in Figure 10.3. This figure is a scatter diagram plotting the relationship between domestic debt levels as a share of GDP and each country's per capita growth rate over the years in

Figure 10.3 Government Domestic Debt and GDP Growth, 1994–2004

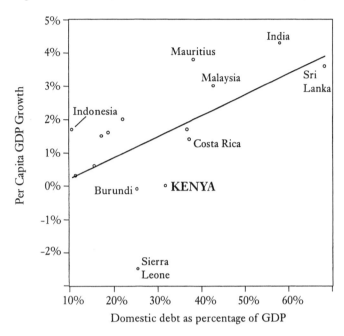

Source: International Monetary Fund (2007a, and prior years). World Bank World Development Indicators (2006).

our sample, 1994–2004. As we can see from Figure 10.3, there is, in fact, a clear positive relationship between domestic debt levels and GDP growth. That is, the figure shows that countries with higher domestic debt/GDP ratios tended to grow somewhat faster.[3] As the figure shows, the countries that have both higher domestic debt levels and faster average growth rates than Kenya include Sri Lanka, India, Mauritius, Malaysia, and Costa Rica.

Even recognizing that Kenya's domestic debt is not high, and that there is no clear relationship between a country's debt levels and its growth performance, it is still the case that the structure of the government matters for managing public financial resources. As we see in Table 10.3, about one-third of Kenya's public debt is held as short-term treasury bills, and the debt servicing costs are high. Public expenditures on domestic interest payments are projected to total Ksh 39 billion in fiscal year 2006–07. In addition, as Table 10.3 also shows, the domestic private banks hold nearly half of all Kenya's public debt. This creates a potential constraint on extending credit for other uses, such as the targeted

Table 10.3 Composition of Kenyan Government Debt as of December 31, 2006 (figures are in billions of Ksh and percentages of total Ksh 372 billion debt)

	Treasury bills (short-term instruments)	Treasury bonds (long-term instruments)	Total govern-ment debt (bills + bonds)
Commercial banks	38.3	115.1	153.9
	(10.4%)	(30.9%)	(41.3%)
Central bank	35.5	0	35.5
	(9.5%)	(0%)	(9.5%)
Parastatals	9.5	23.8	33.3
	(2.6%)	(6.4%)	(8.9%)
All others	50.4	99.1	149.5
	(13.5%)	(26.6%)	(40.2%)
TOTALS	134.2	238.0	372.2
	(36.1%)	(63.9%)	(100%)

Source: Central Bank of Kenya.

credit policies we have proposed. Banks have an incentive to hold relatively risk-free public securities instead of riskier loans, particularly when the yield on government treasury bills is relatively high. Finally, it is also true that a very large domestic deficit is a prime factor that leads to bouts of hyperinflation.[4]

However, relatively modest increases in debt will not, in themselves, induce hyperinflation or any approximation to it. The Kenyan fiscal budget is presently under control, and it would remain under control even if, at least over a period of two to three years, the Treasury were to maintain borrowing at a level of around 2 percent as opposed to cutting back to 0.8 percent of GDP. At the same time, the introduction of new, longer-term maturity bonds would improve the capacity for fiscal financial management. Specifically, lengthening the maturity structure of the public debt could lower recurrent servicing costs over time by reducing the need to constantly turn over the public debt.

EXTERNAL SOURCES OF INCREASED FUNDING

Increased External Borrowing

According to the National Treasury, Kenya's total outstanding external debt stock currently stands at approximately 23.1 percent of GDP. Debt servicing payments are budgeted at around Ksh 6.6 billion for the 2006–07 fiscal year

(Government of Kenya 2006a). Although Kenya's external debt is considered to be sustainable relative to the country's level of exports, there are nevertheless sound reasons for Kenya to avoid increasing the dependence on foreign borrowing. Such borrowing exposes fiscal policy to the risk of exchange rate volatility that can dramatically influence debt servicing costs and add an additional element of uncertainty to budget planning processes. Although external debt servicing costs are not currently excessive, the stock of external debt is significant and could squeeze fiscal resources excessively in the future, given the potential variability in the costs of such credit.

Debt Relief

As mentioned earlier, Kenya's external debt is considered to be "sustainable" given the country's export performance. Therefore, Kenya was not included in the debt relief initiatives of the "Highly Indebted Poor Countries" (HIPC). External debt servicing costs are estimated to be between Ksh 6–7 billion annually over the next several years. Therefore, complete external debt relief would give the Kenyan government a modest amount of additional resources to use for developmental spending. Nevertheless, the decision to grant debt relief is not the decision of the Kenyan government. Therefore, there is no clear policy recommendation in this regard, other than a general advocacy for debt forgiveness. Success in this endeavor would, in any case, not generate a large additional flow of available public funds.

Overseas Development Assistance (ODA)

In recent years, donors had been reluctant to provide direct budget support to Kenya, primarily due to concerns about government corruption. They were rather providing support for specific projects, and channeling this support through non-government agencies. Such procedures were eroding the administrative capacity of Kenya's public sector. In addition, the level of assistance has fallen from around 8 percent of government expenditure in the mid-1990s to its current level of 5 percent.

In September 2007, 17 donor countries and the Kenyan government announced a major shift in policy. Under what is termed the Kenya Joint Assistance Strategy 2007–12, the major donors agreed to resume channeling most of their donor assistance directly through the Kenyan Treasury. This is a highly positive development, enabling government civil servants to administer projects directly. It is also expected that this measure will speed up the disbursement and use of aid funds and reduce their transaction costs.[5]

At least in the initial announcement of this policy shift, there was no mention of the level of donor assistance also increasing. Increased ODA in the form of direct budget support would certainly increase the resources available to implement the development strategies outlined in this report. However, ODA flows can be uncertain and volatile, undermining the budget planning process. Without a commitment to long-term ODA, governmental policy planning that assumes a particular level of assistance remains speculative.

Like debt relief, increased ODA does not represent a policy decision to be taken by the Kenyan Government. The Kenyan developmental planning process will certainly be enhanced by the new Joint Assistance Strategy. At the same time, without long-term commitments to increased ODA levels, the Kenyan government should assume that increases in long-term funding are likely to be modest.

NOTES

1. Government of Kenya 2006a, pp. 19-20.
2. See the discussions in McKinley 2007 on sub-Saharan Africa in general and Weeks and McKinley 2006 on Zambia.
3. The straight line trending upward in the diagram is the slope of the bivariate regression of the domestic debt/GDP ratio, the explanatory variable, on per capita GDP growth, the dependent variable.
4. Bruno and Easterly (1998) carefully document this point.
5. Justus Ondari, "Kenya Signs Joint Aid Strategy," *Daily Nation*, September 11, 2007.

11. A Restatement of Goals and Strategies

The purpose of this study, as we have emphasized throughout, is to outline a workable set of policies for greatly expanding decent employment opportunities in Kenya. Promoting decent employment is the single most effective tool for Kenya to achieve the United Nations' Millennium Development Goals (MDGs) for poverty reduction and, more generally, to spread prosperity in Kenya widely. The study ranges over a large number of topics and proposals. It is therefore especially important to see how these various proposals come together to advance this basic end of expanding decent employment.

Kenya does have a serious problem of unemployment, with 10.4 percent of labor market participants unemployed in 2005–06. But as we have stressed in this study, the more serious problem is that a majority of Kenyans in the workforce are employed—in most cases working more than 40 hours per week—and still living at or near the official poverty line. Unfortunately, the data available to us to support this view does not include income figures from the 2005–06 KIHBS on the 50 percent of the labor force engaged in agricultural self-employment. But it is likely that average income levels for the agricultural self-employed are at or below the average income level of the 35 percent of working Kenyans employed in the informal sector.

The single most important need in Kenya therefore is to raise income levels for those who are working. This can be done through several channels. The ones on which we focus on this study are:

1. increasing the number of available formal sector jobs;
2. raising productivity levels for existing areas of employment, in agriculture as well as both the informal and formal sectors. The main channel for achieving higher productivity is to increase the levels of both public and private investment;
3. expanding the size of the domestic and foreign markets for goods and services produced by Kenyans;
4. improving access to both domestic and foreign markets, for large-scale and small businesses; and

5. maintaining decent labor standards as well as cooperation arrangements between business and labor through institutions to deal with issues such as inflation control and the costs of regulation.

These priority channels for expanding decent employment in Kenya are reflected in the spending priorities we have proposed for the government. This includes, for example, our proposal to significantly increase spending on roads and water infrastructure beyond the levels of growth that the government has already budgeted. As we have seen with these proposals, the increased spending will itself create roughly 350,000 formal sector jobs, paying an average of Ksh 5,000 per month. At the same time, these investments will promote significant improvements in productivity, beginning with the rural areas, where roughly half of Kenya's labor force now resides.

However, improving productivity does not in itself raise incomes. For the self-employed—either in agriculture, or in informal or formal non-agricultural enterprises—they must also be able to sell the larger yield from this rise in productivity. This is why increased government extension services, marketing cooperatives, and an expansion of grain storage facilities are all necessary. They are all ways of expanding opportunities for the self-employed and other businesses to succeed in marketing.

For workers who are employees receiving wage income, it also does not automatically hold that improvements in productivity will lead to higher incomes. We have noted the situation within the horticultural export sector where firms are evidently operating at a globally competitive level of productivity, yet workers, at least at some firms, are still paid poverty-level wages. Improvements in productivity must therefore be shared equitably among workers and owners. This point reinforces the significance of decent labor standards and, as appropriate, union representation for workers.

Note here that a virtuous cycle can be formed around these policy measures. Raising productivity and better market access can lead to broadly-shared improvements in incomes. Workers with higher incomes will then create an expanding domestic market, since they will have more money to spend on raising their living standards. The expanding domestic market will produce more employment.

The other major area that we have proposed for increased expenditure is for government to make credit much more affordable for businesses of all sizes, including informal household enterprises. The principal idea is for the large commercial banks to form business alliances with microfinance enterprises, with loans from the commercial banks to the microenterprises guaranteed to a substantial degree—up to 75 percent—by the government. We have worked out in Chapter 9 the details as to how much such a program would cost, operating at a very large scale within Kenya's economy. We have also discussed measures that can establish controls within the program to minimize corruption.

This program should also create virtuous cycles of business expansion, employment expansion, and market expansion. Thus, the commercial banks will be given new market opportunities. They will be able to operate in the market for small-scale loans at substantially reduced levels of risk. Kenya's already extensive system of microfinance enterprises will then also be able to expand, given their much larger base of loanable funds. As we have seen, at present, household enterprises begin with virtually no access to credit from any kind of lending institution. This greatly restricts their capacity to operate at a size large enough to be productive. Under the program we have outlined, these businesses should have much greater access to credit. They can thereby grow faster and their average earnings will increase. Employment and the domestic market both expand as a result.

Beyond our proposals for increased government spending, we have also proposed measures for creating a macroeconomic environment that is more conducive to expanding decent employment. Formally speaking, macroeconomic policy in Kenya is still focused on maintaining an inflation target of 5 percent. As we have seen, in practice, this 5 percent inflation target has been achieved only once in the past ten years. At the same time, in the past two years, real GDP growth has averaged a relatively healthy 6 percent per year while inflation has remained a bit over 10 percent.

We support what appears to be a more defacto expansionary approach being practiced by Kenya's monetary authorities. If the authorities had insisted on pushing the inflation rate below 5 percent, even while energy and food price shocks have been the major source of the economy's inflationary pressures, this would have certainly led to slower real growth and a less favorable employment situation. At the same time, as long as access to credit remains highly restricted—indeed virtually out of reach for small enterprises—the fact that monetary policy is more expansionary will not itself create adequate new borrowing opportunities for small businesses and agricultural enterprises. This is why government policy needs to combine a more expansionary monetary policy with a large-scale program of targeted credit allocation.

We have also argued that Kenya does have significant new opportunities for expanding its export markets. Significant successes have already been attained in areas such as tea and horticulture. But a targeted exchange rate could be an important tool for diversifying Kenya's export base. In particular, Kenya is at present a net exporter within Africa. Kenyan business firms of all sizes should be able to build on this within the framework of a supportive exchange rate regime, operating in conjunction with the productivity-enhancing public investments and credit programs we have outlined.

Overall then, we hold that decent employment in Kenya can be greatly expanded as long as the country's economic policies are focused directly on that aim and these policies are implemented with care. Of course, other concerns must also be addressed. Inflation needs to be held within a reasonable range, roughly, as we have said before, within or close to single digits. Business costs and regulations cannot be made burdensome. The government cannot operate with excessive fiscal deficits. Programs need to be designed in ways that hold corruption in check, as has been done by the Kenya Roads Board with the country's road maintenance program. But none of these concerns are positively focused on expanding decent employment. These concerns should therefore all be seen as supplemental features of a broader program whose overarching focus is expanding decent employment.

Finally, as we have discussed, expanding decent employment in Kenya will be the single most effective means for the country to meet its Millennium Development Goals, particularly with regard to poverty reduction. This will happen because more decent employment opportunities will, first of all, mean higher incomes for families. It will also mean more government revenues, enabling more domestic funds to be devoted to fighting hunger and extreme poverty, universalizing primary education, equalizing opportunities for women, and improving health outcomes.

Appendix 1: Earnings Function for Household Enterprises

We estimated an earnings function for household enterprises based on the KIHBS. For all the earnings functions, the natural logarithm of estimated monthly earnings was the dependent variable. Monthly earnings were calculated as the total estimated monthly revenues minus total estimated monthly costs for the month prior to the survey. In cases where actual earnings in the previous month were estimated to be negative, usual monthly earnings (based on the prior six months) were used instead. The estimates of the earnings functions reported here are conditional on the household enterprise reporting positive earnings.

Table A1.1 lists all the independent variables used in the earnings functions with a brief description of each one. Table A1.2 presents the estimated coefficients for the earnings function. Estimates for two equations are shown in the table. Equation 1 presents estimates for an earnings function that includes all the independent variables listed in Table A1.1. Equation 2 presents similar estimates, but drops certain variables based on their statistical significance. In some cases, statistically insignificant variables are retained in Equation 2 because of the number of household enterprises that exhibit that particular characteristic. The earnings functions include a number of dummy variables. The default represents a household enterprise for which all the dummy variables take on a value of zero (e.g. an informal enterprise managed by a male outside of the manufacturing and service sectors whose start up capital came from a different source from those sources listed in Table A1.1). P-values, showing the statistical significance of the estimates, are included in the table.

The results can be summarized as follows. The earnings of formal household enterprises remain higher than informal enterprises, controlling for other factors. Earnings tend to grow with the number of paid employees. Access to financing through a SACCO appears to increase earnings. More highly educated managers earn more than less educated operators of household enterprises, all other factors being equal. A gender bias in earnings is evident in the sense that women who operate household enterprises earn less than men. Manufacturing enterprises generate less income compared to other types of enterprises. Household enterprises that have forged links with the formal business sector—i.e. the domestic business sector is their main market—enjoy higher earnings.

Table A1.1 Independent variables used in the estimation of household enterprise earnings functions

Variable	Description
Formal	Whether the enterprise is registered
Employees	Number of paid employees
Manufacturing	Enterprise is in the manufacturing sector
Services	Enterprise is in the service sector
Export market	Enterprise sells primarily on export markets
Consumer market	Enterprise sells primarily on consumer markets
Business market	Enterprise sells primarily to domestic businesses
Government market	Enterprise sells primarily to government
Longevity	How long the business has been operating
Family workers	Number of unpaid contributing family workers
Capital: savings	Start-up capital from savings
Capital: family	Start-up capital from family member
Capital: SACCO	Start-up capital from SACCO
Capital: asset sale	Start-up capital from the sale of an asset
Capital: bank	Start-up capital from a commercial bank
Capital: money lender	Start-up capital from a money lender
Contingent	Enterprise is seasonal/not steady activity
Manager's sex	0=manager is male, 1=manager is female
Manager's age	Age of the manager
Age squared	Age of the manager squared
Manager's education	Years of schooling

Table A1.2 Estimated coefficients for the household enterprise earnings function (dependent variable: logarithm of monthly earnings, P-values in parentheses)

	Equation 1		Equation 2	
Constant	6.3	(<0.01)	6.47	(<0.01)
Formal	0.63	(<0.01)	0.62	(<0.01)
Employees	0.08	(<0.01)	0.08	(<0.01)
Manufacturing	-0.62	(<0.01)	-0.64	(<0.01)
Services	-0.17	(0.15)	-0.16	(0.18)
Export market	-1.78	(0.16)		
Consumer market	0.06	(0.84)		
Business market	0.36	(0.22)	0.31	(0.02)
Government market	1.75	(0.24)	1.47	(0.33)
Longevity	0.00	(0.45)		
Family workers	0.05	(0.38)		
Capital: savings	0.16	(0.11)	0.16	(0.09)
Capital: family	0.13	(0.22)	0.15	(0.16)
Capital: SACCO	0.59	(<0.01)	0.60	(<0.01)
Capital: asset sale	-0.03	(0.85)	-0.03	(0.85)
Capital: bank	0.10	(0.77)		
Capital: money lender	0.16	(0.65)		
Contingent	0.92	(<0.01)	0.89	(<0.01)
Manager's sex	-0.61	(<0.01)	-0.59	(<0.01)
Manager's age	0.01	(0.47)		
Age squared	0.00	(0.25)		
Manager's education	0.08	(<0.01)	0.09	(<0.01)
N	3,546		3,546	
R-squared (adjusted)	0.23		0.22	

Appendix 2: Supply Shock Inflation

Sometimes a distinction is made between "headline inflation" (i.e. the rate of increase of the overall CPI) and "core inflation" (i.e. the rate of increase of the CPI excluding food and energy components). It is unclear that this distinction is overly useful in the Kenyan context. First, food and energy comprise a large fraction of the consumption basket of households in Kenya, particularly low-income households. After excluding these components, the remaining components of CPI may not give socially meaningful measurements of inflation. Second, shocks to food and energy prices may cause price increases for the other components of the CPI. Therefore, it is unclear that measures of "core inflation" actually remove the effects of food and energy prices.

It is useful to see how a shock to one component of the CPI affects other components. For example, how do food price shocks affect other prices in the economy? Are these effects transitory or long-lived?

We used a Vector Autoregression (VAR) model to examine how an exogenous shock to one component of the Kenyan CPI affects other prices in the economy. Price indices for ten expenditure categories were used: food, beverages and tobacco, clothing and footwear, housing, energy, household goods and services, medical goods and services, transportation, education and recreation, and personal goods and services. Monthly price data from January 1991 to December 2005 were included in the analysis. The National Bureau of Statistics kindly supplied the relevant data.

The price indices of the ten components are non-stationary. Therefore, the first differences of the log transformation of the components are used in the analysis.[1] Sequential modified likelihood ratio tests suggest that a lag length of 11 months is appropriate for our VAR specification. We used the estimated VAR model to trace the impacts of an exogenous price shock to one of the CPI components on all the other CPI components. These "impulse responses" are calculated using generalized impulses over 24 months. Asymptotic standard errors are estimated for the impulse responses.

Figure A2.1 shows the impulse response analysis associated with a one-standard deviation shock to the rate of increase of food prices. Note that the responses to the initial impulse are cumulative over the 24 month period. To avoid clutter, only the responses of food, clothing, housing, energy, personal services, and transporta-

Figure A2.1 Accumulated Response to Generalized One Standard Deviation Innovations—Food Prices (± 2 Standard Errors)

Accumulated Responses Are Over 24 Quarters

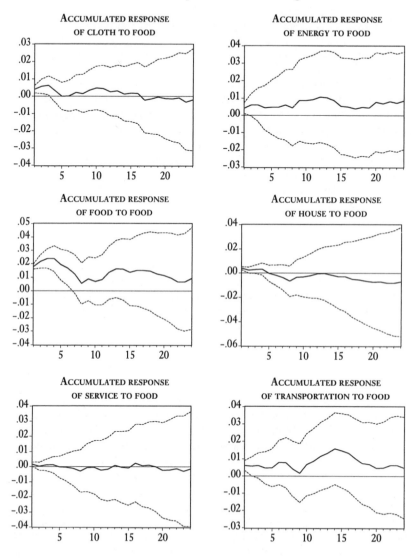

tion are shown.[2] Interestingly, food price shocks appear to have few systematic effects on inflation rates in the rest of the economy. Even within the food sector itself, the cumulative impact of the shock to food price inflation dwindles significantly after two years. The only other sector that shows any significant response to an exogenous increase in food prices is the transportation sector. Food price shocks—a relevant issue given the recent drought—appear to be fairly transitory with little systemic impact on inflationary dynamics in Kenya.

The picture is different if we consider energy price shocks. Figure A2.2 presents the response to a one-standard deviation shock to the rate of increase of energy prices. A once-off energy inflation shock raises the inflation rates of the other CPI components and these higher inflation rates are often sustained over time. Only food and housing inflation appears to be transitory after 24 months, returning more or less to their initial levels prior to the energy shock.

In addition to food and energy prices, shocks to transportation costs have systemic effects on other prices in the Kenyan economy. Figure A2.3 illustrates the impact of a once-off, one standard deviation shock to the inflation rate of transportation costs. Note that the index of transportation prices includes both fuel and non-fuel components. A transportation price shock unleashes inflationary pressures throughout Kenya's economy. Not only does the once-off shock raise inflation rates of other components of the CPI, the shock also appears to lead to accelerating inflation, even after two years, in certain cases – e.g. clothing and services. This analysis suggests that lowering transportation costs will contribute to sustainable lower inflation rates over all.

From this analysis, it appears that although food price shocks have a direct impact on headline inflation in the short run, they tend to be transitory with little or no long-run systemic effect. Energy price shocks do appear to have a more sustained, systemic impact on inflation in Kenya.

NOTES

1. The first difference of the log transformed variables corresponds to the percent change of these variables—or the inflation rates of the individual components of the CPI.
2. The impulse responses of other components of the Kenyan CPI do not differ significantly from those featured in Figures A2.1–A2.3.

Figure A2.2 Accumulated Response to Generalized One Standard Deviation Innovations—Energy Prices (± 2 Standard Errors)

Accumulated Responses Are Over 24 Quarters

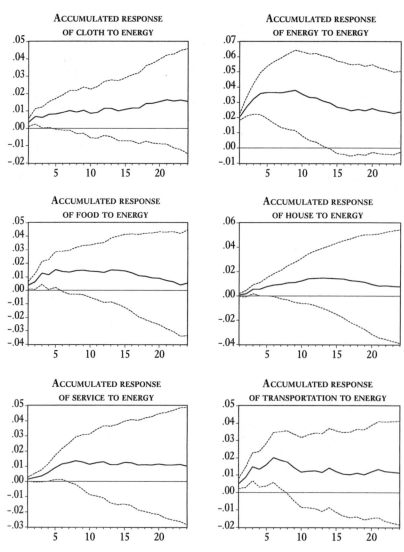

Figure A2.2 Accumulated Response to Generalized One Standard Deviation Innovations—Transportation Prices (± 2 Standard Errors)

Accumulated Responses Are Over 24 Quarters

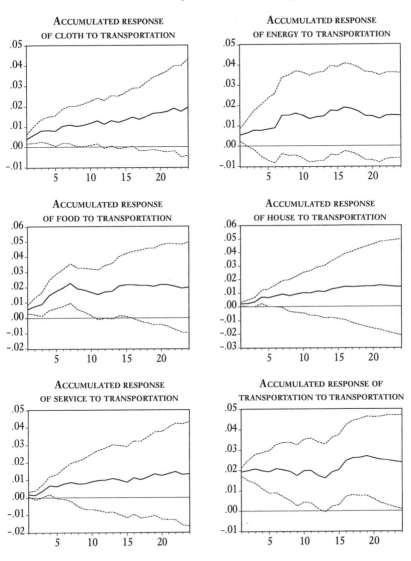

Appendix 3: Exchange Rate Overvaluation Model

We use two different methods for assessing the degree of potential exchange rate misalignment in Kenya: (1) the price parity approach; and (2) econometric estimates of long-run exchange rate equilibria. Both methods have advantages and disadvantages. Therefore, it is useful to use both techniques and compare the results.

We begin with the price parity method for evaluating exchange rate misalignment. Price parity approaches compare domestic prices, expressed in foreign currencies, to the average foreign price level. If exchange rates adjust perfectly to eliminate price differentials, then the exchange rate can be said to be at the correct level. If foreign prices are high relative to domestic prices, the exchange rate may be undervalued. If, on the other hand, foreign prices are low relative to domestic prices, the exchange rate would tend to be overvalued.

Figure A3.1 compares the natural logarithm of the foreign price level to that of domestic prices expressed in foreign currency. Trade-weighted measures of foreign prices and the nominal exchange rate are used to compute the two series. The series are adjusted so that their means over the time period illustrated are identical. Figure A3.1 suggests that, following liberalization, the shilling has become modestly overvalued. Interestingly, during the period in which exchange rates were managed, the exchange rate appears to have been more competitive. Since the means of the two series depicted in Figure A3.1 are the same, we are implicitly assuming that, on average over this period, the exchange rate was at its "correct" level. This assumption may not hold. However, if the exchange rate were overvalued on average throughout this period, then the extent of overvaluation post-liberalization would be more severe than is indicated in Figure A3.1.

The price parity comparison of foreign and domestic prices may not accurately represent the degree of exchange rate misalignment. This is because the price of non-tradables may increase at different rates in Kenya and in the country's major trading partners. Specifically, Balassa (1964) suggests that faster rates of productivity growth may raise the price of non-tradables (largely through improvements in the real wage) and lead to a decline in the measured real exchange rate. When Balassa effects are present, observed real exchange rate appreciations may simply reflect productivity improvements and not an inappropriate exchange rate.

Figure A3.2 examines whether Balassa effects are a significant concern in Kenya. The graph shows changes in relative productivity between Kenya and a trade-weighted average of the productivity of its three largest trading partners. These pro-

Figure A3.1 Average Foreign Price Level and Domestic Prices in Kenya, Adjusted by the Nominal Exchange Rate, 1980–2005

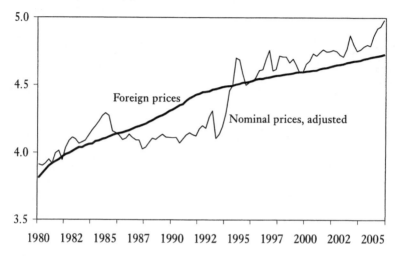

Source: Authors' calculations based on International Monetary Fund (2007a) and (2007b), and World Bank (2005b).

ductivity changes are compared with changes in the real exchange rate index, presented in the main text. Real per capita income (PPP-adjusted) is used to proxy for productivity in the relevant countries.

Figure A3.2 casts doubt on the existence of strong Balassa effects in Kenya. Throughout the period, Kenya's productivity growth lagged behind that of its major trading partners. If Balassa effects were operating in Kenya, this should have led to a relative decline in the price of non-tradables and a depreciation of the real exchange rate. The real exchange rate did depreciate in the 1980s. However, the exchange rate shows a marked appreciation in the 1990s following liberalization, even though the productivity differential widens relative to the earlier period. If Balassa effects are present and strong in Kenya, this suggests that the real exchange rate has been even more overvalued in recent years than the price parity measure would suggest. However, it is likely that Balassa effects are relatively weak or even non-existent in Kenya—that is, wages and the price of non-tradables are not closely linked to productivity trends.

Improvements in labor productivity may have a positive effect on real exchange rates (i.e. lead to a depreciation) if higher productivity lowers unit labor costs and leads to lower prices for non-tradables relative to tradables. This is likely to happen when wages are not sensitive to changes in productivity, as appears to be the case in Kenya.

Price parity techniques provide one approach for evaluating the extent of misalignment. However, there are problems with these methods. Perhaps most sig-

Figure A3.2 Changes in Kenya's Real Exchange Rate and Difference in Productivity Growth between Kenya and Major Trading Partners, 1983–2003 (three-year moving average)

Source: Authors' calculations based on International Monetary Fund (2007a) and (2007b), and World Bank (2005b).

nificantly, the methodology assumes that the "correct" value of the real exchange rate does not change over time or, alternatively, follows a deterministic time trend (Chinn 2005).[1] An alternative way of measuring the degree of exchange rate misalignment is to specify and estimate the relationships between the long-run real exchange rate and its determinants. The degree of misalignment can then be measured as a deviation from this equilibrium level. This technique is often called single equation time series econometric estimation (see Edwards 2001, for a more detailed discussion).

We develop such a model for Kenya. The variables typically identified as determinants of the long-run equilibrium real exchange rate include: interest rates (global and domestic), cross-border transfer payments, productivity growth, the terms of trade, and various policy variables, e.g. government spending, taxes and subsidies (Edwards 1989). The model we develop for Kenya incorporates variables that represent these various influences. Price indices of coffee, tea, and petroleum are used to capture terms of trade effects. The measurement of productivity differentials with Kenya's major trading partners has already been described. The real interest rate differential between 3-month t–bills in Kenya and the U.S. is used to assess differences in global and domestic interest rates. Net current transfers, normalized by GDP, are used to measure cross-border transfer payments. Finally, the fiscal balance as a percent of GDP, seasonally adjusted, enters as a policy variable. Table A3.1 presents a summary of the variables used.

Table A3.1 Variable Definitions Used in the Estimate of the Equilibrium Real Exchange Rate

Variable name	Description
rer	Kenyan real exchange rate index (as described in the text)
coffee	Commodity price index, coffee, New York
tea	Commodity price index, tea, London
petrol	Commodity price index, spot market, average crude price
t-bill gap	Differential between the real interest rates on U.S. and Kenyan 3-month treasury bills
prod dif	Difference in the productivity growth rate between Kenya and its major trading partners (as described in the text)
budget	Budget surplus(+)/deficit(-) as a percent of GDP
transfer	Cross-border transfers as a percent of GDP

In single-equation time series models, the long-run equilibrium relationship between the real exchange rate and its determinants is estimated as a cointegrating relationship among the variables. Variables must be integrated of the same order, if the existence of a cointegrating relationship is to be established. Unit root tests of the variables in Table A3.1 show that all variables are integrated of the first order with the sole exception of the budget surplus/deficit, which is stationary.[2]

Equation 1 of Table A3.2 presents OLS estimates of the cointegrating relationship between all the variables that are integrated of the first order.[3] A cointegrating relationship exists if a linear combination of the non-stationary variables is itself stationary. Unit root tests of the residuals from equation 1 show no indication of a unit root. Therefore, the OLS coefficient estimates can be taken as estimates of the cointegrating relationship (i.e. the long-run equilibrium relationship). The coefficients on two of the variables, tea prices and current transfers, are not statistically significant. These variables are dropped from the estimation and equation 2 of Table A3.2 presents the resulting estimates of the long-run cointegrating relationship.

The coefficient on coffee prices is negative, but its statistical significance is marginal. Nevertheless, this suggests that substantial increases in coffee prices— a major export—may result in "Dutch disease" effects, causing an appreciation of the equilibrium real exchange rate. The coefficient on petroleum prices is also negative. Increases in petroleum raise the average price level and overall rates of inflation in Kenya. These inflationary pressures contribute to a real exchange rate appreciation.

The coefficient on the interest rate differential is negative, as expected. Higher domestic interest rates relative to foreign rates attract short-term capital inflows and lead to an appreciation of the shilling. Interestingly, the coefficient on the productivity differential is positive and highly significant. This suggests that, contrary to the predictions of Balassa (1964), higher rates of productivity growth in Kenya relative to its trading partners, improves competitiveness by reducing unit

Table A3.2 Estimates of the Long-Run Cointegrating Relationship Between the Real Exchange Rate and its Determinants

Variable	Equation 1		Equation 2	
rer_{t-1}	0.764	(p<0.001)	0.785	(p<0.001)
$coffee_t$	-0.018	(0.093)	-0.011	(0.135)
tea_t	-0.016	(0.700)		
$petrol_{t-1}$	-0.101	(0.004)	-0.098	(0.003)
t-bill gap_{t-1}	-0.147	(0.015)	-0.164	(0.004)
prod dif_t	4.579	(0.001)	4.972	(p<0.001)
$transfer_{t-1}$	-2.231	(0.334)		
constant	44.206	(p<0.001)	36.620	(4.860)
adj. - R^2	0.87	0.87		
Durbin-Watson	1.83	1.83		
Dickey Fuller unit root test of residuals	-8.76	(p<0.001)	-8.75	(p<0.001)

Note: Dependent variable: real exchange rate index, p-values in parentheses.
Source: Quarterly data, 1980–2003.

production costs (and, by implication, prices), leading to a depreciation of the real exchange rate.

To estimate the long-run equilibrium real exchange rate, we use the model estimated in equation 2, Table A3.2. The independent variables included in the model are themselves subject to short-run shocks and fluctuations. Therefore, we use a Hodrik-Prescott filter to generate estimates of the long-run trends for each of the independent variables. We then use the estimated model to generate values for the equilibrium real exchange rate and compare them to the actual real exchange rate index. Both series are illustrated in FigureA3.3.[4]

The difference between the actual and equilibrium exchange rates gives us a measure of the extent of exchange rate misalignment. If the actual rate falls below the equilibrium level, the exchange rate is overvalued. If the actual rate lies above the equilibrium, it is undervalued. Therefore, subtracting the actual value from the equilibrium value, and expressing the difference as percent of the equilibrium exchange rate gives us a measure of overvaluation (i.e. the higher the number, the greater the overvaluation). Figure A3.4 presents estimates of the degree to which the Kenyan shilling is overvalued.

The single equation estimates of overvaluation look remarkably similar to the patterns of overvaluation indicated by the price parity technique. If we take the difference between the measure of domestic prices, adjusted by the nominal exchange rates, and the measure of foreign prices generated by the price parity analysis as an indicator of overvaluation, the correlation coefficient between the two estimates of overvaluation is 0.84. The fact that two very different approaches to measuring the

Figure A3.3 Actual Real Exchange Rate Index and Estimates of the Equilibrium Exchange Rate, 1980–2005

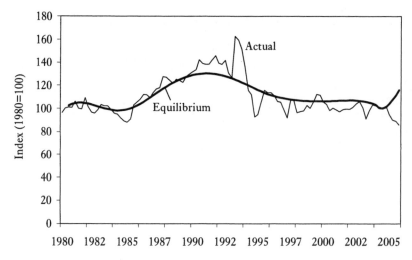

Source: Authors' calculations based on International Monetary Fund (2007a) and (2007b), and World Bank (2005b).

degree of misalignment produce very similar estimates reinforces our confidence in the analysis of exchange rate dynamics in Kenya.

Many of the observations made with regard to the price parity analysis hold true for the single-equation estimates of overvaluation. That is, when exchange rates were managed by a crawling peg regime, the actual exchange rate remained at a more competitive level (i.e. closer to its equilibrium value) when compared to the post-liberalization period. This conclusion is reinforced by the observation that the large nominal devaluation, prior to liberalization, produced only a temporary real de-valuation. The real exchange rate returned quickly to its earlier levels, suggesting that the real exchange rate was more or less in equilibrium prior to the devalua-tion.

TRADE AND EXCHANGE RATE MODEL

In order to better understand the determinants of Kenyan imports and exports, we estimated an export function and an import function for the economy as a whole. The specifications of these functions follow standard economic theory. The export function is given by:

$$x_t = \alpha_0 + \alpha_1 x_{t-1} + \alpha_2 \varepsilon_t + \alpha_3 p_t^x + \alpha_4 y_t^f + \mu_t$$

Figure A3.4 Estimate of the Extent of Overvaluation (percent), 1980–2005

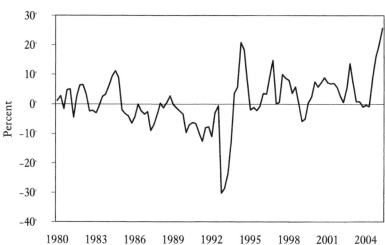

Source: Authors' calculations based on International Monetary Fund (2007a) and (2007b), and World Bank (2005b).

in which ε represents the real exchange rate, p^x the price of major export commodities, y^f aggregate income in Kenya's major trading partners over the period examined (U.K., U.S., and Germany), and μ is a stochastic error term. The import function is:

$$m_t = \beta_0 + \beta_1 m_{t-1} \beta_2 \varepsilon_t + \beta_3 p_t^m + \beta_4 y_t^k + \omega_t$$

in which ε is the real exchange rate, p^m the price of major imported commodities, y^k aggregate income in Kenya, and ω represents the stochastic error term for the import function.

Commodity prices of coffee and tea are included as the major export prices and world petroleum prices are used as the primary imported commodity. Real gross national income in Kenya's three largest trading partners is used to measure Kenya's potential export market. Similarly, Kenya's gross domestic product is used to indicate domestic national income. Exports and imports are measured by their U.S. dollar value as reported in the IMF's *Direction of Trade Statistics* database (2007b).

Several of the variables possess unit roots. Therefore, the variables are transformed and first differences of the natural logarithms are used in the estimations. In addition, a dummy variable is added to the model to control for the pre- and post-liberalization period (using the fourth quarter of 1993 as the reference point). The functions are estimated with quarterly data from 1980 to 2003.

Table A3.3a Coefficient Estimates, Export Function (p-values in parentheses)

Variables	Coefficient	
x_{t-1}	-0.280	(0.008)
ε_t	0.252	(0.132)
ε_{t-1}	0.219	(0.190)
p_t^{coffee}	0.206	(0.009)
p_{t-1}^{coffee}	0.083	(0.303)
p_t^{tea}	0.079	(0.309)
p_{t-1}^{tea}	0.143	(0.070)
y_t^f	1.337	(0.346)
y_{t-1}^f	0.557	(0.696)
d_t	0.026	(0.188)
constant	-0.008	(0.658)
adj.-R^2	0.202	

Table A3.3b Wald test, Coefficient Sums (p-values in parentheses)

Variable	Elasticity	
ε	0.470	(0.039)
p^{coffee}	0.290	(0.002)
p^{tea}	0.222	(0.043)
y^f	1.893	(0.232)

Table A3.3a presents estimates of coefficients on the export function and Table A3.3b contains Wald coefficient tests to determine if the sums of the coefficients on the contemporaneous and lagged variables are statistically significant. Therefore, the estimates in Table A3.3b represent short-run export elasticities.

Along similar lines, Table A3.4a presents estimates of coefficients on the import function and Table A3.4b contains Wald coefficient tests to determine if the sums of the coefficients on the contemporaneous and lagged variables are statistically significant.

Table A3.4a Coefficient Estimates, Import Function (p-values in parentheses)

Variables	Coefficient	
m_{t-1}	-0.196	(0.050)
ε_t	-0.209	(0.225)
ε_{t-1}	-0.153	(0.381)
p_t^{petrol}	-0.097	(0.198)
p_{t-1}^{petrol}	0.173	(0.024)
y_t^k	2.137	(0.002)
y_{t-1}^k	-0.613	(0.390)
d_t	0.014	(0.498)
constant	-0.008	(0.565)
adj.-R^2	0.184	

Table A3.4b Wald Test, Coefficient Sums (p-values in parentheses)

Variable	Elasticity	
ε	-0.362	(0.122)
p^{petrol}	0.076	(0.445)
y^k	1.523	(0.028)

NOTES

1. In the price parity assessment of misalignment presented here, the implicit assumption is that the equilibrium exchange rate does not change over time and does not follow a deterministic trend. Unit root tests suggest that such an assumption is only partly true: the Kenyan real exchange rate series developed for this analysis does not follow a deterministic time trend but it is also non-stationary.
2. Augmented Dickey-Fuller tests were used to determine whether the variables are stationary or non-stationary (i.e. whether the series has a unit root or not). The hypothesis that a unit root exists could not be rejected, at the 1% level, for all the variables examined here except for the budget deficit as a percent of GDP. The first differences of the variables, however, showed no indication of possessing a unit root (at a significance level of 1%). Therefore, these variables are integrated of the first order.
3. In all cases, the lagged dependent variable (rert-1) is included as a regressor. Estimates of the model with both contemporaneous independent variables and independent variables lagged one period were generated (not shown). The lag structure in Table A3.2 was generated by retaining those variables with the greatest statistical significance.
4. The real exchange rate equilibrium model is estimated for the period 1980–2003. Estimates of the equilibrium exchange rate and the extent of misalignment for 2004 and 2005 represent out-of-sample forecasts.

Acronyms

ASCRA	Accumulating Savings and Credit Associations
CD	certificate of deposit
COMESA	Common Market for Eastern and Southern Africa
CPI	Consumer Price Index
EPZ	export processing zones
ERS	*Economic Recovery Strategy for Wealth and Employment Creation*
FAOSTAT	Food and Agriculture Organization (of the United Nations) Statistics
GDP	Gross Domenstic Product
HCDA	Horticultural Crops Development Authority
HIPC	Highly Indebted Poor Countries
ILO	International Labour Organization
IMF	International Monetary Fund
IPO	Initial Public Offering
ICDC	Industrial and Commercial Development Corporation
KACE	Kenya Agriculture Commodities Exchange
KARI	Kenya Agricultural Research Institute
KERUSSU	Kenya Rural Savings and Credit Societies Union
KCC	Kenya Cooperative Creameries
KFA	Kenya Farmers Association
KGGCU	Kenya Grain Growers Cooperative Union
KIHBS	Kenya Integrated Household Budget Survey
KMC	Kenya Meat Commission
KNBS	Kenya's National Bureau of Statistics
KPCU	Kenya Planters and Cooperative Union
KRB	Kenya Roads Board
KREP	Kenya Rural Enterprise Program
Ksh	Kenyan shillings
KTDA	Kenyan Tea Development Authority
MDG	UN Millennium Development Goals
MFI	microfinance institutions

MMFA   member-based micro finance agencies
MSE   micro and small enterprise(s)
MTBSP   medium-term budget strategy paper
ODA   Overseas Development Assistance
ROSCA   Rotating Savings and Credit Associations
SACCO   Savings and Credit Cooperatives
SME   Small and Medium-sized Enterprise
T&V   Training and Visit
UNDP   United Nations Development Programme
VAR   vector autoregression

Bibliography

Aidt, Toke and Zafiris Tzannatos (2002) *Unions and Collective Bargaining: Economic Effects in a Global Environment*, Washington DC: World Bank.

Aidt, Toke and Zafiris Tzannatos (2003) *Unions and Collective Bargaining: Economic Effects in a Global Environment*, Washington DC: World Bank.

Alby, Philippe, Jean-Paul Azam, and Sandrine Rospabé (2005) "Labor Institutions, Labor-Management Relations, and Social Dialogue in Africa," Washington, DC: World Bank.

Amsden, Alice (2001) *The Rise of "The Rest": Challenges to the West from late-industrializing economies*, Oxford and New York: Oxford University Press.

Argwings-Kodhek, Gem (2004) "Feast and Famine: Financial Services for Rural Kenya," Nairobi, Kenya: Tegemeo Institute of Agricultural Policy and Development.

Aryeetey, Ernest (2001) "Strengthening Ghana's Financial Market: An Integrated and Functional Approach," Legon, Ghana: Institute of Statistical, Social and Economic Research (ISSER).

Alatas, Vivi and Lisa Cameron (2003) "The Impact of Minimum Wages on Employment in a Low Income Country: An Evaluation Using the Difference-in-differences Approach," Policy Research Working Paper 2985, Washington, DC: World Bank.

Atieno, Rosemary (2001) "Formal and Informal Institutions' Lending Policies and Access to Credit by Small-Scale Enterprises in Kenya: An Empirical Assessment," AERC Research Paper 111, Nairobi: African Economic Research Consortium.

Baker, Dean (2003) "Tobin Taxes: Are They Enforceable?" in James Weaver, Randall Dodd, and Dean Baker, eds. *Debating the Tobin Tax: New Rules for Global Finance*, Washington, DC: New Rules for Global Finance Coalition.

Balassa, Bela (1964) "The purchasing power parity doctrine: a reappraisal," *Journal of Political Economy* 6: 584–96.

Bigsten, Arne (2002) "The History and Policy of Manufacturing in Kenya" in A. Bigsten and P. Kimuyu, eds. *Structure and Performance of Manufacturing in Kenya*, New York: Palgrave, pp. 7–30.

Bruno, Michael (1993) *Crisis, Stabilization, and Economic Reform: Therapy by Consensus*, Oxford: Clarendon Press.

Bruno, Michael (1995) "Does inflation really lower growth?" *Finance and Development* 3: 35–38.

Bruno, Michael and William Easterly (1998) "Inflation crises and long-run growth," *Journal of Monetary Economics*, 1: 3-26.

Burdekin, Richard C.K., Arthur T. Denzau, Manfred W. Keil, Thitithep Sitthiyot, and Thomas D. Willett (2004) "When does inflation hurt economic growth? Different nonlinearities for different economies," *Journal of Macroeconomics* 3: 519–32.

Calmfors, Lars (1993) "Centralization of wage bargaining and macroeconomic performance," *OECD Economic Studies* 21: 161–91.

Campbell, John and Tuomo Vuolteenaho (2004) "Inflation Illusion and Stock Prices," NBER Working Paper 10263, Cambridge, MA: National Bureau of Economic Research.

Central Bank of Kenya (2005) *Statistical Bulletin 2005*, Nairobi: Central Bank of Kenya.

Central Bank of Kenya (2006) *Statistical Bulletin 2006*, Nairobi: Central Bank of Kenya.

Central Bank of Kenya (various years) *Annual Report*, Nairobi: Central Bank of Kenya.

Chinn, Menzie (2005) "A Primer on Real Effective Exchange Rates: Determinants, Overvaluation, Trade Flows, and Competitive Devaluation," NBER Working Paper 11521, Cambridge, MA: National Bureau of Economic Research.

Cottani, Joaquin, Domingo Cavallo, and M. Khan (1990) "Real exchange rate behavior and economic performance in LDCs," *Economic Development and Cultural Change*, 1: 61–76.

Cukierman, Alex, Martin Rama, and Jan van Ours (2001) "Long-run Growth, the Minimum Wage and Other Labor Market Institutions," Unpublished paper.

Deaton, Angus (1999) "Commodity Prices and Growth in Africa," *Journal of Economic Perspectives*, 3: 23–40.

Dollar, David (1992) "Outward-oriented developing economies really do grow more rapidly: evidence from 95 LDCs, 1976–1985," *Economic Development and Cultural Change*, 3: 523–44.

Dornbusch, Rudiger and Stanley Fischer (1991) "Moderate Inflation," NBER Working Paper 3896, Cambridge, MA: National Bureau of Economic Research.

Easterly, William (2001) "The lost decades: developing countries' stagnation in spite of policy reform, 1980–98," *Journal of Economic Growth*, 2: 135–57.

Edwards, Sebastian (1989) "Exchange rate misalignment in developing countries," *World Bank Research Observer*, 1: 3–21.

Edwards, Sebastian (2001) "Exchange Rate Regimes, Capital Flows, and Crisis Prevention," NBER Working Paper 8529, Cambridge, MA: National Bureau of Economic Research.

Export Processing Zones Authority (EPZ) (2005) *Horticulture Industry in Kenya 2005*, Athi River, Kenya: EPZ.

Export Processing Zones Authority (EPZ) (2006) *Sugar Industry in Kenya 2006*, Athi River, Kenya: EPZ.

European Commission (2004) *Assessment of the Value Added Opportunities in the Kenyan Coffee Industry*, Nairobi, Kenya: European Commission.

Evans, Anna Cora and Geza Radu (2002) "The Unpaved Road Ahead: HIV/AIDS & Micro Finance. An Exploration of Kenyan Credit Unions (SACCOs)," World Council of Credit Unions Research Monograph 21, Madison, Wisconsin: World Council of Credit Unions.

Fafchamps, Marcel, Tyler Biggs, Jonathan Conning, and Pradeep Srivastava (1994) "Enterprise Finance in Kenya," draft, World Bank Regional Program on Enterprise Development, Africa Region.

Flanigan, Robert J. (1999) "Macroeconomic performance and collective bargaining: an international perspective," *Journal of Economic Literature*, 3: 1150–175.

Forteza, Alvaro and Martin Rama (2006) "Labor market 'rigidity' and the success of economic reforms across more than 100 countries," *The Journal of Policy Reform*, 1: 75–105.

Freeman, Richard (2005) "Labor market institutions without blinders: The debate over flexibility and labour market performance," *International Economic Journal*, 2: 129–145.

Freeman, Richard B. (1993) "Labor market institutions: Help or hindrance," *Proceedings of the World Bank Annual Conference on Development Economics*, Washington DC: World Bank.

Frenkel, Roberto and Lance Taylor (2005) "Real Exchange Rate, Monetary Policy, and Employment: Economic Development in a Garden of Forking Paths," paper presented at the conference *Alternatives to Inflation Targeting Monetary Policy for Stable and Egalitarian Growth in Developing Countries*, May 13–15, Buenos Aires: Centre for Studies on State and Society (CEDES).

Gala, Paulo and Claudio Lucinda (2006) "Exchange rate misalignment and growth: old and new econometric evidence," mimeo, São Paulo, Brazil: São Paulo School of Business Administration and São Paulo School of Economics.

Gautam, M. (2000) *Agricultural Extension: The Kenyan Experience*, Washington DC: World Bank.

Gautam, M. and J. Anderson (1999) "Reconsidering the Evidence on the Returns to T&V in Kenya," Working Paper, Washington DC: World Bank.

Gebeyehu, Worku (2000) "Does type of tenure impact on technical efficiency of farmers?," *Ethiopian Journal of Economics*, 1: 58–92.

Gerdin, Anders, (2002) "Productivity and Economic growth in Kenyan agriculture, 1964–1996," *Agricultural Economics*, 27: 7–13.

Ghosh, Atish and Steven Phillips (1998) "Warning: Inflation may be harmful to your growth," *International Monetary Fund Staff Papers* 4: 672–86.

Ghura, Dhaneshwar and Thomas Grennes (1993) "The real exchange rate and macroeconomic performance in sub-Saharan Africa," *Journal of Development Economics*, 1: 155–74.

Gĩthĩnji, M. and C. Perrings (1993) "Social and ecological sustainability in the use of biotic resources in Sub-Saharan Africa," *Ambio*, 2–3: 110–16.

Griffin, Keith (2003) "Problems of poverty and marginalization," *Indicators: The Journal of Social Health*, vol. 2, pp. 22–48.

Government of Kenya (1966) *Statistical Abstract 1966*, Nairobi: Kenya National Bureau of Statistics.

Government of Kenya (1977) *Statistical Abstract 1977*, Nairobi: Kenya National Bureau of Statistics.

Government of Kenya (1986) *Statistical Abstract 1986*, Nairobi: Kenya National Bureau of Statistics.

Government of Kenya (1989) *Rural Labour Force Survey 1988 Database.* Nairobi: National Bureau of Statistics.

Government of Kenya (1991) *Statistical Abstract 1991*, Nairobi: Kenya National Bureau of Statistics.

Government of Kenya (1996) *Statistical Abstract 1996*, Nairobi: Kenya National Bureau of Statistics.

Government of Kenya (1999) *Rural Labour Force Survey 1998 Database.* Nairobi: National Bureau of Statistics.

Government of Kenya (2002) *The New Kenya Consumer Price Index Users' Guide*, Nairobi: Kenya National Bureau of Statistics.

Government of Kenya (2003a) *Statistical Abstract 2003*, Nairobi: Kenya National Bureau of Statistics.

Government of Kenya (2003b) *Task Force Report on Coffee Marketing*, Nairobi: Ministry of Agriculture.

Government of Kenya (2003c) *Economic Recovery Strategy for Wealth and Employment Creation*, Nairobi: Ministry of Planning.

Government of Kenya (2004a) *Public Expenditure Review*, Nairobi: Government of Kenya.

Government of Kenya (2004b) *Strategy for the Revitalization of Agriculture: 2004–2014*, Nairobi: Kenyan Ministry of Agriculture & Ministry of Livestock and Fisheries Development.

Government of Kenya (2005b) *Poverty Reduction Strategy Paper*, Washington DC: International Monetary Fund.

Government of Kenya (2005c) *Summary of District Annual Reports*, Memo provided to the authors, Nairobi: Ministry of Cooperative Development.

Government of Kenya (2006a) *Medium-Term Budget Strategy Paper*, Nairobi: Ministry of Finance.

Government of Kenya (2006b) *Physical Infrastructure Sector Medium-Term Expenditure Framework Report, 2006/7–2008/9*, revised draft, Nairobi: Ministry of Finance.

Government of Kenya (2006c) *Economic Survey 2006*, Nairobi: Ministry of Planning.

Government of Kenya (2007a) *Basic Report on Poverty in Kenya*, Nairobi: Kenya National Bureau of Statistics.

Government of Kenya (2007b) *Labour Force Analytical Report*, unpublished draft, Nairobi: Kenya National Bureau of Statistics.

Grosh, B. (1991) *Public Enterprise in Kenya*, Boulder, Colorado: Lynne Reinner Press.

Heckman, James (2007) "Comments on 'Are protective labor market institutions really at the root of unemployment? A critical perspective on the statistical evidence, by David Howell, Dean Baker, Andrew Glyn, and John Schmidt,'" *Capitalism and Society*, 2(1).

Horticultural Crops Development Authority (HCDA) (2006) "Memo on Employment Led Growth," Nairobi: HCDA.

Horticultural Crops Development Authority (HDCA) (various years) *Export Statistics*, Nairobi: HCDA.

Holden, Stein and Hailu Yohannes (2002) "Land redistribution, tenure insecurity and intensity of production: a study of farm households in Southern Ethiopia," *Land Economics*, 4: 573–90.

Howell, David R., Dean Baker, Andrew Glyn, and John Schmitt (2006) "Are Protective Labor Market Institutions Really at the Root of Unemployment? A Critical Perspective on the Statistical Evidence," CEPR Reports and Issue Briefs 2006–14, Washington, DC: Center for Economic and Policy Research.

Hospes, Otto, Muli Musinga, and Milcah Ong'ayo (2002) "An Evaluation of Micro-Finance Programmes in Kenya as Supported through the Dutch Co-Financing Programme, with a Focus on KWFT," Study commissioned by the Steering Committee for the Evaluation of the Netherlands' Co-financing Programme.

Humphrey, J., N. McCulloch, and M. Ota (2004) "The impact of European market changes on employment in the Kenyan horticulture sector," *Journal of International Development*, 1: 63–80.

Husbands, Kaye G., Thomas Pinckney, and Tobias Konyango (1996) "Education and Agricultural Productivity in Kenya," in H. Bruton and C. Hill, eds. *The Evaluation of Public Expenditure in Africa*, Washington, DC: World Bank.

International Food Policy Research Institute (2004) *Assuring Food and Nutritional Security*, All Africa Conference Proceedings, Kampala, Uganda: IFPRI.

Infante, Ricardo, Andrés Marinakis, and Jacobo Velasco (2003) "Minimum Wage in Chile: An Example of the Potential and Limitations of this Policy Instrument," International Labour Organization Employment Paper 52, Geneva: ILO.

Institute for Economic Analysis (1998) *Our Problems Our Solutions,* Nairobi: IEA.

Institute of Economic Affairs (2000) "Reassessing Kenya's land reform," *The Point,* vol. 40.

International Labour Organization (1972) *Employment, Incomes, and Equality: A Strategy for Increasing Productive Employment in Kenya,* Geneva: ILO.

International Monetary Fund (2007a) *International Financial Statistics* CD-ROM (June), Washington, DC: International Monetary Fund.

International Monetary Fund (2007b) *Direction of Trade Statistics* CD-ROM (May), Washington, DC: International Monetary Fund.

Islam, Iyanatul and Suahasil Nazara (2000) "Minimum Wage and the Welfare of Indonesian Workers," International Labour Organization Occasional Discussion Paper, Jakarta: ILO.

Iversen, T., Jonas Pontusson, and David Soskice, eds. (2000) *Unions, Employers, and Central Banks,* Cambridge: Cambridge University Press.

Jayne, Thomas S., Takashi Yamano, and James Nyoro (2004) "Interlinked credit and farm intensification: evidence from Kenya," *Agricultural Economics,* 2–3: 209–218.

Jenkins, Rhys (2005) "Globalisation of production, employment, and poverty: three macromeso-micro studies," *European Journal of Development Research* 4: 601–25.

Khan, Mohsin S. and Abdelhak S. Senhadji (2001) "Threshold effects in the relationship between inflation and growth," *International Monetary Fund Staff Papers,* 1: 1–21.

Kimuyu, Peter, and John Omiti (2000) "Institutional Impediments to Access to Credit by Micro and Small Scale Enterprises in Kenya," Institute of Policy Analysis and Research Discussion Paper 26, Nairobi: IPAR.

Layard, Richard, Stephen Nickell, and Richard Jackman (1994) *The Unemployment Crisis,* Oxford and New York: Oxford University Press.

Layard, Richard, Stephen Nickell, and Richard Jackman (2005) *Unemployment: Macroeconomic Performance and the Labour Markets,* Oxford: Oxford University Press.

Lewis, Blane D. and Erik Thorbecke (1992) "District-level economic linkages in Kenya: evidence based on a small regional Social Accounting Matrix," *World Development* 6: 881-97.

Lewis, Jeffrey D. (2001) "Policies to Promote Growth and Employment in South Africa," World Bank Discussion Paper 16, Informal Discussion Papers on Aspects of the Economy of South Africa, Washington DC: World Bank Southern Africa Department.

Lindström, Susanna and Per Roonäs (2005) *An Integrated Economic Analysis for Pro-Poor Growth in Kenya,* Country Economic Report 8, Nairobi: Society for International Development.

Lofchie, Michael (1993) "Trading Places" in Thomas M. Callaghy and John Ravenhill, eds. *Hemmed in: Responses to Africa's Economic Decline,* New York: Columbia University Press.

Lustig, Nora and Darryl McLeod (1997) "Minimum Wages and Poverty in Developing Countries: Some empirical evidence" in Sebastian Edwards and Nora Lustig, eds. *Labor Markets in Latin America*, Washington, D.C.: Brookings Institution Press, pp. 62–103.

Manda, D.K. and K. Sen (2004) "The labour market effects of globalization in Kenya," *Journal of International Development*, 1: 29–44.

Manda, D.K., Arne Bigsten, and Germano Mwabu (2005) "Trade union membership and earnings in Kenyan manufacturing firms," *Applied Economics*, 15: 1693–704.

Marshall, Mike (1994) "Lessons from the Experience of the Swedish Model" in P. Arestis and M. Marshall, eds. *The Political Economy of Full Employment*, Aldershot: Edward Elgar.

Migott, Adhola *et al.* (1991) "Indigenous land rights in Sub Saharan Africa: constraint on productivity?" *World Bank Economic Review*, 5: 155–75.

Modigiliani, Franco and Richard Cohn (1979) "Inflation, rational valuation and the market," *Financial Analysts Journal*, 2: 24–44.

Montenegro, Claudio E. and Carmen Pagés (2003) "Who Benefits from Labor Market Regulations? Chile 1960–1998," NBER Working Paper 9850, Cambridge, MA: National Bureau of Economic Research.

Mude, Andrew (2006) "Imperfections in Membership Based Organizations of the Poor," Ph.D. manuscript, Cornell University.

Muendo, K.M. and D. Tschirley (2004) "Improving Kenya's Domestic Horticultural Production and Marketing Systems," Nairobi, Kenya: Tegemeo Institute of Agricultural Policy and Development.

Murithi, Muriuki "Postbank May Soon Give Loans in the Villages," *The Nation*, July 6, 2006, http://allafrica.com/stories/printable/200607060622.html.

Muriuki, H., A. Omore, N. Hooten, M. Waithaka, R. Ouma, S.J. Staal, and P. Odhiambo (2003) "The Policy Environment in the Kenya Dairy Sub-sector," SDP Research and Development Report 2, Nairobi: Smallholder Dairy Project.

Musila, Jacob Wanjala (2004) "The Common Market for Eastern and Southern Africa and Kenya's export trade," *International Journal of Social Economics*, 1–2: 67–77.

Nam, Sang-woo (1984) "Korea's Stabilization Efforts since the Late 1970s," Working Paper 8405, Korea Development Institute, OECD (Organisation for Economic Co-operation and Development).

Ndung'u, Njuguna (2000) "The exchange rate and monetary policy in Kenya," *African Development Review*, 1: 24–51.

Ndung'u, Njuguna and Rose Ngugi (1999) "Adjustment and liberalization in Kenya: the financial and foreign exchange markets," *Journal of International Development*, 3: 465–91.

Ngotho, Kamau (2005) "Kenya's wealth in foreign hands," *Sunday Standard*, April 5, Nairobi.

Ngugi, Rose (2000) "Financial reform process in Kenya," *African Development Review*, 1: 52–77.

Ngugi, Rose (2001) "An Empirical Analysis of Interest Rate Spread in Kenya," AERC Research Paper 106, Nairobi: African Economic Research Consortium.

Nissanke, Machiko and Ernest Aryeetey (1998) *Financial Integration and Development: Liberalization and Reform in sub-Saharan Africa*, London and New York: Routledge.

Nyoro, James (2002) "Agricultural and Rural Growth in Kenya," Nairobi, Kenya: Tegemeo Institute of Agricultural Policy and Development.

Nyoro, James and T.S. Jayne (1999) "Trends in Regional Agricultural Productivity in Kenya," Nairobi: Tegemeo Institute of Agricultural Policy and Development.

Obare, G. (2000). "The impacts of rural infrastructure on farm productivity in Nakuru District, Kenya," unpublished Ph.D. Dissertation, Egerton University.

Odhiambo, M.O., P. Kristanson, and J. Kashangaki (1996) *Comparative Costs of Production Analysis in East Africa*, Washington DC: AMEX International.

Omamo, S.W. (1998) "Transport costs and smallholder cropping choices: an application to Siaya District, Kenya," *American Journal of Agricultural Economics*, 1:116–23.

Omamo, S.W. and L. Mose (2001) "Fertilizer trade under market liberalization: Preliminary evidence from Kenya," *Food Policy*, 1:1–10.

Omolo, Jacob and John Omati (2004) "Is Minimum Wage Policy Effective in Kenya?," Institute of Policy Analysis and Research Discussion Paper 54, Nairobi: IPAR.

Ouma, J. (1989) *Development in Kenya through Co-operatives*, Nairobi: Shirikon Publishers.

Ouma, Shem., Dickson Khainga, Willia Wasala, and Jacob Oduor (2006) "Monetary Policy Reaction Function for Kenya," KIPRA Discussion Paper 58, Nairobi: Kenya Institute for Public Policy Research and Analysis.

Pekkarinen, P., M. Pohjola, and B. Rowthorn (1992) *Social Corporatism: A Superior Economic System?*, Oxford and New York: Oxford University Press.

Phillips, S.D., R.T. Mccutcheon, S.J. Emery, R. Little, and M.R. Kwesiga (1995) "Technical analysis of the employment creation potential of a National Public Works Programme," *Journal of the South African Institution of Civil Engineers*, 3: 18–24.

Pollin, Robert (2003) *Contours of Descent: U.S. Economic Fractures and the Landscape of Global Austerity*, New York and London: Verso Press.

Pollin, Robert (2006) "Globalization and the Transition to Egalitarian Development" in James Boyce, Stephen Cullenberg, Prasanta Pattanaik, and Robert Pollin, eds. *Human Development in the Era of Globalization*, Cheltenham, UK and Northampton, MA: Edward Elgar Publishing, 211–38.

Pollin, Robert, Gerald Epstein, James Heintz, and Leonce Ndikumana (2006) *An Employment-Targeted Economic Program for South Africa*, Brasilia: International Poverty

Centre of the United Nations Development Program and Cheltenham, UK and Northampton, MA: Edward Elgar Publishing.

Pollin, Robert and Marc Schaberg (1998) "Asset exchanges, financial market trading, and the M1 income velocity puzzle," *Journal of Post Keynesian Economics*, 1: 135–62.

Pollin, Robert and Andong Zhu (2006) "Inflation and economic growth: A cross-country non-linear analysis," *Journal of Post Keynesian Economics*, 4: 593–614.

Rama, Martin (2001) "The consequences of doubling the minimum wage: The case of Indonesia," *Industrial and Labor Relations Review*, 4: 864–81.

Reinhart, Carmen M. and Ioannis Tokatlidis (2003) "Financial liberalisation: the African experience," *Journal of African Economies*, 1: 53–88.

Rolfe, R.J., D.P. Woodward and B. Kagira (2004) "Footloose and tax free: incentive preferences in Kenyan export processing zones," *South African Journal of Economics*, 4: 784–807.

Sacerdoti, Emilio (2005) "Access to Bank Credit in Sub-Saharan Africa: Key Issues and Reform Strategies," IMF Working Paper 166, New York: International Monetary Fund.

Saget, Catherine (2001) "Is the Minimum Wage an Effective Tool to Promote Decent Work and Reduce Poverty? The experience of selected developing countries," ILO Employment Paper 13, Geneva: International Labour Organization.

Schwartz, August L. (1994) "The role of the private sector in agricultural extension," ODA Network Paper 94, London: Overseas Development Administration.

Shem Migot-Adholla, Peter Hazell, Benoît Blarel, and Frank Place (1991) "Indigenous land rights systems in Sub-Saharan Africa: a constraint on productivity?," *World Bank Economic Review*, 5(1):155–75.

Shiferaw, Bekele and Stein T. Holden (2001) "Farm-level benefits to investment for mitigating land degradation: empirical evidence from Ethiopia," *Environment and Development Economics*, 6: 335–358.

Stern, N.H. (1972) *An Appraisal of Tea Production on Small Holdings in Kenya*, Paris: OECD.

Teal, Francis (2000) "Real wages and the demand for skilled and unskilled male labour in Ghana's manufacturing sector, 1991–1995," *Journal of Development Economics*, 2: 447–61.

Tiffen, Mary, Michael Mortimore, and Francis Gickuki (1994) *More People, Less Erosion: Environmental Recovery in Kenya*, London: John Wiley and Sons.

United Nations Development Programme (2001) *Human Development Report 2001 Kenya*, Nairobi: UNDP.

US Department of Agriculture (2006) *Kenya Sugar Update 2006*, Gain Report KE6004, Washington, DC: USDA.

Wagacha, Mbui (2003) "Analysis of Liberalization and Economic Growth in Kenya" in M. Kimenyi, J.M. Mbaku, and N. Mwaniki, eds. *Restarting and Sustaining Economic Growth and Development in Africa*, Aldershot: Ashgate.

Wasike, W. (2001) "Road Infrastructure Policy in Kenya," KIPPRA Working Paper 58, Nairobi: Kenya Institute for Public Policy Research and Analysis.

Weeks, John and Terry McKinley (2006) "Does Debt Relief Increase Fiscal Space in Zambia?" United Nations Development Programme, International Poverty Centre, UNDP: Brazilia, Brazil.

World Bank (1995) *World Development Report 1995: Workers in an Integrating World*, New York: Oxford University Press.

World Bank (2005a) "Jobs in Kenya: Concept Note," Manuscript, Washington, DC: World Bank.

World Bank (2005b) *World Development Indicators*, Washington, DC: World Bank.

World Bank (2005c) *World Development Report: Workers in an Integrating World*, Washington, DC: World Bank.

World Bank (2007) *World Development Indicators*, CD-ROM, Washington, DC: World Bank.

Index

About the Authors

Robert Pollin (Project Director) is Professor in the Department of Economics and founding Co-Director of the Political Economy Research Institute at the University of Massachusdetts-Amherst. He received a Ph.D. in Economics from the New School for Social Research in New York City in 1982. His research centers on macroeconomics, conditions for low-wage workers in the U.S. and globally, and the analysis of financial markets. His recent books include *Contours of Descent: U.S. Economic Fractures and the Landscape of Global Austerity* (Verso 2003), *An Employment-Targeted Economic Program for South Africa* (co-authored, United Nations Development Program and Edward Elgar, 2006), *A Measure of Fairness: The Economics of Living Wages and Minimum Wages in the United States* (co-authored, Cornell University Press, 2008) and the edited volumes *The Macroeconomics of Saving, Finance, and Investment* (University of Michigan Press 1997), *Globalization and Progressive Economic Policy* (co-edited, Cambridge University Press 1998), and *Human Development in the Era of Globalization* (co-edited, Edward Elgar 2006). He has worked previously with the United Nations Development Program in South Africa and Bolivia. With James Heintz, he is now conducting research under commission with the UN Economic Commission on Africa (UNECA) on economic growth and the expansion of decent employment throughout sub-Saharan Africa. He consults extensively throughout the United States on the viability of "living wage" policies. He has previously worked with the Joint Economic Committee of the U.S. Congress and as a member of the Capital Formation Subcouncil of the U.S. Competitiveness Policy Council.

Mwangi wa Gīthīnji earned his Ph.D. from the University of California at Riverside in 1997. His primary interests are in the areas of Development Economics, Political Economy, and Environmental Economics with particular attention to Africa. He is most interested in issues of class, gender, and income distribution in relation to agrarian transition. Mwangi is the author of *Ten Millionaires and Ten Million Beggars* (Ashgate Press, 2000) which examines issues of income distribution, class, and gender in Kenya. In addition, he has published journal articles and book chapters on economic development in Africa. He has consulted widely for UN agencies on economic issues in specific African countries and the region as a whole. Mwangi was Chair of Africana Studies and Associate Professor of Economics at Gettysburg College, before moving to University of Massachusetts-Amherst in 2006 where he is an Assistant Professor of Economics.

James Heintz is Associate Research Professor and Associate Director at the Political Economy Research Institute, University of Massachusetts-Amherst. He received his Ph.D. in Economics from the University of Massachusetts in 2001 and an M.S. in Economics in 1992 from the University of Minnesota. He has written on a wide range of economic policy issues, including job creation, informal employment, egalitarian macroeconomic strategies, and investment behavior. In addition to the current study of Kenya, he has researched employment-oriented development policy for a variety of countries, including South Africa, Ghana, The Gambia, and Cambodia. He has served as a consultant for various UN agencies including the ILO, the UNDP, UNRISD, UNIFEM, and UNECA. He is co-author of *The Ultimate Field Guide to the U.S Economy* (The New Press 2000) and *An Employment-Targeted Economic Program for South Africa* (UNDP and Edward Elgar 2006). His current work focuses on employment policies for low- and middle-income countries; informal employment and labor market segmentation; and the links between macroeconomic policies and distributive outcomes.